Dictionary of Synonyms & Antonyms

Dictionary of Synonyms & Antonyms

Anil Kumar Mishra

PRABHAT PRAKASHAN

Published by
PRABHAT PRAKASHAN PVT. LTD.
4/19 Asaf Ali Road,
New Delhi-110 002 (INDIA)
e-mail: prabhatbooks@gmail.com

ISBN 978-93-5048-503-3
DICTIONARY OF SYNONYMS & ANTONYMS
by Anil Kumar Mishra

Edition
2025

Price
₹ 600.00 (Rupees Six Hundred only)

Printed at
Narula Printers, Delhi

Preface

The concept of 'Dictionary of Synonyms & Antonyms' is to provide illustrated examples to show how words of less obvious sense are used, and markers such as 'informal,' 'derogatory,' and 'obsolete' highlight the usage style. It is replete with appropriate words that will help improve the vocabulary to a great extent. A person who has to use words to express himself or his thoughts in a better manner will benefit from owning a Dictionary of Synonyms and Antonyms. It is a handy reference book for better choice of words to enhance and improve language skills. This book serves this purpose more than any other. This useful reference goes beyond a thesaurus, explaining the fine shades of meaning that differentiate synonyms. Alphabetical arrangement of terms makes it easy to find the right words.

Similarly Antonyms, meanings and their usages have also been provided.

This is a good book to have if you are a poet, writer, student, or just a word-lover. It will serve as a useful guide to find and use the most appropriate word.

A

Abandon: abdicate, waive, discontinue, relinquish, resign, surrender, vacate, desert, forsake, leave, quit, give up, forgo, withdraw, maroon, discard, drop.
ant.- defend, maintain, occupy.

Abase: degrade, disgrace, cast-down, demean, dishonour.
ant.- dignify, elevate, honour, praise.

Abate: assuage, decrease, diminish, lessen, mitigate, moderate, reduce, subside, allay, slacken, subdue, curtail, remit.
ant.- enlarge, increase, intensify, prolong, enhance.

Abbreviate: abridge, condense, contract, curtail, lessen, reduce, shorten, digest, truncate, prune.
ant.- enlarge, expand, extend, lengthen.

Abbreviation: abridgement, contraction, curtailment, reduction, shortening.
ant.- enlargement, expansion, extension.

Aberrant: abnormal, deviate, eccentric, peculiar, unusual.
ant.- normal, ordinary, regular, usual.

Abet: excite, fan, stirup, provoke, rouse, stimulate, incite, support.
ant.- deter, discourage, hinder, oppose, resist.

Abeyance: adjournment, post-ponement, deferment, inactivity, suspension.
ant.- action, enforcement, renewal, revival.

Abhor: despise, detest, dislike, execrate, hate, loathe.
ant.- admire, desire, esteem, like, relish, respect .

Ability: aptitude, aptness, capability, capacity, dexterity, efficiency, faculty, qualification, talent, knowledge, power, skill, competency.
ant.- inability, incapability, incapacity, incompetence.

Abnormal: aberrant, erratic, irregular, unusual, eccentric, anomalous.
ant.- normal, regular, usual.

Abolish: eradicate, abrogate, annul, cancel, invalidate, nullify, finish, end, revoke, exterminate, wipe out.
ant.- confirm, continue, establish, institute, legalize, restore.

Abominable: detestable, foul, hateful, loathsome, odious, repugnant, revolting.
ant.- agreeable, enjoyable, delightful, pleasant.

Abominate: abhor, detest, dislike, hate, loathe.
ant.- admire, cherish, like, love.

Abrupt: precipitate, short, unexpected, occurring by chance, sudden, curt, rude, precipitous, sharp, sheer.
ant.- anticipated, expected, gradual.

Absent: missing, non-attendant, not present, non-resident, lost, wanting, omitted, gone, away, lacking, truant.
ant.- attendant, present.

Absolute: complete, entire, infinite, perfect, total, ultimate, full, filled, whole, supreme, unrestricted, thorough, sheer, fixed, positive, unbounded, plenary.
ant.- incomplete, imperfect.

Absolve: cleanse, discharge, acquit, exonerate, pardon, release, shrive, forgive.
ant.- bind, blame, charge, convict, incriminate.

Absorb: assimilate, consume, engulf, imbibe, incorporate, merge, swallow, engross, take in, integrate, preoccupy, obsess.
ant.- discharge, dispense, eject, emit, exude.

Abstinence: abstention, continence, moderation, self-restraint, sobriety, temperance.
ant.- excess, gluttony, greed, intemperance, self-indulgence.

Abstract: detach, dissociate, isolate, remove, separate, abridge.
ant.- add, combine, insert, unite, inject.

Abstracted: appropriated, detached, parted, removed, separated, excluded, abridged.
ant.- added, combined, united, injected.

Absurd: inconsistent, irrational, ludicrous, nonsensical, self-contradictory, preposterous, ridiculous, comic, senseless, unreasonable, illogical, paradoxical, extravagant, fantastic, silly, unmeaning, fatuous, laughable.

ant.- rational, reasonable, logical, sensible, sound.

Abundant: bountiful, copious, lavish, opulent, plentiful, profuse, rich.
ant.- insufficient, rare, scant, scarce.

Abuse: dishonour, disparage, insult, maltreat, revile, upbraid, asperse, defame, harm, malign, persecute, vilify.
ant.- commend, laud, respect, cherish, favour, praise, sustain.

Academic: bookish, erudite, learned, literary, pedantic, scholarly, theoretical, scholastic, collegiate, educational.
ant.- commonsense, simple, ignorant, practical.

Accede: agree, assent, consent, acquiesce, yield, comply, attain.
ant.- dissent, protest, refuse.

Accelerate: expedite, forward, hasten, hurry, push, dispatch, quicken, rush, speed up, anticipate.
ant.- block, hinder, impede, obstruct, resist, retard.

Accentuate: emphasize, stress, exaggerate, heighten, intensify, underline.
ant.- minimize, moderate, subdue.

Acclaim: applaud, cheer, extol, honour, glorify, laud, praise, hail, salute.
ant.- berate, dishonour, jeer, revile.

Accommodate: adapt, adjust, arrange, conform, harmonize, oblige, serve, fit, suit.
ant.- embarrass, disarrange, obstruct, prevent.

Accompany: attend, chaperon, conduct, convoy, escort, join, follow.
ant.- desert, leave.

Accomplice: assistant, abettor, accessory, ally, associate, confederate, crony.
ant.- adversary, enemy, opponent, rival.

Accomplish: achieve, attain, complete, consummate, execute, fulfil, manage, finish, perform.
ant.- block, defeat, fail, frustrate, spoil.

Accord: agree, allow, assent, concede, permit, agreement, acquiescence, harmony, grant, reconciliation, unison.
ant.- contend, disallow, dispute, question, dissension, opposition, strife.

Accost: address, approach, greet, speak to, hail.
ant.- avoid, evade, passby.

Accrue: accumulate, amass, gather, grow, increase, store, collect.
ant.- diminish, disperse, dissipate.

Accumulate: accrue, amass, assemble, collect, gather, hoard, increase, pile, store, aggregate, bank.
ant.- diminish, disperse, dissipate, spend, waste.

Accuse: blame, censure, denounce, incriminate, indict, charge.
ant.- absolve, exonerate, acquit, vindicate.

Achieve: accomplish, execute, fulfil, gain, realize, win, attain, reach.
ant.- abandon, fail, lose, miss.

Achievement: performance, accomplishment, deed, feat, attainment, execution, realization.
ant.- neglect, omission, defeat, failure, misfortune.

Acquaintance: cognizance, companion, experience, ken, familiarity, friendship, intimacy, knowledge.
ant.- ignorance, inexperience, unfamiliarity.

Acquire: attain, collect, earn, get, obtain, procure, reach, secure, win.
ant.- fail, lose, surrender, miss.

Act: accomplishment, action, deed, do, doing, execute, operation, feat, perform, transaction.
ant.- abstain, discontinue, cease, stop.

Action: work, achievement, activity, deed, exploit, motion, movement, performance.
ant.- idleness, inactivity, inertia, repose.

Active: operative, working, busy, industrious, agile, alert, brisk, energetic, lively, mobile, nimble, quick, sprightly, activeness, business, vigil, animation, wakefulness.
ant.- dormant, inactive, idle, indolent, passive.

Activity: action, activeness, business, vigil, activation, wakefulness, agility, alertness, briskness, energy, enterprise, exercise, intensity, liveliness, motion, progress, quickness, rapidity.
ant.- dullness, idleness, inactivity, inertia.

Actuality: certainty, fact, reality, truth, event, incident, occurrence.
ant.- fiction, supposition, theory, unreal.

Adapt: accommodate, adjust, conform, modify, fit, suit, regulate, convert, reconcile.
ant.- derange, misapply, misfit.

Add: adjoin, annex, append, attach, augment, increase.
ant.- deduct, detach, reduce, remove, subtract, withdraw.

Adequate: ample, capable, commensurate, qualified, satisfactory, sufficient, suitable, fitting, enough, serviceable.
ant.- deficient, insufficient, lacking, scant.

Adhere: attach, clasp, cleave, cling, fasten, grasp, grip, have, hold, keep, maintain, support, check, carry, accommodate, confine, contain.
ant.- leave, loosen, unfasten.

Adjacent: adjoining, beside, bordering, close, near, next, neighbouring.
ant.- far away, beyond, distant, separate.

Admire: appreciate, approve, esteem, praise, respect, venerate, idolize, regard.
ant.- abhor, despise, detest, dislike, hate.

Admissible: allowable, justifiable, permissible, tolerable, acceptable, suitable.
ant.- inadmissible, irrelevant, unacceptable, unsuitable.

Admit: accept, allow, assent, concede, grant, permit, sanction.
ant.- debar, deny, dismiss, refuse, reject.

Advance: accelerate, elevate, forward, further, improve, move, promote, bring forward, offer, propose, propound, proceed, suggest.
ant.- halt, oppose, retreat, withdraw.

Advantage: benefit, profit, gain, interest.
ant.- detriment, harm, disadvantage.

Adverse: antagonistic, hostile, contrary, opposed, opposite, unfavourable.
ant.- favourable, cooperative, assisting, approving.

Advise: admonish, counsel, instruct, recommend, suggest, inform, notify, prescribe, exhort.

ant.- deceive, misdirect, misinform.

Affect: alter, change, influence, modify, concern, regard, impress, melt, move, soften, subdue, touch, adopt, assume, feign, pretend.

ant.- unalter, still, unmodify, disregard, frozen, stuck.

Affection: attachment, friendliness, goodwill, kindness, love, tenderness.

ant.- animosity, antipathy, aversion, dislike, indifference, repugnance.

Affirm: assert, aver, declare, maintain, state, swear.

ant.- contradict, demur, deny, oppose, nullify.

Afraid: alarmed, cowardly, fearful, frightened, scared, timid, timorous.

ant.- brave, courageous, bold, valourous.

Aggravate: impair, intensify, spoil, magnify, worsen, annoy, embitter, exasperate, irritate, provoke.

ant.- appease, improve, mitigate, soften, soothe.

Aggregate: amount, entirety, collection, conglomeration, mass, sum, total, whole.

ant.- element, part, particular, unit.

Agility: activity, briskness, energy, enterprise, liveliness, movement, quickness, rapidity.

ant.- dullness, idleness, inactivity, inertia.

Agitate: arouse, disturb, excite, perturb, provoke, rouse, ruffle, shake, stir, trouble.

ant.- calm, ease, placate, soothe, quite.

Agony: ache, anguish, distress, misery, pain, suffering, trial, ferment, torture, anxiety.

ant.- comfort, happiness, health, mitigation, ease, relief.

Agree: acquiesce, approve, assent, accede, comply, concur, consent, harmonize.

ant.- contradict, differ, disagree, dispute, dissent.

Agreeable: acceptable, amiable, gratifying, pleasant, pleasing, suitable, willing, congenial, compatible, harmonious.

ant.- disagreeable, obnoxious, offensive, unpleasant.

Aim: aspiration, design, endeavour, goal, intention, purpose.

ant.- aimless, carelessness.

Alarm: consternation, dismay, fear, signal, terror, warning, fright, panic, scare, alert, warn.
ant.- assurance, composure, peace, security, tranquillity, calm.

Alien: foreign, strange, foreigner, stranger, immigrant, exterior, unconformity.
ant.- citizen, countryman, dweller, inhabitant.

Allege: affirm, aver, cite, claim, declare, maintain, state, assert.
ant.- contradict, dissent, refute, repudiate, deny.

Alleviate: abate, diminish, extenuate, lighten, mitigate, relieve, soften, soothe, lessen.
ant.- aggravate, augment, increase, intensify.

Alliance: association, coalition, combination, confederacy, federation, partnership, union, compact, treaty.
ant.- divorce, secession, schism, separation.

Allot: apportion, dispense, distribute, divide, mete, allocate, assign, give, grant, measure.
ant.- confiscate, deny, refuse; retain, withhold.

Allow: empower, permit, sanction, authorize, give, grant, yield, acknowledge, admit, concede.
ant.- deny, forbid, protest, refuse, resist.

Allude: hint, imply, insinuate, intimate, refer, suggest.
ant.- declare, specify.

Allure: attract, bewitch, captivate, charm, coax, entice, seduce, tempt.
ant.- dissuade, discourage, repel, threaten.

Ally: accessory, accomplice, assistant, associate.
ant.- adversary, enemy, opponent.

Alone: deserted, desolate, isolated, lonely, secluded, unaccompanied, lone, only, solitary, apart, individually, single, solely, singly.
ant.- accompanied, attended, together.

Also: besides, likewise, moreover, furthermore, in addition.
ant.- apart, unlike, excluding.

Alternative: choice, elective, option.
ant.- obligation, required.

Always: ceaselessly, forever, constantly, continually, ever, eternally, perpetually.
ant.- never, occasionally, rarely, sometimes.

Amalgamate: blend, coalesce, combine, consolidate, fuse, mingle, merge, unite.
ant.- separate, divide.

Amateur: apprentice, learner, beginner, neophyte, non-professional, novice.
ant.- authority, expert, master, professional.

Ambiguous: dubious, vague, equivocal, indefinite, obscure.
ant.- explicit, unequivocal, clear.

Ambition: aspiration, desire, eagerness, goal.
ant.- contentment, laziness, indifference, satisfaction.

Amend: better, change, repair, correct, improve, reform.
ant.- blemish, corrupt, debase, spoil.

Amiable: agreeable, engaging, friendly, good-natured, gracious, pleasant.
ant.- disagreeable, hateful, ill-natured.

Among: amidst, between, amid, mingle, mixed.
ant.- apart, alone, separate.

Amorous: erotic, loving, lustful, lovesick.
ant.- frigid, unsexual.

Amount: aggregate, sum, total, quantity.
ant.- segregate.

Ample: large, great, extensive, broad, sufficient, copious, wide, plenty, expansive, spacious.
ant.- limited, narrow.

Amuse: entertain, recreate, cheer, regale.
ant.- bore, irk.

Analogy: similarity, parity, resemblance, similitude.
ant.- disparity.

Ancient: old, primitive, pristine, not modern, hoary, venerable, antique, archaic.
ant.- new, modern.

Angel: spirit, supernatural being, seraph, cherub, archangel, celestial being, invisible choir, heavenly host, ministering, spirit, guardian angel.
ant.- devil, fiend.

Anger: wrath, rage, fury, ire, resentment.
ant.- calm, calmness, peace, pacify.

Angry: provoked, irritated, irate, angered, wrathful.
ant.- happy, pleased, pleasant.

Announce: publish, proclaim, promulgate, declare.
ant.- conceal, hide.

Annual: yearly, seasonal, yearlong, anniversary.
ant.- daily.

Answer: reply, make answer, respond, response, rescript.
ant.- question, inquiry, query.

Anxious: restless, unquiet, solicitous, eager, worried.
ant.- calm, cool, assured.

Apex: top, summit, acme, zenith, pinnacle, highest point, peak, climax.
ant.- base, bottom, depths.

Appear: be visible, present itself, show itself.
ant.- disappear, vanish.

Appease: pacify, satisfy, propitiate, mollify, soothe, placate, slake.
ant.- provoke, dissatisfy, vex.

Applaud: cheer, clap, praise, laud.
ant.- condemn, criticize.

Approve: accept, appreciate, grant, sanction, confirm, make valid.
ant.- disallow, veto.

Ardent: burning, passionate, hot, fervent, keen, warm, zealous.
ant.- cold, cool, frigid.

Arrange: adjust, settle, set in order.
ant.- disarrange.

Arrest: detention, capture, apprehension, seizure, seize, apprehend.
ant.- free, release.

Arrive: come, get here, reach attain.
ant.- depart, leave.

Artificial: unnatural, factitious, made by art, fake, hand-made, handcrafted, synthetic.
ant.- genuine, true, natural.

Ashamed: abashed, humiliated, sorry, embarrassed, mortified, shy.
ant.- honoured, proud.

Ask: question, inquire, require, claim, demand.
ant.- answer, reply.

Assemble: collect, muster, gather, congregate.
ant.- break up, disassemble, disband.

Assent: agree, concur, accede, give consent.
ant.- deny, dissent.

Assistance: help, aid, support, succour.
ant.- opposition, resistance.

Assurance: assuredness, comfort, consolation, pledge.
ant.- distrust, mistrust, suspicion.

Attach: fasten, tie, join, connect, affix, fix, annex.
ant.- detach, disconnect, untie.

Attack: assail, assault, invade, aggress.
ant.- defend, guard.

Attest: certify, endorse, give evidence, testify, prove, witness, depose, bear, swear vouch.
ant.- prove false, rebut, refute.

Attractive: charming, fascinating, winsome, lovely.
ant.- displeasing, ugly.

Augury: omen, auspice, precursor, herald, prophecy.
ant.- bad omen, ill-omen.

Authentic: genuine, real, true, uncorrupted, authoritative, pure, trustworthy.
ant.- unreal, untrue.

Avoid: escape, keep away from, shun.
ant.- pursue, seek out.

Awful: dread, fearful, horrible, horrid, terrible, alarming, dreadful, dire, tremendous.
ant.- bold, fearless.

Aback: hinder part, posterior portion, backside, rear, hindquarters.
ant.- face, fore, front.

❑

B

Backward: regressive, dull, retrogressive, retrograde, revisionary, sluggish, stupid, disinclined, indisposed, loath, reluctant.
ant.- advanced, civilized, forward, progressive.

Bad: base, deleterious, evil, immoral, noxious, pernicious, rotten, vile, sinful, unsound, spurious, villainous, wicked.
ant.- excellent, honourable, moral, right, good, virtuous.

Balance: equilibrium, poise, harmony, excess, stability, steadiness, proportion, symmetry, remainder, reside, remains.
ant.- imbalance, instability, unsteadiness.

Baleful: deleterious, harmful, noxious, pernicious, wicked, evil, hurtful, injurious.
ant.- excellent, honourable, good, beneficial.

Banal: common, fatuous, hackneyed, insipid, ordinary, trite, vapid.
ant.- exciting, fresh, novel, original, striking.

Banish: debar, deport, dismiss, eject, exclude, exile, expatriate, expel, ostracize, oust.
ant.- accept, admit, forgive, receive, repatriate.

Barbarous: atrocious, crude, barbaric, brutal, merciless, savage, inhuman, ruthless, cruel, uncivilized.
ant.- civilized, cultured, humane, kind, polite.

Barren: unprolific, sterile, infertile, unproductive.
ant.- fecund, fertile, productive.

Barrier: blockade, bulwark, impediment, hindrance, obstacle, obstruction, bar, rampart.
ant.- admittance, entrance, opening, passage.

Base: abject, contemptible, degraded, despicable, mean, ignominious, inferior, low, shameful, sordid, vile, vulgar.
ant.- esteemed, exalted, lofty, moral, righteous, superior, noble.

Bashful: abashed, coy, diffident, modest, sheepish, shy, timid, timorous.
ant.- adventurous, daring, fearless, bold.

Basic: fundamental, primary, indispensable, principal, vital.
ant.- additional, extra, secondary.

Batter: demolish, disfigure, mar, dent, pound, pummel, smash, thrash, beat, belabour, bruise.
ant.- protect, secure, treat gently.

Battle: combat, conflict, contest, fight, fray, skirmish, strife, struggle.
ant.- accord, agreement, peace, truce.

Bear: allow, maintain, permit, suffer, endure, tolerate, carry, convey, transport, produce, spawn, yield.
ant.- avoid, cast aside, dodge, evade, refuse.

Beat: batter, belabour, buffet, castigate, flog, hit, knock, pound, pummel, punch, strike, thrash, defeat, overpower, overthrow, rout, subdue, vanquish, whip, palpitate, pulsate, pulse, throb.
ant.- assist, held, defend, shield.

Beautiful: attractive, pretty, beauteous, charming, comely, elegant, graceful, handsome, lovely.
ant.- foul, hideous, ugly, homely, repulsive, unsightly.

Becoming: suitable, decent, appropriate, befitting, comely, decorous, fitting, pleasing, seemly.
ant.- unbecoming, unseemly, displeasing.

Before: ahead, earlier, prior, forward, sooner, foremost, beforehand.
ant.- after, afterward, later, behind.

Beg: adjure, ask, beseech, crave, entreat, implore, importune, petition, pray, request, solicit, supplicate.
ant.- assist, bestow, cede, give grant.

Begin: commence, enter, inaugurate, initiate, originate, start.
ant.- complete, end, finish, terminate.

Beginning: commencement, inauguration, inception, opening, outset, source, start.
ant.- closing, completion, conclusion, end, finish, termination.

Belief: confidence, conviction, credence, opinion, persuasion, reliance, faith, trust, credit, assurance, presumption, troth.
ant.- denial, doubt, heresy, incredulity, mistrust.

Beloved: dear, darling, dearest, loved, pet.
ant.- despised, unwanted.

Below: beneath, lower, under, underneath.
ant.- above, aloft, overhead, over.

Bend: bow, contract, crook, curve, deflect, divert, flex, incline, lean, stoop, turn, twist, influence, mold.
ant.- stiffen, straighten.

Beneficial: advantageous, gainful, helpful, profitable, salutary, useful, wholesome.
ant.- detrimental, pernicious, harmful, disadvantageous.

Benefit: advantage, avail, gain, good, interest, profit.
ant.- distress, injury, trouble, harm.

Benevolence: altruism, beneficence, charity, generosity, goodwill, humanity, kindness, liberality, magnanimity, munificence, philanthropy.
ant.- cruelty, malevolence, selfishness, unkindness.

Beyond: above, distant, far, farther, more, over superior, yonder.
ant.- closeby, here, near.

Bias: bent, disposition, inclination, leaning, partiality, penchant, predilection, predisposition, prejudice, slant, proneness, propensity, tendency.
ant.- fairness, impartiality, equity, equality, neutrality.

Big: bulky, colossal, enormous, extensive, giant, great, huge, hulking, immense, large, massive, monstrous, vast.
ant.- little, petite, slight, small, tiny.

Bigotstad: dogmatic, fanatic, illiberal, intolerant, narrow-minded, opinionated, hide-bound, prejudiced.
ant.- broad-minded, open-minded, unbigoted.

Bitter: acrid, biting, distasteful, pungent, sharp, sour, tart, galling, grievous, painful, poignant, fierce, acrimonious, caustic, harsh, sardonic, cruel, severe.
ant.- pleasant, sweet, sugary.

Blame: censure, condemn, implicate, rebuke, reprehend, accuse, reproach, reprove, upbraid.
ant.- absolve, exonerate, acquit, praise.

Blank: bare, barren, empty, vacant, unfilled, vacuous, void.
ant.- filled, full, occupied.

Bleak: bare, chilly, desolate, unsheltered, dreamy, dismal, cold, dull, gloomy.
ant.- cheerful, pleasant, warm, serene.

Blemish: blot, mark, speck, stain, defect, disfigurement, disgrace, dishonour, fault, flaw, imperfection.
ant.- adornment, decoration, embellishment, perfection.

Blend: adjoin, amalgamate, coalesce, combine, commingle, conjoin, consolidate, fuse, merge, mingle, mix, unite.
ant.- decompose, disintegrate, separate.

Blind: sightless, unseeing, visionless, unsighted, stone-blind.
ant.- farsighted, perceiving, sensible, seeing, sighted.

Bliss: blessedness, ecstasy, blissfulness, gladness, joy, happiness, rapture, pleasure.
ant.- grief, misery, pain, sadness, wretchedness.

Bluff: deceive, defraud, delude, mislead, humbug.
ant.- faithfulness, loyalty.

Blunt: dull, edgeless, obtuse, pointless, unsharpened, abrupt, bluff, brusque, impolite, outspoken, harsh, rough, unceremonious.
ant.- edgy, pointed, sharp.

Boast: bluster, brag, exult, gloat, vaunt, puff.
ant.- disavow, disclaim, deprecate.

Bold: adventurous, audacious, brave, courageous, daring, fearless, intrepid, strong.
ant.- bashful, cowardly, timid, retiring, shy, fearful.

Bondage: vassalage, enslavement, subjugation, thraldom, thrall, serfdom, servitude, slavery, subjection.

ant.- freedom, liberation.

Border: boundary, brink, edge, extremity, fringe, frontier, limit, margin, outskirts, rim, trim, verge.

ant.- center, inside, interior, core, mainland, region.

Boredom: doldrums, dullness, ennui, tedium, weariness.

ant.- amusement, entertainment, excitement, stimulus.

Bother: annoy, disturb, harass, irritate, haunt, inconvenience, molest, perplex, pester, plague, tease, trouble, upset, worry.

ant.- gratify, please, relieve, soothe.

Bottom: base, foot, foundation, groundwork, framework, sole, lowest part.

ant.- apex, peak, summit, top, upper part.

Bound: hop, jump, leap, skip, spring, vault, circumscribe, confine, curb, define, limit.

ant.- crawl, walk.

Bountiful: abundant, ample, copious, opulent, overflowing, plenteous, plentiful, profuse, rich.

ant.- deficient, insufficient, scant, scarce, incomplete.

Brag: boasting, bluster, boast, flaunt, flourish, vaunt.

ant.- debase, degrade, demean, denigrate.

Brave: adventurous, outrageous, daring, fearless, hardy, heroic, intrepid, undaunted, valiant, bold, valorous, venturesome.

ant.- cowardly, afraid, fearful, timid, weak.

Break: burst, crack, demolish, destroy, fracture, pound, rack, crush, rend, rupture, sever, shatter, shiver, smash, split, squeeze.

ant.- join, mend, repair, restore, unite, attach, connect.

Breed: produce, generate, procreate, beget, conceive, create, engender, start, propagate.

ant.- abort, kill, murder.

Brief: concise, curt, laconic, pithy, short, succinct, terse, fleeting, momentary, passing, short-lived, transient.

ant.- extended, lengthy, long, prolonged, protracted.

Bright: brilliant, gleaming, glistening, lucid, luminous, lustrous, radiant, scintillating, shining, translucent, intelligent, sunny, smart, witty.
ant.- dark, dull, gloomy.

Bring: bear, carry, conduct, convey, draw, fetch, impart, transfer, transport, transmit.
ant.- abandon, relinquish, leave.

Brisk: alert, quick, lively, animated, sprightly.
ant.- lazy, slow, sluggish.

Briskness: activity, agility, energy, enterprise, intensity, liveliness, quickness, rapidity, vigour.
ant.- dullness, idleness, inactivity.

Brittle: breakable, crisp, crumbling, delicate, fragile, frail, frangible, friable, gimcrack, shivery, splintery.
ant.- durable, enduring, tough, strong, unbreakable.

Broad: comprehensive, extensive, large, sweeping, vast, wide.
ant.- confined, light, limited, narrow, restricted.

Broken: crushed, destroyed, fractured, interrupted, reduced, ruptured, separated, shattered, smashed.
ant.- repaired, united, whole.

Brotherhood: brotherliness, fellowship, kinship, family, solidarity, unity, association, clan, fraternity, society.
ant.- acrimony, discord, opposition, strife.

Brusque: abrupt, gruff, blunt, curt, rude, harsh, precipitous, rough, rugged, steep.
ant.- gentle, courteous.

Brutal: barbarous, bestial, brutish, carnal, coarse, cruel, ferocious, inhuman, rude, merciless, rough, ruthless, savage.
ant.- civilized, courteous, gentle, humane, kind, soft-hearted.

Build: construct, erect, establish, found, make, manufacture, put up.
ant.- demolish, destroy, end.

Buoyant: blithe, cheerful, elated, joyful, happy, jaunty, lively, spirited, vivacious.
ant.- dejected, depressed, despondent, sullen, unhappy.

Burden: encumbrance, load, weight, overload.
ant.- alleviate, console, ease, mitigate.

Burn: blaze, char, cremate, flame, incinerate, ignite, scald, scorch, sear, singe.
ant.- extinguish, subdue, quench.

Bury: conceal, cover, entomb, hide, immure, inhume.
ant.- display, exhume, expose, reveal.

Business: commerce, concern, employment, engagement, enterprise, job, occupation, profession, pursuit, trade, vocation, work.
ant.- avocation, hobby.

Busy: active, assiduous, hard working, diligent, industrious, occupied, engaged.
ant.- apathetic, indifferent, lethargic.

Buy: acquire, invest, negotiate, procure, purchase, bargin for.
ant.- market, sell, transfer.

❑

C

Calamitous: disastrous, cataclysmic, catastrophic, ruinous, fatal.
ant.- favourable, helpful.

Calamity: adversity, casualty, catastrophe, disaster, misfortune, mishap, ruin.
ant.- advantage, benefit, blessing, fortune.

Calculate: compute, consider, count, enumerate, estimate, figure, reckon.
ant.- assume, conjecture, guess, miscalculate.

Call: address, assemble, clamour, command, convoke, cry demand, designate, exclaim, invite, name, phone, proclaim, rally, roar, scream, shout, shriek, summon, utter, yell.
ant.- call off, cancel, dismiss.

Callous: hard, impenitent, indifferent, soulless, indurate, insensible, obdurate, tough, insensitive, unfeeling, unsusceptible.
ant.- soft, compassionate, sensitive, tender.

Calm: composed, peaceful, cool, dispassionate, peaceful, placid, quiet, sedate, self-possessed, serene, tranquil, undisturbed, unperturbed.
ant.- agitated, angry, excited.

Calumny: aspersion, lying, detraction, defamation, libel, scandal, slander, vilification.
ant.- charity, commendation, defence, flattery, kindness, praise.

Cancel: abolish, abrogate, annul, delete, eliminate, erase, expunge, invalidate, nullify, obliterate, quash, repeal, rescind, revoke.
ant.- approve, confirm, enforce, ratify.

Candid: frank, free, ingenuous, sincere, straightforward, outspoken, truthful, fair, open, impartial, blunt, unbiased.
ant.- artful, insincere, sly, scheming.

Candour: fairness, frankness, impartiality, openness, rectitude, sincerity, truthfulness, uprightness.
ant.- artifice, cheating, deceit, dishonesty, fraud, guile, stratagem.

Capability: ability, aptitude, aptness, capacity, dexterity, efficiency, faculty, qualification, skill, talent.
ant.- incapacity,

incompetency, incapability, inefficiency.

Capable: able, competent, efficient, fitted, qualified, skilful, suitable, proficient.
ant.- inadequate, incapable, incompetent, unable, unfit.

Capacity: ability, aptitude, aptness, capability, faculty, power, skill, talent, content.
ant.- impotence, inability, incapacity.

Capitulate: yield, abandon, acquiesce, relinquish, renounce, submit, surrender.
ant.- conquer, overcome.

Capricious: changeful, fickle, idiosyncratic, inconstant, variable, whimsical, fantastic, quaint, bizarre, fanciful.
ant.- constant, dependable, stable, steady.

Captivity: bondage, confinement, custody, detention, imprisonment, servitude, slavery, subjection.
ant.- freedom, independence, liberty.

Capture: apprehend, arrest, catch, grasp, grab, seize, snare, trap.
ant.- free, liberate, release, set free.

Care: concern, caution, carefulness, worry, attention, caution, regard, precaution, vigilance, wariness, watchfulness, guardianship, ward.
ant.- disregard, indifference, neglect.

Career: avocation, business, calling, life-work, experience, line, occupation, profession, pursuit, sphere, vocation.
ant.- idleness, retirement.

Careful: attentive, meticulous, prudent, scrupulous, thoughtful, cautious, circumspect, discreet, guarded, vigilant, wary, watchful.
ant.- careless, improvident, indifferent, lax, negligent.

Careless: inattentive, indiscreet, reckless, thoughtless, unconcerned, negligent.
ant.- accurate, careful.

Caress: cuddle, embrace, fondle, hug, kiss, pamper, pet.
ant.- annoy, buffet, neglect, spurn, tease, vex.

Caricature: burlesque, travesty, parody, cartoon, exaggeration, farce,

imitation, mimicry, ridicule.
ant.- accuracy, exactitude, reality, truth.

Carnal: bodily, earthly, physical, fleshly, concupiscent, corporeal, lascivious, lustful, sensual, voluptuous, worldly.
ant.- chaste, ethereal, intellectual, spiritual.

Carping: captious, cavilling, disparaging, fault finding, hypercritical, pedantic.
ant.- appreciative, approving, commendatory, encouraging.

Carry: bring, bear, convey, move, remove, support, sustain, transmit, transport.
ant.- abandon, drop, leave.

Casual: chance, haphazard, cursory, incidental, informal, nonchalant, offhand, random, accidental, unconcerned, unpremediated.
ant.- expected, formal, intended, planned, intentional.

Casualty: accident, adversity, calamity, mishap, disaster, misadventure, misfortune.
ant.- design, intention, prosperity, purpose.

Catastrophe: adversity, affliction, blow, calamity, casualty, cataclysm, disaster, mishap, misery, ruin, upheaval, paroxysm, destruction.
ant.- benefit, blessing, happiness.

Catch: apprehend, arrest, nab, grab, capture, clasp, grasp, grip, overtake, seize, snare, trap.
ant.- cast aside, free, liberate, loose, release, drop.

Catching: attractive, magnetic, communicable, contagious, infectious, pestilential, infective, transmittable, noxious, contaminative.
ant.- healthful, hygienic, non-communicable.

Cause: agent, antecedent, determinant, inducement, motive, origin, originator, principle, reason, source, create, effect, evoke, incite, induce, occasion, originate, prompt.
ant.- effect, consequence, development, end result.

Caustic: burning, inflammatory, incendiary, acrid, bitter, biting, distasteful, pungent, sour, tart, acrimonious, harsh, sardonic, severe.
ant.- mellow, pleasant, sweet.

Caution: alert, care, heed, prudence, vigilance, warning, wariness, watchfulness, admonish, injunction.
ant.- carelessness, recklessness, rashness.

Cautious: attentive, heedful, prudent, wary, scrupulous, thoughtful, alert, careful, circumspect, discreet, vigilant.
ant.- heedless, impetuous, hasty, careless.

Cease: conclude, discontinue, stop, terminate, finish, halt, desist, end.
ant.- continue, initiate, persist, start.

Cede: assign, convey, delivery, handover, grant, relinquish, surrender, transfer, yield.
ant.- gain, receive, win.

Celebrate: commemorate, keep, hallow, honour, observe, solemnize, commend, extol, laud, praise.
ant.- disregard, ignore, neglect, disgrace, dishonour, profane.

Celebrated: distinguished, eminent, famous, glorious, illustrious, renowned, noted.
ant.- unknown, unpopular, ignominious.

Celerity: alacrity, quickness, rapidity, speed, velocity, haste, swiftness.
ant.- slowness, sluggishness.

Celestial: divine, ethereal, eternal, supernal, unearthly, empyreal, Godlike, heavenly, supernatural, transcendant, holy.
ant.- earthly, infernal, mortal.

Censure: blame, condemn, criticize, denounce, reprimand, rebuke, reproach, reprove, upbraid, chide.
ant.- approve, commend, endorse, praise.

Center: core, focus, middle, midpoint, midst, nucleus.
ant.- border, periphery, rim.

Certain: assured, definite, incontrovertible, indubitable, inevitable, positive, reliable, secure, sure, true, undeniable, fixed, unquestionable.
ant.- doubtful, false, probable, questionable.

Certainty: assuredness, self-reliance, confidence, surety, conviction, firmness, sureness, certitude, assurance.
ant.- disbelief, uncertainty, doubt.

Certify: assure, attest, aver, declare, demonstrate, inform, prove, state, testify, verify, vouch.

ant.- deny, disown, repudiate.

Chance: opportunity, possibility, probability, occasion.

ant.- impossibility, improbability.

Change: alteration, alternation, innovation, modification, mutation, revolution, substitution, transition, variation, permutation, modulation.

ant.- permanence, stability, uniformity.

Changeable: changefule, fickle, inconstant, shifting, unstable, vacillating, variable, wavering, alterable, kaleidoscopic, ever-changing, mutable.

ant.- stable, unchangeable, steady.

Chaos: anarchy, confusion, disorder, disorganization, jumble, muddle, shambles, snarl.

ant.- system, orderliness, organization, tidiness.

Characteristic: attribute, feature, idiosyncrasy, individuality, mark, peculiarity, singularity, quality, trait.

ant.- uncharacteristic, unrepresentative.

Charge: accuse, arraign, blame, impeach, incriminate, indict.

ant.- absolve, exonerate, acquit.

Charity: altruism, benefaction, benevolence, bounty, generosity, humanity, kindness, liberality, magnanimity, philanthropy, tenderness.

ant.- inhumanity, malevolence, selfishness, miserliness.

Charming: attractive, bewitching, captivating, delightful, winning, enchanting, ravishing.

ant.- unattractive, unpleasant, unlikeable.

Chase: follow, hunt, persist, pursue, seek, track, trail.

ant.- avoid, elude, escape, flee.

Chaste: clean, clear, genuine, undefiled, immaculate, pure, unadulterated, uncontaminated, guiltless, innocent, sincere, uncorrupted, virgin, virtuous.

ant.- foul, polluted, tainted,

corrupt, defiled, lewd, wanton.

Chastise: castigate, correct, discipline, punish, reprove, reprimand, strike, whip.
ant.- comfort, forgive, pardon, reward.

Cheap: inexpensive, low-priced, beggarly, common, inferior, mean, petty, shabby, contemptible, despicable, underpriced, cutrate, reduced-rate, half-price.
ant.- costly, dear, expensive, valuable.

Check: analyze, audit, examine, compare, confirm, inspect, probe.
ant.- disregard, hasten, neglect, omit.

Cheer: comfort, console, soothe, encourage, gladden, solace, sympathize.
ant.- antagonize, depress, dishearten.

Cheerful: cheery, jolly, buoyant, genial, glad, smiling, sunny, gay, happy, joyous, light-hearted, merry, sprightly.
ant.- dejected, gloomy, morose, sad, sullen.

Cherish: appreciate, revere, hold dear, prize, treasure, value, foster, nurture, nourish, nurse, protect, shelter.
ant.- abandon, dislike, disregard, neglect.

Chicanery: deception, duplicity, fraud, intrigue, machination, subterfuge, trickery.
ant.- fair dealing, honesty.

Chief: boss, president, captain, chieftain, commander, head, leader, master, principle rule, fundamental source, ruler.
ant.- attendant, servant, subordinate.

Chivalrous: brave, courageous, courteous, gallant, heroic, knightly, spirited, valiant, bold, valorous.
ant.- cowardly, timorous, rude, unmannerly.

Choice: liking, precedence, taste, selection, option, pick, desire.
ant.- dislike, unacceptance.

Choose: select, elect, opt, pick, prefer, cull.
ant.- refuse, reject, dismiss.

Chronic: confirmed, inveterate, persistent.
ant.- occasional, temporary.

Circuitous: devious, indirect, roundabout, swerving, tortuous, wandering, winding.

ant.- straight, undeviating, direct.

Circumspection: anxiety, care, concern, solicitude, worry, attention, caution, discreetness, heed, regard, vigilance, wariness.

ant.- audaciousness, negligence, disregard, indifference.

Circumvent: encircle, entrap, balk, evade, check, foil, forestall, frustrate, outwit, prevent, thwart.

ant.- aid, help.

Civil: affable, considerate, courteous, cultivated, well-mannered, gracious, polite, refined, urbane.

ant.- boorish, ill-mannered, rude.

Civilization: breeding, culture, cultivation, education, enlightenment, illumination, polish, refinement.

ant.- ignorance, illiteracy, vulgarity.

Claim: advance, affirm, allege, assert, aver, contend, declare, demand, express, maintain, state, defend, support, uphold.

ant.- contradict, deny, refute.

Clamour: blare, cry, hubbub, hullabaloo, noise, din, outcry, racket, uproar, tumult.

ant.- quiet, silence, stillness.

Clandestine: concealed, covert, furtive, hidden, private, secret, stealthy, sly, undercover, surreptitious.

ant.- conspicuous, exposed, unmasked, revealed, open.

Clarify: explain, illustrate, interpret, make clear, clear up, purify, refine, unravel.

ant.- confuse, muddy, obscure.

Classic: antique, elegant, firstrate, model, neat, pure, refined, simple, trim.

ant.- barbaric, baroque, mixed.

Clean: unadulterated, cleanse, purify, scrub, spotless, stainless, sweep, wash.

ant.- dirty, soiled, stained.

Clear: cloudless, fair, sunny, limpid, transparent, apparent, distinct, evident, intelligible, lucid, obvious, perspicuous, unmistakable, plain, vivid, open, unobstructed.

ant.- overcast, ambiguous, cloudy, obscure, vague.

Clemency: charity, mercy, compassion, forgiveness, leniency, mildness, pity.

ant.- inhumanity, pitilessness, cruelty.

Clever: adroit, dexterous, keen, quick, quickwitted, skillful, canny, cunning, talented, witty, bright, ingenious, expert, intelligent, sharp, smart.
ant.- awkward, clumsy, slow, unskilled, foolish, ignorant, stupid.

Cleverness: canniness, shrewdness, smartness, intellect, intelligence, perspicacity, sagacity, sense, understanding.
ant.- stupidity, dullness, witlessness.

Climax: acme, apex, pinnacle, consummation, culmination, height, peak, summit, vertex, zenith.
ant.- anticlimax, depth, floor.

Climb: ascend, mount, rise, scale, clamber, soar.
ant.- descend, fall, drop, sink.

Cloak: cloth, cape, wrap, sleevless outer garment, mantle, robe, domino.
ant.- bare, expose, reveal, unveil.

Close[1]: abutting, adjacent, adjoining, contiguous, near, nearby, neighbouring.
ant.- away, distant, faraway, far off.

Close[2]: bar, enclose, fence in, occlude, seal, shut, clog, complete, conclude, end, finish, terminate.
ant.- open, unlock, begin, commence, start.

Clothes: apparel, array, attire, clothing, dress, garb, garments, raiment, wear, costume, outfit.
ant.- nakedness, nudity.

Cloudy: dark, dim, indistinct, dusky, sunless, murky, obscure, shadowy.
ant.- bright, clear, distinct, sunny, uncloudy.

Clumsy: inept, awkward, cumbersome, maladroit, ponderous, unwieldy, lumbering, bungling, bumbling.
ant.- adroit, dexterous, skillful.

Clutch: catch, embrace, clasp, grapple, grasp, grip, seize, snatch.
ant.- free, release.

Coalition: alliance, association, combination, confederacy, federation, league, partnership, union.
ant.- disunity, division, separation.

Coarse: crass, vulgar, gross, harsh, rough, unrefined, bawdy, immodest, indelicate, inelegant, rude, unpolished, crude, vulgar.
ant.- fine, refined, smooth.

Coax: cajole, entice, inveigle, beguile, invite, persuade, wheedle, allure.
ant.- bully, force, coerce, harass.

Coerce: compel, constrain, drive, enforce, force, impel, oblige.
ant.- allure, convince, induce, persuade.

Coercion: compulsion, force, constraint, pressure, violence.
ant.- persuasion, conviction.

Cogent: convincing, effective, forceful, weighty, forcible, persuasive, potent, powerful, sound, strong.
ant.- ineffective, unconvincing, weak.

Cognizance: acquaintance, awareness, information, knowing, knowledge, learning, perception, scholarship, understanding, wisdom.
ant.- ignorance.

Coincide: accord, harmonize, agree, collude, concur, equal, match, square, synchronize, tally.
ant.- differ, disagree, diverge, separate, contradict.

Cold: arctic, bleak, chilly, cool, freezing, frigid, frosty, frozen, icy, wintry, indifferent, stoical, passionless, unconcerned, reserved, unfeeling.
ant.- heated, hot, warm, sunny, torrid.

Colleague: ally, associate, collaborator, companion, comrade, confederate, consort, friend, mate, partner, teammate, workmate.
ant.- adversary, opponent, stranger.

Collect: accumulate, amass, assemble, concentrate, congregate, consolidate, gather, gain, hoard, obtain, heap, pile.
ant.- disperse, distribute, scatter.

Collected: calm, composed, cool, placid, quiet, sedate, tranquil, unperturbed.
ant.- agitated, excited, perturbed.

Collision: clash, crash, shock, accident, conflict, impact, encounter, meeting, discord, struggle, contention, controversy, clashing, interference, opposition.
ant.- accord, agreement, concord, harmony.

Colossal: elephantine, vast, enormous, gargantuan, gigantic, huge, immense, large, mammoth, prodigious, tremendous, mountainous.
ant.- little, small, tiny.

Comatose: drowsy, faint, lethargic, stuporous, torpid, unconscious.
ant.- conscious, sensible, awake, aware.

Combat: battle, brawl, conflict, contest, duel, encounter, fight, skirmish, struggle, controversy, discord, opposition.
ant.- accord, peace, truce, armistice.

Combine: accompany, adjoin, associate, attach, conjoin, connect, couple, join, link, unite, mix, blend.
ant.- detach, dissociate, separate, divide.

Comely: beautiful, charming, elegant, fair, fine, graceful, handsome, lovely, pleasing, pretty, attractive, good-looking, fair.
ant.- ugly, unattractive, unsightly.

Comfort: cheer, console, encourage, gladden, relieve, solace, soother, support, succour, sympathize.
ant.- antagonize, depress, dishearten, trouble.

Comfortable: acceptable, agreeable, commodious, contented, cozy, gratifying, warm, pleasurable, protected, relaxed, restful, well off.
ant.- miserable, wretched, uneasy, uncomfortable.

Comical: amusing, diverting, farcical, funny, humorous, laughable, droll, ludicrous, ridiculous, witty.
ant.- serious, sober, solemn, grave, humourless.

Command: bidding, decree, dictate, direction, injunction, instruction, mandate, order, ordinance, dictum, behest, nod.
ant.- appeal, request, ask, beg.

Commemorate: memorialize, celebrate, honour, observe, solemnize.
ant.- disdain, dishonour, neglect, disregard.

Commence: arise, begin, enter, inaugurate, initiate, institute, introduce, originate, start.
ant.- cease, complete, finish, terminate, end.

Commencement: beginning, incipience, inception, opening, outset.
ant.- termination, completion, consummation, end.

Commend: applaud, cite, acclaim, approve, extol, eulogize, praise.
ant.- censure, criticize, condemn, rebuke.

Commensurate: appropriate, proper, fit, suitable, well-suited, to the point.
ant.- incompatible, improper.

Commiseration: compassion, sympathy, condolence.
ant.- coldness, indifference, disdain.

Commit: promise, bind, obligate, pledge, perform, perpetrate, do, commend, consign, entrust, trust.
ant.- fail, neglect, release, renounce, free, loose.

Commodious: spacious, roomy, ample, capacious, huge, large.
ant.- cramped, narrow, poky, small.

Common: habitual, frequent, ordinary, prevalent, public, usual.
ant.- noble, aristocratic, extraordinary, rare, refined, uncommon, unusual.

Commotion: agitation, chaos, confusion, disarray, disorder, disturbance, stir, ado, fuss, turbulence, ferment, tumult, turmoil.
ant.- calmness, tranquillity, peace.

Communicate: convey, tell, disclose, divulge, impart, inform, promulgate, reveal, transmit.
ant.- conceal, keep secret, suppress, withhold.

Communion: association, concord, fellowship, intercourse, sacrament, harmony, closeness, union.
ant.- alienation, contention, discord.

Compact[1]: close, condensed, constricted, contracted, dense, firm, narrow, pressed, snug, stretched, tense, tight.
ant.- diffuse, loose, relaxed, slack.

Compact[2]: compress, condense, cram, pack down, tamp.
ant.- disperse, loosen, separate.

Companion: associate, crony, colleague, comrade, consort, fellow, friend, mate, partner.
ant.- adversary, enemy, foe, rival, stranger.

Company: companionship, intimacy, association, fellowship, society, corporation.
ant.- dispersion, loneliness, seclusion, solitude.

Comparable: alike, allied, analogous, correlative, corresponding, like, parallel, similar.
ant.- dissimilar, opposed, incomparable, divergent, incongruous.

Compassion: commiseration, tenderness, kindness, mercy, pity, sympathy.
ant.- cruelty, inhumanity, ruthlessness, severity, tyranny, mercilessness.

Compatible: accordant, well-matched, agreeable, congruous, consonant, harmonious, suitable.
ant.- contradictory, unsuitable, incompatible, incongruous, inconsistent.

Compel: coerce, constrain, drive, enforce, force, impel, oblige.
ant.- deter, hamper, impede, obstruct.

Compensation: recompense, reward, payment, indemnity, indemnification, wages.
ant.- forfeiture, loss, penalty.

Competent: capable, efficient, fitted, proficient, qualified, skillful.
ant.- inadequate, unqualified, incapable, incompetent, inept.

Complain: deplore, grouse, grumble, lament, repine, whine.
ant.- applaud, approve, praise, sanction.

Complete: all, entire, full, whole, thorough, total, unbroken, undivided.
ant.- abandon, neglect, withdraw, deficient, lacking, unfinished.

Complex: complicated, manifold, compound, intricate, involved, obscure, knotty.
ant.- apparent, plain, simple, easy.

Complexion: colour, pigment, shade, tincture, tinge, hue, tint.
ant.- paleness, transparency.

Compliant: humble, meek, modest, submissive, unpretentious, unassuming.
ant.- arrogant, boastful,

haughty, ostentatious, proud, vain.

Compliment: adulation, praise, honour, admiration, tribute, commendation, endorse, flattery.
ant.- censure, criticism, denounce, reprehend.

Comply: follow, obey, accede, acquiesce, agree, assent, consent, coincide, concur, conform, submit.
ant.- disagree, dessent, disobey, oppose.

Compose: construct, create, fashion, formulate, forge, produce, shape, constitute, form, arrange, combine, organize, devise, frame, invent.
ant.- agitate, destroy, disfigure, dismantle.

Composed: calm, collected, comfortable, imperturbed, peaceful, placid, quiet, sedate, serene, tranquil.
ant.- agitated, excited, perturbed.

Composure: balance, calmness, equilibrium, poise, self-possession, placidity, serenity.
ant.- impatience, agitation, excitement, rage, turbulence.

Compound: alloy, amalgamate, mix, unite, blend, combine, complex, mingle, composite, fraternize, join.
ant.- elemental, simple, single, unmixed.

Comprehend: apprehend, conceive, discern, embrace, grasp, know, learn, perceive, realize.
ant.- exclude, misapprehend, misinterpret.

Comprehension: cognizance, discernment, insight, understanding.
ant.- ignorance, insensibility, misconception.

Compress: condense, digest, consolidate, abridge, reduce, constrict, compact, squeeze.
ant.- expand, extend, increase, ratify, stretch, swell, loosen, separate.

Comprise: consist, contain, embody, include, embrace, encompass, hold, involve.
ant.- except, fall, short, lack, reject.

Compromise: accommodation, settlement, adjustment, agreement, arbitration, concession, conciliation.
ant.- controversy, dissention, disagreement, dispute.

Compute: calculate, count, enumerate, estimate, figure, reckon.
ant.- conjecture, guess, surmise.

Comrade: associate, friend, colleague, mate, companion, consort, partner.
ant.- adversary, stranger.

Conceal: bury, camouflage, cover, disguise, hide, mask, screen, secrete, veil.
ant.- disclose, divulge, expose, lay bare, reveal, unveil, uncover.

Concede: assent, acquiesce, consent, allow, give in, permit, sanction, surrender, authorize, grant, relinquish, yield, acknowledge, admit.
ant.- object, protest, refuse, reject.

Conceit: egotism, pride, self-glorification, self-esteem, vanity.
ant.- humility, meekness, modesty.

Concept: conception, notion, idea, view, thought.
ant.- entity, matter, substance.

Concern: company, institution, profession, establishment, business, institute, occupation, employment.
ant.- unconcern.

Concise: compact, condensed, incisive, pithy, succinct, terse, short, laconic, epigrammatic, brief, summary.
ant.- lengthy, redundant, repetitive, verbose, wordy.

Conclusion: completion, consummation, determination, termination, decision, result, deduction, inference.
ant.- inception, beginning, commencement, introduction, preamble, prelude, start.

Concord: accordance, amity, agreement, harmony, unity.
ant.- difference, disagreement, discord, dissension, variance.

Concrete: firm, hard, solidified, actual, definite, material, particular, specific, tangible.
ant.- abstract, immaterial, indefinite, intangible.

Concur: agree, approve, assent, certify, comply, consent, coincide, conform, endorse.
ant.- argue, contradict, differ, disapprove, dispute, dissent, oppose, reject.

Condemn: blame, censure, denounce, reprehend, reprove, reproach, reprobate, upbraid.
ant.- approve, commend, condone, praise, acclaim, applaud.

Conditional: contingent, dependent, relying, subject, subordinate.
ant.- absolute, autonomous, independent, unconditional.

Condone: excuse, forgive, overlook, pardon, remit.
ant.- condemn, forbid, punish, denounce, censure.

Confederate: aide, accessory, accomplice, ally, assistant, associate, colleague, partner, supporter.
ant.- adversary, opponent, enemy, opposition.

Confederation: alliance, union, coalition, confederacy, league, federation, treaty, entente.
ant.- schism, separation.

Confess: acknowledge, admit, allow, concede, disclose, avow, grant.
ant.- deny, disclaim, disown, repudiate, disagree, oppose.

Confidence: assurance, self-possession, assuredness, trust, conviction, belief, reliance, self-reliance.
ant.- disbelief, distrust, mistrust.

Confine: bind, circumscribe, bound, enclose, encompass, fence, limit, restrict.
ant.- develop, free, release, unfetter.

Confirm: corroborate, verify, substantiate, establish, settle, approve, fix, ratify, sanction, strengthen, validate.
ant.- annul, abrogate, cancel, destroy, shatter, void.

Confiscate: commandeer, take, capture, grip, seize.
ant.- free, give back, restore, return, release.

Conflict: battle, combat, duel, encounter, fight, struggle, contention, discord, strife, dissension, opposition, war, variance.
ant.- concord, harmony, peace, repose, tranquillity, treaty, truce.

Conform: adapt, adjust, assent, comply, submit.
ant.- dissent, contrary, against, opposed.

Confront: combat, encounter, face, meet, squarely, oppose.
ant.- sidestep, flee, avoid, evade.

Confuse: bewilder, complicate, confound, derange, disconcert, obscure, perplex, puzzle.
ant.- clarify, illumine, organize.

Confusion: befuddlement, bemusement, bewilderment, perplexity, puzzlement.
ant.- enlightenment.

Confute: show up, rebut, disprove, refute.
ant.- affirm, confirm, prove, endorse, verify.

Congruous: proper, apt, fit, right, suitable, suited.
ant.- unsuitable, inept, incongruous.

Conjecture: guess, hypothesis, presumption, speculation, supposition.
ant.- certainty, fact, proof, truth.

Connect: adjoin, affiliate, affix, annex, append, attach, join, link, unite.
ant.- detach, disconnect, disengage, separate, unfasten.

Conquer: beat, checkmate, defeat, master, overcome, overthrow, prevail, quell, rout, sudue, subjugate, surmount, vanquish.
ant.- cede, forfeit, lose, retreat, succumb, surrender.

Conquest: subjugation, victory, triumph, success.
ant.- defeat, failure.

Conscientious: careful, just, exacting, incorruptible, honest, scrupulous, trusty, meticulous, upright, faithful, honourable.
ant.- corrupt, dishonest, unjust.

Conscious: apprised, aware, certain, cognizant, informed, mindful, percipient, sensible.
ant.- ignorant, insensible, oblivious, senseless, unaware, unwitting.

Consent: accede, acquiesce, agree, allow, assent, comply, concede, concur, conform, yield, grant, deign.
ant.- demur, disagree, dissent, refuse.

Consequence: effect, end, fruit, issue, outcome, product, sequel, upshot.
ant.- beginning, cause, commencement, origin, start.

Conserve: maintain, save, retain, keep, guard, protect, nurse, preserve.
ant.- discard, relinquish, reject, neglect.

Consider: contemplate, deliberate, meditate, ponder, reflect, weigh, brood.

ant.- abandon, dismiss, forget, ignore, neglect, overlook.

Considerate: thoughtful, humane, kind, meditative, solicitous, sympathetic, unselfish.
ant.- harsh, repressive, scornful, thoughtless.

Consideration: attention, care, mindfulness, watchfulness, reflection, thought, deliberation, contemplation, rumination.
ant.- disregard, failure, indifference, oversight.

Consign: commit, condemn, delegate, deliver, dispatch, send, ship.
ant.- hold, receive, retain.

Consistent: accordant, regular, compatible, conforming, undeviating, agreeing, harmonious, compatible, uniform, conforming, consonant, constant, equable, coherent, congruous.
ant.- contradictory, contrary, discrepant, incongruous, inconsistent, varying.

Console: cheer, comfort, ease, freshen, gladden, invigorate, soothe, solace.
ant.- depress, grieve, wound, hurt, sadden.

Consolidate: affiliate, fuse, amalgamate, blend, coalesce, combine, compact, compress, condense, conjoin, merge, join, pool, solidify, unite.
ant.- disjoin, disperse, separate.

Conspicuous: clear, apparent, discernible, eminent, patent, perceptible, manifest, notable, noticeable, obvious, plain, prominent, visible.
ant.- concealed, covered, hidden, obscure, unknown, unseen, secret.

Constancy: firmness, fixedness, permanence, reliability, resolution, stability, steadiness.
ant.- capriciousness, fickleness, fluctuation, instability, vacillation.

Constantly: always, continually, eternally, evermore, forever, incessantly, perpetually, unceasingly.
ant.- fitfully, occasionally, never, rarely, sometimes.

Consternation: alarm, awe, dread, fright, dismay, fear, horror, panic, terror.
ant.- calm, peacefulness, quietness, repose, tranquillity.

Constrain: compel, drive, force, oblige, press.
ant.- ask, implore, plead, supplicate.

Constrict: bind, choke, limit, strangle, compress, cramp, hamper, shrink, squeeze, tighten.
ant.- expand, free, loosen, release, untie.

Construct: build, compose, erect, fabricate, form, frame, make, produce.
ant.- demolish, destroy, dismantle, raze.

Consume: use, use up, utilize, spend, employ.
ant.- accumulate, collect, gather, hoard, store.

Consummate: accomplish, end, close, achieve, complete, conclude, execute, finish, fulfil, perfect, terminate, absolute.
ant.- incomplete, second rate, unfinished.

Contagious: catching, noxious, communicable, pestilential, transmitable, contaminative, infectious, epidemic.
ant.- incommunicable.

Contaminate: befoul, dirty, deband, corrupt, debase, defile, deprave, infect, poison, pollute, soil, stain, taint, vitiate.
ant.- disinfect, decontaminate, purify.

Contemplate: think, meditate, muse, ponder, reflect, consider, study, intend, view.
ant.- discard, neglect, reject.

Contemporary: coequal, coeval, synchronous, new, coincident, contemporaneous, current, modern, simultaneous.
ant.- ancient, antiquated, bygone, old, out-of-date, obsolete.

Contempt: derision, disdain, disregard, disrespect, disparagement, mockery, scorn, slight, slur.
ant.- honour, esteem, regard, respect.

Contemptible: depraved, low, degenerate, despicable, mean, scurrilous, sordid, vile.
ant.- admirable, dignified, gracious, pleasing, respectable, worthy.

Contend: battle, combat, cope, compete, contest, dispute, fight, grapple, maintain, struggle, vie.
ant.- cease, cede, desert, halt, stop, quit.

Contention: competition, emulation, rivalry, altercation, animosity, battle, combat, conflict, duel, enmity, feud, fight, struggle, controversy, discord, opposition, quarrel, strife, variance, contest, contestation.
ant.- amity, benevolence, concord, goodwill, harmony, kindness, regard, respect, sympathy.

Contentment: content, delight, ease, gladness, happiness, joy, satisfaction, serenity.
ant.- despair, discomfort, dissent, grief, misery, regret, sadness, sorrow.

Continent: abstemious, self-restrained, austere, abstinent, celibate, ascetic.
ant.- unrestrained, intemperate.

Continual: ceaseless, constant, continuous, endless, incessant, invariable, perpetual, persistent, steady, unbroken, unceasing, uninterrupted, unremitting, repeated, frequent, unvarying.
ant.- checked, concluded, intermittent, interrupted, stopped.

Continuance: continuation, duration, existence, extension, prolongation.
ant.- arrest, finish, hindrance, impediment, stoppage.

Continue: go ahead, maintain, proceed, keep up, uphold, persevere, persist, sustain.
ant.- arrest, check, complete, desist, end, finish, interrupt.

Contradict: correct, belie, controvert, deny, overthrow, demur, disclaim, disprove, oppose, recall, recant, rectify, contravene, refute.
ant.- acquiesce, accept, approve, agree, confirm, sanction, seal, sign, verify, vouch.

Contrary: adverse, antagonistic, opposed, opposite, counter, conflicting, contradictory, counteractive, dissimilar, unlike.
ant.- unopposed, agreeing, alike, similar, correspondent, homogeneous.

Contrast: differentiate, discriminate, distinguish, antithesis, disparity, dissimilarity, divergence, incongruity, variation, difference, opposition, unlikeness.
ant.- unseparatedness, integral unity.

Contravene: violate, hinder, contradict, infringe, oppose, interpose, nullify, obstruct, thwart, void.
ant.- agree, approve, assent, assist, concur, consent.

Contribute: add (to), aid, assist, befriend, benefit, cooperate, donate, favour, furnish, help, share, subscribe, supply.
ant.- counteract, disapprove, harm, ignore, neglect, oppose, shun, withhold.

Contrite: penitent, regretful, remorseful, repentant, sorrowful.
ant.- impenitent, obdurate, remorseless.

Control: command, direct, dominate, guide, govern, hold, manage, regulate, rule, superintend, check.
ant.- abandon, forsake, ignore, relinquish, renounce, resign.

Controversy: altercation, debate, argument, bickering, contention, disagreement, dispute, quarrel, squabble, wrangling.
ant.- agreement, concord, forbearance, harmony, peace, restraint.

Convalesce: improve, rally, recover, recuperate, revive.
ant.- die, fail, falter, regress.

Convene: assemble, collect, congregate, convoke, gather, meet, muster.
ant.- adjourn, disperse, scatter.

Convenient: commodious, accessible, handy, adapted, appropriate, available, suitable, favourable, fitting, opportune.
ant.- inaccessible, inconvenient, inexpedient, troublesome, unsuitable.

Conventional: traditional, accepted, customary, formal, ordinary, orthodox, prevalent, social, stipulated, usual.
ant.- extraordinary, foreign, informal, irregular, strange, unconventional, unusual, unorthodox.

Convergence: assemblage, concourse, confluence, focal, approach, conjunction, point, meeting.
ant.- disjunction, divergence, division.

Convert: adapt, alter, change, metamorphose, modify, shift, transfigure, transform, veer, transmute, turn (from).

ant.- retain, continue, keep, maintain, persist, preserve.

Convey: bear, bring, carry, communicate, impart, transmit, transport.
ant.- hold, keep, preserve, retain.

Convict: criminal, culprit, felon, malefactor, offender, transgressor, censure, condemn, doom, sentence.
ant.- innocent, blameless, guiltless.

Convince: affect, clarify, coax, exhort, induce, influence, persuade, prevail upon, satisfy, sway, touch, win over.
ant.- deprecate, dissuade, warn.

Convivial: cordial, jolly, merry, sociable, gay, cheery.
ant.- dismal, severe, solemn, staid.

Convoke: assemble, call, meet, congregate, collect, convene, gather, muster, summon.
ant.- adjourn, disband, discharge, dismiss, disperse, dissolve, separate.

Convolution: circumvolution, coil, curl, involution, sinuosity, twist, wave, winding line.
ant.- level, surface, straight, line, uncurved.

Convoy: accompany, attend, chaperon, escort, go with, protect, support, guard, watch over.
ant.- abandon, avoid, desert, ignore, leave, neglect, quit.

Cool: calm, chill, ice, freeze, frigid, refrigerate, frosty, gelid, shivery.
ant.- sultry, sunny, warm.

Cooperate: aid, assist, coexist, connive, help, encourage, fraternize, support.
ant.- disturb, encumber, delay, handicap, hinder, impede, prevent.

Copious: abundant, ample, abounding, bountiful, overflowing, exuberant, plentiful, plenteous, profuse, rich.
ant.- deficient, meagre, scant, scarce, sparse.

Cordial: amicable, earnest, friendly, genial, gracious, hearty, heartily, kindly, pleasant, sincere, sociable, warm.
ant.- aloof, cool, hostile, indifferent, inhospitable, taciturn, unfriendly.

Corporal: physical, bodily, anatomical, carnal, corporeal, fleshly, somatic, material.

ant.- immaterial, incorporeal, spiritual.

Corpulent: beefy, fat, fleshy, obese, paunchy, plump, portly, rotund, stocky, stout, thickset.

ant.- gaunt, lean, slender, thin.

Correct: accurate, faultless, impeccable, precise, proper, exact, right, true.

ant.- erroneous, inaccurate, incorrect, false, faulty, untrue, wrong.

Correlation: correspondence, likeness, reciprocation, correlativity, reciprocity, mutuality, interrelation, analogy.

ant.- disparagement, unlikeness, divergence.

Corroborate: affirm, approve, assure, back, certify, confirm, endorse, sanction, support.

ant.- contradict, deny, disallow, disclaim, disprove, oppose, refute.

Corrupt: base, fraudulent, contaminated, contemptible, corrupted, crooked, debased, demoralized, depraved, dishonest, impure, infected, lewd, low, perverted, profligate, putrid, rotten, spoiled, tainted, unprincipled, unscrupulous, venal, vitiated.

ant.- clean, decent, honourable, noble, wholesome, pure.

Corruption: baseness, graft, criminality, degradation, depravity, guiltiness, infamy, perversion, swindling, vice, wickedness.

ant.- honesty, integrity, morality, soundness, uprightness.

Counsel: admonish, advise, apprise, guide, inform, instruct, recommend, suggest, exhort, prescribe.

ant.- conceal, misinform, mislead, withhold.

Count: calculate, compute, enumerate, figure, number, reckon, score, tally.

ant.- conjecture, estimate, guess, miscalculate.

Counterfeit: artificial, bogus, ersatz, fake, false, feigned, fictitious, forged, fraudulent, phony, sham, spurious, synthetic, unreal.

ant.- genuine, natural, real, true.

Couple: join, tie, adjoin, link, unite, brace, yoke, pair, two, marry.

ant.- detach, disconnect, disjoin, separate.

Courage: boldness, bravery, chivalry, daring, dauntlessness, fearlessness, fortitude, mettle, gallantry, hardihood, heroism, intrepidity, prowess, spirit, valour.
ant.- cowardice, timidity, fear, pusillanimity, cowardliness, weakness.

Courteous: affable, agreeable, amiable, cordial, gracious, civil, considerate, cultivated, genteel, mannerly, obliging, polished, polite, refined, suave, urbane, well-bred, well-mannered.
ant.- boorish, discourteous, impertinent, rude, uncivil, uncouth.

Covenant: agreement, alliance, concord, understanding, bargain, compact, contract, pact, stipulation.
ant.- difference, disagreement, variance.

Cover: cloak, conceal, curtain, disguise, envelop, guard, hide, mask, overlay, overspread, protect, screen, shield, veil, comprise, embody, embrace.
ant.- bare, divulge, expose, reveal, uncover, unveil.

Covert: clandestine, concealed, sheltered, disguised, furtive, hidden, secret, sly, underhand, unseen.
ant.- candid, conspicuous, evident, explicit, frank, open, overt, unconcealed, visible.

Covetousness: avarice, craving, cupidity, desire, envy, greed, greediness, jealousy.
ant.- benevolence, generosity, liberality, munificence.

Coward: afraid, chicken-hearted, effeminate, faint-hearted, shy, sissy, spiritless, timid, timorous, poltroon, dastard, sneak, craven, recreant, scared.
ant.- bold, brave, daring, courageous, dauntless.

Crafty: cunning, deceitful, foxy, furtive, guileful, plotting, scheming, shrewd, stealthy, surreptitious, sly, calculating, underhand, wily, tricky.
ant.- candid, ingenuous, honest, simple, undesigning, naive.

Crass: slow-witted, dull, obtuse, stupid, witless, foolish.

ant.- brilliant, intelligent, prudent.

Craving: appetite, desire, longing, passion, yearning.
ant.- disgust, distaste, repugnance.

Crazy: crazed, delirious, demented, frenzied, mad, deranged, idiotic, insane, lunatic, maniacal.
ant.- rational, reasonable, sane, sensible, wise.

Create: cause, engender, form, generate, invent, make, originate, produce, appoint, ordain.
ant.- annihilate, destroy, disband, terminate.

Credible: believable, plausible, probable, reasonable, reliable, trustworthy.
ant.- improbable, incredible, unbelievable, unreliable.

Crime: guilt, sin, atrocity, depravity, felony, immorality, infringement, injustice, misdeed, misdemeanour, offense, outrage, vice, wrong, transgression, wickedness.
ant.- benevolence, benignity, innocence, morality, virtue, uprightness.

Criminal: convict, culprit, vile, sinner, delinquent, felon, malefactor, offender, wrong, transgressor, abominable, blamable, felonious, sinful, vicious, iniquitous.
ant.- faultless, good, honest, innocent, just, legal, sinless, virtuous.

Crisis: critical, juncture, crucial point, emergency, exigency, strait, turning point, extremity, pinch, crux, crunch, climax.
ant.- calm, equilibrium, normality.

Crisp: breakable, brittle, crumbling, fragile, frail, splintery.
ant.- flexible, unbreakable, tough.

Criterion: gauge, yardstick, measure, model, norm, proof, rule, standard, touchstone, test.
ant.- chance, possibility, guess, probability, supposition.

Critical: discerning, acute, discriminating, exacting, fastidious, particular, urgent, captious, carping, caviling, censorious, disapproving, faultfinding, crucial,

decisive, momentous, pressing.
ant.- cursory, superficial, approving, commendatory, encouraging, insignificant, unimportant.

Crooked: abased, adulterated, corrupt, criminal, deceitful, defiled, degraded, depraved, dishonest, fraudulent, law-breaking, bent, bowed, curved, deformed, winding, wry, zigzag.
ant.- honest, law-abiding, mortal, respectable.

Crowd: assembly, horde, mass, mob, multitude, populace, throng, compress, cramp, jostle, press, shove, squeeze, swarm, gathering, concourse.
ant.- secluded place.

Cruel: barbarous, brutal, cold-blooded, ferocious, harsh, inhuman, merciless, pitiless, ruthless, savage, sadistice.
ant.- benevolent, charitable, compassionate, considerate, humane, kind, merciful.

Cull: choose, pick, select, elect, separate, opt, specify.
ant.- refuse, reject.

Culmination: acme, apex, climax, conclusion, height, consummation, crown, end, peak, summit, zenith.
ant.- beginning, inception, base.

Culprit: criminal, delinquent, felon, malefactor, offender, sinner, transgressor, evil-doer, wrongdoer.
ant.- innocent, blameless, guiltless, honest.

Culture: civilization, customs, lifestyle, mores, society, way of life.
ant.- boorishness, ignorance, illiteracy, pretension, stupidity, vulgarity.

Cultured: cultivated, educated, enlightened, polished, refined, well-bred.
ant.- crude, ignorant, simple, uncouth.

Cunning: calculating, crafty, devious, plotting, scheming, sly, artful, clever, shrewd, canny, skillful, tricky.
ant.- honest, clumsy, dull, inept, stupid.

Curb: bridle, check, constrain, control, hinder, hold back, inhabit, limit, repress, restrain, stop, subdue, suppress.
ant.- incite, instigate, aid, encourage.

Curious: examining, inquiring, inquisitive, interesting, interrogative, meddling, prying, searching.

ant.- disinterested, dull, incurious, indifferent, unconcerned.

Cursory: hastily, rapidly, quickly, briskly, swiftly, speedily.

ant.- slowly, unhurriedly.

Curt: abrupt, unexpected, hasty, precipitate, sudden, blunt, brusque, rude, harsh, rough, sharp, snappish, tart.

ant.- gradual, smooth, courteous.

Curtail: abbreviate, clip, cut, abridge, condense, contract, diminish, lessen, limit, reduce, restrict, retrench, shorten.

ant.- elongate, enlarge, extend, lengthen, prolong.

Custom: convention, fashion, habit, manner, mores, practice, precedent, ritual, usage, wont.

ant.- deviation, difference, divergence, irregularity.

Cynical: contemptuous, doubtful, distrustful, pessimistic, petulant, satirical, testy, misanthropic, sneering, sarcastic, cutting, disdainful, censorious.

ant.- believing, calm, good-natured, pleasant.

❑

D

Daily: diurnal, quotidian, everyday, circadian.
ant.- sometimes, occasionally.

Dainty: delicate, tasty, delicious, exquisite, palatable, toothsome.
ant.- tasteless, insipid.

Dally: prolong, dawdle, idle, loiter, loaf, waste time.
ant.- hasten, hurry.

Dam: dike, seawall, levee, break-water, embankment, floodgate.
ant.- open, release, unblock.

Damage: deface, harm, hurt, impair, injure, mar, spoil, detriment, disadvantage, evil, injury, loss.
ant.- enhance, improve, perfect, award, benefit, mend, repair, reward, advantage, recompense.

Damn: criticize, censure, denunciate, condemn, denounce.
ant.- bless, exalt, favour, praise, promote.

Danger: defenselessness, exposure, hazard, insecurity, jeopardy, menace, peril, precariousness, threat, risk.
ant.- carefulness, certainty, confidence, preservation, security, sureness.

Daring: adventurous, brave, audacious, bold, chivalrous, courageous, enterprising, fearless, intrepid, stout-hearted.
ant.- chicken-hearted, cowardly, diffident, hesitating, modest, retiring, shy, timid.

Dark: black, clouded, dim, gloomy, lurid, murky, obscure, opaque, overcast, shady, dusky.
ant.- bright, clear, distinct, illumined, brilliant, pleasant, apparent, transparent, visible.

Daunt: appall, discourage, dishearten, dismay, frighten, intimidate, scare, dash, depress.
ant.- aid, animate, inspire, embolden, encourage, help, stimulate, succour.

Dazzle: amaze, astonish, astound, bewilder, dumfound, daze, impress, overpower.
ant.- befog, dampen, darken.

Dead: deceased, defunct, departed, extinct, gone, inanimate, lifeless, perished, spiritless.

ant.- alive, animate, being, continuing, enduring, existent, existing, living.

Deadly: lethal, fatal, destructful, destructive, mortal, noxious, poisonous, virulent.
ant.- animating, energizing, invigorating, preservative, stimulating, strengthening, wholesome.

Dear: beloved, darling, dearie, honey, sweetheart, costly, exorbitant, expensive, high-priced, valuable.
ant.- unloved, unloving.

Debase: adulterate, degrade, contaminate, corrupt, defile, deprave, pollute, impair, lower, pervert, shame, taint, vitiate.
ant.- purify, refine.

Debt: arrears, charge, debit, deficit, liability, obligation, score, indebtedness.
ant.- asset, excess, overage.

Decay: decompose, dwindle, degenerate, ebb, molder, rot, putrefy, spoil, mortify, wane, waste.
ant.- bloom, flourish, grow, increase, luxuriate, rise.

Deceit: artifice, beguilement, cheating, chicanery, cunning, deceitfulness, deception, delusion, duplicity, falseness, guile, fraud, sham, treachery, trickery.
ant.- authenticity, candour, honesty, openness, sincerity, truthfulness, uprightness.

Deceive: beguile, cheat, circumvent, defraud, delude, dupe, entrap, lie to, mislead, outwit, trick.
ant.- advise, aid, assure, be candid, be frank, be truthful, counsel, help, succour.

Decent: meek, humble, coy, simple, chaste, modest.
ant.- inadequate, indecent, reprehensible, unsuitable, coarse, improper, obscene, lewd, vulgar.

Deception: beguilement, deceit, chicanery, craftiness, cunning, deceitfulness, dishonesty, duplicity, equivocation, fabrication, fraud, falsehood, trickery, guile, prevarication, sham, wiliness.
ant.- candour, frankness, honesty, openness, simplicity, square dealing, sincerity, truthfulness, veracity.

Decide: adjudicate, conclude, determine, judge, resolve, end, settle.

ant.- defer, delay, postpone, procrastinate, suspend, vacillate, wait, waver.

Decision: determination, finding, judgement, outcome, resolution, conclusion, settlement, verdict.
ant.- deferment, delay, indefiniteness, indetermination, postponement, procrastination.

Declaration: affirmation, announcement, assertion, proclamation, profession, avowal, statement.
ant.- denial, retraction, silence.

Decline: descent, droop, slant, slope, decay, decrease, degenerate, depreciate, deteriorate, diminish, dwindle, ebb, fail, lessen, retrogress, sink, wane, weaken.
ant.- incline, improve, increase.

Decompose: decompound, rot, decay, disintegrate, disperse, spoil, putrefy, fester.
ant.- grow, flourish.

Decorate: adorn, beautify, bedeck, embellish, enrich, garnish, ornament, trim.
ant.- strip, uncover.

Decorum: dignity, etiquette, propriety, sedateness, seemliness.
ant.- impropriety, indecency, rudeness.

Decoy: beguile, entice, entrap, lure, seduce, mislead, tempt.
ant.- guide, lead, reveal, show.

Decrease: abate, contract, curtail, decline, deduct, diminish, dwindle, lessen, minimize, narrow, reduce, shorten, shrink, subtract, wane.
ant.- add, develop, dilate, enlarge, expand, extend, grow, increase, widen.

Decry: belittle, blame, censure, condemn, criticize, depreciate, derogate, discredit, disparage.
ant.- acclaim, approve, commend, exalt, extol, magnify.

Dedicate: apportion, bless, consecrate, devote, enshrine, give, hallow, offer, set apart.
ant.- alienate, desecrate, misapply, misconvert, misuse.

Deface: blemish, mutilate, deform, disfigure, impair, mar, spoil.
ant.- restore, mend, repair.

Defeat: beat, checkmate, conquer, thwart, outwit, crush, foil, frustrate, overcome, quell, rout, subdue, subjugate, surmount, triumph, vanquish, whip, win.

ant.- capitulate, cede, lose, retreat, surrender, yield.

Defect: blemish, deficiency, drawback, lack, error, failure, fault, flaw, imperfection, incompleteness.

ant.- advantage, completeness, excellence, faultlessness, perfection.

Defence: guard, protection, ward, safeguard, shelter, shield, vindication.

ant.- abandonment, betrayal, capitulation, desertion, surrender.

Defend: cover, fortify, guard, insure, protect, safeguard, plead, save, screen, secure, shelter, shield, advocate, espouse, justify, maintain, uphold, vindicate.

ant.- abandon, abdicate, attack, desert, forsake, oppose, relinquish, renounce, resign, surrender.

Defer: adjourn, break up, delay, stay, hinder, postpone, procrastinate, put off, restrain, retard, suspend.

ant.- accelerate, advance, expedite, forward, further, hasten, quicken, stimulate.

Deficient: defective, faulty, imperfect, inadequate, incomplete, insufficient, lacking, wanting.

ant.- adequate, perfect, ample, satisfactory, sufficient.

Defile: befoul, contaminate, dirty, tarnish, blacken, corrupt, debauch, infect, seduce, soil, spoil, stain, sully, taint.

ant.- clean, cleanse, disinfect, glorify, purify, sanctify, wash.

Define: describe, determine, elucidate, explain, interpret, specify.

ant.- confuse, derange, distort, mix, tangle, twist.

Definite: certain, circumscribed, clear, definitive, determined, exact, explicit, fixed, limited, positive, precise, specific.

ant.- confused, equivocal, indefinite, indistinct, vague.

Definition: commentary, description, determination, elucidation, explanation, exposition, interpretation, meaning, rendering,

significance, specification.
ant.- absurdity, confusion, nonsense, vagueness.

Deflate: empty, exhaust, void, reduce, puncture.
ant.- blow up, fill, inflate, raise.

Deflect: avert, deviate, diverge, bend, curve, divert, swerve, turn, twist.
ant.- hit, strike.

Deform: contort, cripple, deface, disfigure, distort, impair.
ant.- beautify, improve, perfect, repair.

Deformed: crippled, twisted, disfigured, distorted, malformed, unseemly, unsightly, misshapen.
ant.- graceful, shapely, symmetrical, well-built, well-formed.

Defraud: beguile, cheat, deceive, dupe, fool, gull, hoodwink, overreach, rob, swindle, trick.
ant.- assist, befriend, help, contribute, remunerate, requite, support.

Defray: clear, discharge, pay, liquidate, reimburse, meet, settle.
ant.- deny, disclaim, disown, embezzle, refuse, repudiate.

Deft: adept, adroit, agile, clever, apt, dexterous, expert, handy, nimble, skilful.
ant.- awkward, clumsy, inept, maladroit.

Defy: disobey, contravene, disregard, flont, violate.
ant.- obey, accept, relent, cooperate, yield.

Degenerate: corrupt, debase, debauch, decay, decline, demoralize, depreciate, deteriorate, diminish, dwindle, sink, weaken, worsen.
ant.- ameliorate, ascend, improve, increase.

Degradation: abasement, decline, baseness, regression, debasement, degeneracy, disgrace.
ant.- ascendancy, elevation, exaltation, reward, superiority.

Degrade: abase, abash, demean, corrupt, crush, debase, demote, discredit, humble, humiliate, mortify, shame, subdue, vitiate.
ant.- elevate, exalt, honour, praise.

Dejection: depression, despair, despondency, discontent, gloom, heaviness, melancholy, pensiveness, sadness, sorrow.
ant.- delight, exhilaration,

cheer, gaiety, hilarity, joy, merriment.

Delay: defer, retard, postpone, put off, arrest, detain, hinder, impede, prolong, protect, stay, dally, dawdle, linger, procrastinate, loiter, tarry.
ant.- dispatch, expedite, facilitate, hasten, precipitate, quicken.

Delectable: agreeable, delightful, exquisite, gratifying, pleasing, enjoyable, pleasurable, pleasant.
ant.- distressfull, distressing, grievous, painful.

Deleterious: bad, injurious, baleful, base, damaging, deadly, destructive, evil, harmful, hurtful, immoral, iniquitous, noxious, pernicious, poisonous, sinful, unsound, unwholesome, villainous, wicked.
ant.- advantageous, healthful, helpful, honourable, moral, reputable, salutary.

Deliberate: considered, designed, intentional, judged, pondered, prudent, reasoned, studied, thoughtful, unhurried, weighed.
ant.- careless, imprudent, hasty, unintentional, discard, neglect, reject.

Delicate: dainty, fastidious, feeble, fine, fragile, frail, slender, slight, soft, tender, weak.
ant.- boisterous, clumsy, coarse, depraved, indelicate, robust, rude, vulgar.

Delicious: appetizing, dainty, toothsome, delectable, sweet, delightful, gratifying, luscious, palatable, pleasing, savoury, tasteful.
ant.- distasteful, nauseous, acrid, unpalatable, unsavoury.

Delightful: agreeable, alluring, charming, enjoyable, glad, gratifying, inspiring, merry, pleasant, pleasing, pleasurable, satisfactory.
ant.- depressing, mournful, offensive, painful, wearisome.

Delirium: aberration, dementia, frenzy, hallucination, insanity, lunacy, madness, mania, raving.
ant.- normality, saneness, sanity.

Deliver: convey, give, hand over, distribute, transport, impart, surrender, transfer, yield, announce, proclaim,

communicate, free, impart, pronounce, discharge, save, emancipate, liberate, rescue, redeem, release.
ant.- convince, withhold, betray, capture, imprison, restrain, restrict.

Delusion: chimera, deception, error, fallacy, fantasy, hallucination, illusion, mirage, misconception, phantom.
ant.- actuality, certainty, fact, materiality, reality, substance, truth.

Demand: ask, beg, beseech, charge, crave, exact, implore, inquire, levy, order, request, require, seek, solicit, supplicate.
ant.- give, offer, present, reply, tender.

Demented: crazy, frenzied, insane, irrational, lunatic, maniacal.
ant.- lucid, normal, rational, reasonable, sane.

Demise: death, decease, end, bereavement, expiration, dying.
ant.- birth, rise, growth.

Demolish: annihilate, destroy, devastate, dismantle, eradicate, exterminate, extinguish, level, obliterate, overturn, ravage, raze, ruin, wreck, wipe out.
ant.- construct, embellish, improve, mend, restore, uphold.

Demonstration: certainty, show, consequence, corroboration, deduction, evidence, exhibition, explanation, exposition, induction, manifestation, proof, rally, presentation, conclusion, verification, substantiation.
ant.- concealment, distortion, falsification, misrepresentation.

Demoralize: disorganize, dishearten, pervert, dispirit, disconcert, discourage, incapacitate, undermine.
ant.- encourage, hearten, exalt, inspire, invigorate, organize.

Demur[1] : balk, delay, object, disapprove, dissent, falter, hesitate, pause, scruple, vacillate, waver.
ant.- accept, agree, assent, consent, decide, persevere, proceed.

Demure[2] : coy, decorous, diffident, modest, prim, prudish, sedate, shy, sober, staid.
ant.- impudent, indecorous, shameless, wanton.

Denounce: accuse, arraign, blame, censure, charge, condemn, curse, decry, indict, reprehend, reprimand, scold, reproach, reprove, upbraid, vilify.
ant.- applaud, commend, praise.

Dense: compact, compressed, concentrated, crowded, close, impenetrable, thick, thickest.
ant.- dispersed, open, rare, scattered, sparse, thin.

Deny: contradict, contravene, gainsay, oppose, rebuff, disprove, discover, refute, abjure, disavow, disclaim, disown, forbid, renounce, refuse, repudiate, withhold.
ant.- admit, affirm, agree, assert, concede, confirm.

Depart: decamp, go, leave, quit, retire, set out, exit, move out, withdraw.
ant.- abide, dwell, linger, remain, stay, tarry.

Dependable: certain, reliable, sure, trustworthy, trusty.
ant.- questionable, uncertain, unreliable, untrustworthy.

Dependent: contingent, relative, reliant, relying, subject.
ant.- absolute, autonomous, independent.

Depict: delineate, draw, illustrate, paint, picture, portray, sketch.
ant.- caricature, confound, confuse, distort.

Deplete: empty, exhaust, lessen, evacuate.
ant.- augment, enlarge, fill, increase, strengthen.

Deplore: regret, be sorry (for), complain, cry (for), grieve, deprecate, lament, mourn, wail, weep.
ant.- boast, cheer, delight, rejoice, revel.

Deposit: hoard, lay down, pledge, place, save, store.
ant.- withdraw, draw out, take away.

Depravity: corruption, degeneracy, depravation, deterioration, immorality, sinfulness, wickedness, turpitude, degradation, perversion.
ant.- integrity, justice, morality, purity, virtue.

Deprecate: condemn, blame, disapprove, censure, damn, up braid.
ant.- approve, praise, applaud.

Depreciate: decrease, deflate, devaluation, devalue, underrate, undervalue.

ant.- increase, magnify, raise, grow.

Depress: abase, debase, lower, degrade, deject, discourage, disgrace, dispirit, humble, humiliate, sink.

ant.- cheer, comfort, praise, encourage, stimulate.

Depression: despair, dejection, gloominess, hopelessness, melancholy, misery.

ant.- contentment, elation, hope, light-heartedness.

Deprive: abridge, bereave, strip, debar, depose, despoil, dispossess, divest, separate.

ant.- assist, confer, endow, enrich, repay, restore.

Derelict: neglected, wrecked, delinquent, negligent, cast-away, stranded, deserted, abandoned.

ant.- accepted, admitted, sanctioned.

Derision: contempt, disdain, disregard, disrespect, insult, irony, jeering, mockery, raillery, ridicule, sarcasm, scorn, slight, slur, sneering.

ant.- adulation, flattery, regard, respect, reference, applaud, praise.

Derivation: beginning, birth, cause, commencement, cradle, foundation, fountain, inception, nucleus, origin, rise, root, source, spring.

ant.- consequence, end, harvest, issue, out-growth, termination.

Derogatory: belittling, defamatory, deprecatory, disparaging, humiliating.

ant.- favouring, helping, lauding, praising.

Descent: debasement, slant, fall, degradation, decline, declivity, slope, descension, declension, declination, inclination.

ant.- ascension, ascent, climb, elevation, rise.

Describe: characterize, define, delineate, explain, express, illustrate, narrate, recite, recount, relate, represent.

ant.- confuse, misrepresent, deceive, exaggerate, distort.

Desecrate: abuse, debase, defile, misuse, pervert, pollute, profane, secularize.

ant.- cleanse, consecrate, hallow, purify, sanctify.

Desert: wasteland, wilderness, waste, solitude, abandon, abdicate, abjure, forsake, leave, quit, relinquish, secede, surrender, vacate.

ant.- garden, oasis, pasture.

Designate: appoint, choose, characterize, denominate, denote, indicate, point out, manifest, name, select, show, signify, specify.
ant.- discharge, dismiss, terminate.

Desire: affection, ambition, appetite, ardour, aspiration, concupiscence, coveting, craving, eagerness, wish, zeal, hungering, inclination, longing, yearning.
ant.- abhorrence, aversion, detestation, repulsion, distaste.

Desirable: acceptable, liked, advisable, agreeable, proper, delightful, enviable, pleasing, profitable, wanted, worthy.
ant.- undesirable, disliked, unwanted, unwished.

Desist: abstain, arrest, bar, cease, give up, leave off, discontinue, drop, end, halt, impede, obstruct, quit, relinquish, seal, stop, terminate.
ant.- continue, endure, wait, proceed, retain.

Desolate: abandoned, alone, bare, bereaved, bleak, dejected, deserted, dismal, dreary, forgotten, forlorn, forsaken, inhospitable, lonely, miserable, secluded, solitary, uninhabited, unpeopled.
ant.- cultivated, enjoyable, fertile, inhabited, pleasant, teeming.

Despair: dejection, depression, desperation, misery, gloom, despondency, discouragement, hopelessness, pessimism, sadness.
ant.- hope, expectation, elation, anticipation, confidence, faith, optimism.

Desperate: despairing, dejected, forlorn, woebegone, despondent, hopeless.
ant.- cautious, composed, confident, hopeful, peaceful, satisfied.

Despicable: abject, base, low, corrupt, contemptible, vile, cowardly, depraved, lying, malicious, nasty, mean, scurrilous, shameless, sordid, worthless.
ant.- exalted, honourable, noble, praise, respectable.

Despise: abhor, abominate, condemn, denounce, deride, detest, disdain, dislike, loathe, scorn, spurn.
ant.- admire, applaud, cherish, commend, love.

Despondent: dejected, low, depressed, despairing, disconsolate, disheartened, dispirited, doleful, melancholy, sad, downcast, wretched, discouraged, prostrate.
ant.- buoyant, ebullient, elated, happy, joyous.

Despotic: absolute, arbitrary, arrogant, autocratic, cruel, tyrannical, tyrant, dictator, autocrat, tyrannous.
ant.- mild, conditional, constitutional, limited, reasonable.

Destiny: chance, doom, fate, fortune, predestination, lot, portion, predetermination.
ant.- choice, freedom, volition, will.

Destitution: beggary, lack, indigence, need, pauperism, penury, poverty, privation, want.
ant.- abundance, affluence, opulence, prosperity, security.

Destroy: annihilate, consume, demolish, devastate, raze, dismantle, dispel, eradicate, exterminate, extirpate, kill, obliterate, overthrow, ravage, ruin, slaughter, terminate.
ant.- construct, fabricate, invigorate, renew, strengthen.

Destruction: abolishment, annihilation, cataclysm, demolition, desolation, devastation, downfall, eradication, extermination, extinction, extirpation, havoc, obliteration, overthrow, subversion.
ant.- recovery, renewal, restitution, restoration, revival.

Desultory: abnormal, loose, discursive, erratic, flighty, irregular, rambling, unsettled.
ant.- steady, constant, firm, methodical, unalterable, stable.

Detach: disconnect, disengage, disjoin, disunite, unfix, part, untie, remove, cut off, cleaver, sunder, separate, sever, unfasten, withdraw.
ant.- adhere, bind, coalesce, link, merge.

Detail: describe, itemize, narrate, particularize, relate, report, tell, account, article, description, item, minutia, narrative, particular, portion, recital, specification, trifle.
ant.- conceal, reserve, stifle, suppress.

Detain: arrest, check, confine, bar, keep, restrain.
ant.- free, hasten, liberate, release.

Detect: ascertain, disclose, discover, espy, expose, ferret out, find out, identify, perceive, uncover, unearth, unmask.
ant.- blunder, miss, omit, overlook, pass by.

Deter: restrain, discourage, disincline, prohibit, put off, disusage, hinder, prevent, stop, warn.
ant.- encourage, promote, stimulate, urge.

Deteriorate: degenerate, atrophy, collapse, corrode, decay, decline, decompose, discolour, disintegrate, ebb, erode, mold, oxidize, recede, retrogress, rot, rust, wane, wear.
ant.- improve, refurbish, renew.

Determined: decided, firm, fixed, immovable, resolute, stable, stubborn, unalterable, unwavering, willful.
ant.- irresolute, fluctuating, uncertain, undecided, wavering.

Detest: abhor, abominate, despise, dislike, execrate, hate, loathe.
ant.- admire, appreciate, cherish, love, respect.

Detour: by way, deviation, by-pass indirect course, side road digression.
ant.- direct route, highway.

Detraction: aspersion, back biting, calumny, defamation, depreciation, derogation, disparagement, libel, slander, vilification.
ant.- admiration, respect, praise, recommendation.

Detriment: damage, harm, deterioration, disadvantage, hurt, impairment, injury, loss.
ant.- advantage, assistance, benefit, gain, profit.

Devastate: demolish, desolate, despoil, pillage, ruin, waste, wreck, ravage, raze, destroy.
ant.- benefit, cultivate, enrich, preserve, restore.

Develop: amplify, cultivate, enlarge, evolve, expand, extend, grow, mature.
ant.- compress, conceal, contract, hide, restrict.

Development: expansion, evolution, growth, improvement, maturing, progress.
ant.- compression, decline, curtailment, degeneration.

Deviate: deflect, diverge, divert, shift, shunt, sidetrack, stray, swerve, wander.
ant.- continue, persevere, direct, persist, remain.

Devious: circuitous, crooked, indirect, mazy, roundabout, swerving, tortuous, wandering, winding.
ant.- direct, straightforward, straight.

Devise: arrange, bequeath, concoct, contrive, invent, make, plan, prepare, will.
ant.- disarrange, fumble, muddle.

Devoid: bare, destitute, empty, sans, lacking, unendowed, unprovided, void, wanting, without.
ant.- abundant, complete, full, possessing, replete.

Devolve: alienate, be handed down, commission, consign, transfer, depute, deliver, fall (upon).
ant.- take back.

Devote: allot, apportion, assign, consign, consecrate, dedicate, give to, employ at, destine.
ant.- return, take back.

Devotion: consecration, Godliness, dedication, devoutness, fidelity, piety, religiousness, sincerity.
ant.- alienation, apathy, aversion, indifference, neglect, unfaithfulness.

Devour: bolt, consume, eat, wolf down, gobble, gorge, prey upon, swallow (up), waste.
ant.- disgorge, vomit.

Devout: devotional, earnest, religious, worshipping, fervent, Godly, holy, moral, pietistic, pious, reverent, righteous, sacred, sincere, spiritual.
ant.- theistic, impious, profane, secular, worldly.

Dexterity: ability, adroitness, aptitude, aptness, art, capability, cleverness, deftness, facility, handiness, skill.
ant.- awkwardness, ineptitude, blundering, clumsiness.

Dialect: accent, idiom, jargon, argot, patois, provincialism, vernacular.
ant.- official language, standard, decree, prescribe.

Dictatorial: dogmatic, arbitrary, domineering, imperious, tyrannical, opinionated, despotic.

ant.- acquiescent, docile, obsequious, submissive, subservient, passive.

Die: decease, demise, expiration, expire, pass away, perish.
ant.- live, survive, begin, endure, flourish, grow.

Difference: deviation, variety, discrepancy, disparity, dissimilarity, variation, distinction, divergence, inequality, separation.
ant.- congruity, similarity, uniformity.

Different: differing, discordant, disparate, eclectic, dissimilar, distinct, distinctive, diverse, heterogeneous, incongruous, unlike, variant, various.
ant.- alike, congruous, same, harmonious, homogeneous.

Differentiate: contrast, set off, set apart, discriminate, isolate, distinguish, particularize, separate.
ant.- confound, group, mingle.

Difficult: arduous, complex, complicated, enigmatical, hard, tough, intricate, involved, laborious, obscure, perplexing, puzzling, rigid, toilsome, troublesome, irksome, trying, unmanageable, unyielding.
ant.- easy, facile, pleasant, simple.

Difficulty: annoyance, anxiety, complication, contention, dilemma, embarrassment, entanglement, impediment, intricacy, obstacle, obstruction, perplexity, problem, trouble, worry.
ant.- comfort, facility, felicity, flexibility, pleasure, satisfaction.

Diffident: bashful, hesitant, modest, shrinking, shy, timid.
ant.- bold, brash, brazen.

Diffuse: scatter, spread, sprinkle, disperse.
ant.- abbreviated, brief, restricted.

Diffusion: broadcasting, circulation, distribution, dispersion, spreading.
ant.- collection, restriction, suppression.

Dignify: adorn, advance, exalt, award, decorate, elevate, ennoble, extol, glorify, honour, magnify, prefer, proclaim, promote.
ant.- belittle, degrade, demean, humiliate, slander.

Dignity: decency, decorum, nobility, eminence, grace,

greatness, propriety, stateliness, worth.

ant.- degradation, lowliness.

Digress: bend, deflect, depart, deviate, diverge, divert, ramble, sidetrack, stray, turn aside, wander.

ant.- continue, persevere, persist, preserve.

Dilapidated: crumbled, battered, broken-down, tumbleddown, ramshackled, decayed.

ant.- rebuilt, renewed, restored.

Dilate: broaden, distend, enlarge, expand, extend, increase, magnify, open, spread, stretch, swell, widen.

ant.- abridge, compress, contract, diminish, reduce.

Dilemma: doubt, difficulty, fix, perplexity, predicament, problem, quandary.

ant.- advantage, freedom, solution.

Diligence: alertness, activity, application, assiduity, attention, care, carefulness, earnestness, heed, industry, intensity, keenness, perseverance, quickness.

ant.- ennui, indolence, laziness, lethargy, slowness..

Dilute: reduce, thin, watery, make thinner, weak.

ant.- concentrated, rich, strong, thick.

Dim: blurred, clouded, dull, giant, gloomy, indefinite, indistinct, misty, obscure, shaded, showy.

ant.- bright, brilliant, clear.

Diminish: abate, abridge, assuage, compress, contract, curtail, decrease, degrade, dwindle, impair, lessen, lower, minimize, moderate, reduce, shorten, shrink.

ant.- amplify, enlarge, increase, intensify, magnify.

Din: clamour, clangour, clash, clatter, hubbub, noise, racket, row, tumult, uproar.

ant.- quiet, silence, stillness.

Diplomatic: artful, courteous, discreet, judicious, politic, tactful.

ant.- blunt, gruff, rude, tactless.

Direct: guide, indicate, head, inform, instruct, lead, manage, order, regulate, supervise, teach, usher.

ant.- deceive, delude, misdirect, misguide.

Dirty: dingy, discoloured, filthy, foul, grimy, muddy, soiled, accolade, indecent, obscene, sordid, base, contemptible, despicable, low, mean, shabby.

ant.- clean, immaculate, spotless, pure, wholesome.

Disability: disqualification, impotence, inability, incompetence, unfitness, weakness.
ant.- ability, capability, capacity.

Disadvantage: detriment, loss, injury, damage, evil, harm, hurt, prejudice.
ant.- advantage, assistance, benefit, profit, utility.

Disagree: differ, dispute, dissent, fight, oppose, quarrel, vary.
ant.- agree, coincide, concur, harmonize.

Disappear: dissolve, vanish, evaporate, fade, melt away, pass, evanesce.
ant.- appear, materialize.

Disappoint: dishearten, fail, frustrate, dismay, let down.
ant.- content, befriend, please, support, relieve, satisfy.

Disapproval: disapprobation, unacceptance, rejection, disallowance.
ant.- approval, sanction.

Disaster: adversity, calamity, casualty, cataclysm, catastrophe, misadventure, mischance, misfortune, mishap, tragedy.
ant.- advantage, fortune.

Disband: break up, demobilize, disperse, dissolve, dismantle, split.
ant.- collect, deposit, receive, retain, save.

Discard: abandon, cancel, cast off, throw aside, discharge, dismiss, divorce, eliminate, reject, repudiate, scrap, shed.
ant.- adopt, embrace, keep, retain.

Discern: descry, detect, discover, discriminate, distinguish, espy, know, observe, perceive, recognize, see, understand.
ant.- disregard, neglect, omit, overlook, slight.

Discerning: acute, ingenious, discriminating, sharp witted, wise, astute, shrewd.
ant.- cursory, shallow, superficial, uncritical.

Discernment: acumen, discrimination, insight, judgment, penetration, perspicuity.
ant.- obtuseness.

Discharge: acquit, clear, deselect, dismiss, eject, emit, exile, expel, free, oust, release, retire.

ant.- load, hire, imprison, retain.

Disciple: adherent, devotee, follower, votary, pupil, catechumen.
ant.- guru, leader, master, teacher.

Discipline: control, regimen, order, regulation, restraint, drill, instruction, method, rule, training, chastisement.
ant.- chaos, confusion, disorder, mutiny, turbulence.

Disclaim: abandon, deny, disallow, disavow, disown, reject, renounce, repudiate.
ant.- acknowledge, claim, own, recognize.

Disclose: betray, declare, discover, divulge, expose, grant, inform, reveal, show, tell, uncover, unfold, unmask, unveil, utter.
ant.- cloak, conceal, cover, withhold.

Disconsolate: broken-hearted, comfortless, hopeless, cheerless, dejected, depressed, despondent, dismal, doleful, gloomy, inconsolable, lugubrious, melancholy, mournful, sad, sorrowful.
ant.- cheerful, glad, happy, joyous, merry.

Discontent: disappointment, displeasure, illusionment, inquietude, dissatisfaction, soreness, uneasiness, vexation.
ant.- content, peace, satisfaction.

Discord: animosity, clash, confusion, contention, difference, disagreement, disharmony, dissension, dissonance, disturbance, harshness, quarrelling, variance, wrangling.
ant.- agreement, amity, concord, harmony.

Discount: allowance, rebate, deduction, reduction, drawback.
ant.- increase, increment, premium, rise.

Discourage: dismay, let-dowm, unnerve, dampen, depress, dishearten, dispirit.
ant.- inspire, encourage, promote.

Discourteous: abusive, vulgar, uncourteous, blunt, boorish, disrespectful, ill-mannered, impolite, impudent, insolent, rough, rude, surly, uncivil, ungracious, unmannerly.
ant.- civil, courteous, genteel, polished, polite.

Discover: ascertain, contrive, descry, detect, disclose, elicit, expose, espy, find, find out, invent, learn, manifest, realize, reveal, uncover, unearth.
ant.- cover, hide, suppress, mask, screen.

Discreet: attentive, careful, wise, cautious, circumspect, considerate, discerning, judicious, sensible, prudent, serious, thoughtful, watchful.
ant.- indiscreet, injudicious, rash, thoughtless.

Discrepancy: contrariety, difference, disagreement, inconsistency, variance.
ant.- accordance, agreement, concurrence, harmony.

Discretion: carefulness, caution, consideration, discernment, circumspection, finesse, foresight, judgment, prudence, sagacity, thoughtfulness.
ant.- foolishness, imprudence, recklessness, thoughtlessness, rashness.

Discrimination: differentiation, difference, distinction, foresight, forethought, heed, perception, perspicacity, prudence, sagacity, vigilance.
ant.- harmony, concord, amity.

Disdain: arrogance, contempt, contumely, derision, pride, detestation, haughtiness, scorn, scornfulness, superciliousness.
ant.- admiration, esteem, regard, respect, reverence.

Disease: affliction, ailment, ailing, disorder, distemper, illness, infirmity, malady, plague, pestilence, sickness, unhealthiness, unsoundness.
ant.- health, healthiness, soundness, sturdiness, vigour.

Disengage: extricate, detach, disentangle, free, liberate, loose, loosen, cut loose, separate, release, unravel, withdraw.
ant.- attach, bind, fasten, tighten, unite.

Disfigure: disfeature, deface, deform, distort, injure, mar, mutilate, blemish, spoil.
ant.- adorn, decorate, repair, restore.

Disgrace: abasement, odium, baseness, disfavour, infamy, dishonour, disrepute, shame, humiliation, ignominy, mortification, opprobrium, scandal, reproach.

ant.- dignity, exaltation, glory, honour, renown, respect.

Disguise: camouflage, cloak, conceal, cover, dissemble, feign, hide, mask, screen, secrete, shroud, suppress, veil, withhold.

ant.- bare, disclose, divulge, expose, reveal, uncover.

Disgust: abhorrence, hatred, abomination, aversion, detestation, dislike, distaste, loathing, nausea, repugnance, revulsion.

ant.- admiration, approbation, esteem, respect, reverence.

Dishonest: cheating, corrupt, corruptible, false, crooked, debased, deceitful, fraudulent, lying, perfidious, unsound, unscrupulous, untrue, venal, untrustworthy, vitiated.

ant.- honest, scrupulous, trustworthy.

Dislike: abhorrence, antipathy, aversion, disaffection, disapproval, disinclination, distaste, hatred, loathing, repugnance, repulsion.

ant.- affection, attachment, devotion.

Disloyal: disloyal, apostate, disaffected, faithless, false, perfidious, unfaithful, unpatriotic.

ant.- faithful, loyal, true, worthy.

Dismal: bleak, cheerless, depressing, doleful, dolorous, dreadful, dreary, dull, sad, funereal, gloomy, horrible, horrid, melancholy, somber, sorrowful, unhappy.

ant.- bright, cheerful, joyous, pleasant.

Dismantle: demolish, raze, strip, take apart, take down.

ant.- assemble, construct, build, raise.

Dismay: alarm, anxiety, apprehension, misgiving, awe, consternation, horror, fright, discouragement, dread, fear, trepidation.

ant.- assurance, confidence, courage, intrepidity.

Dismiss: banish, depose, discard, discharge, expel, oust, remove, repudiate, suspend.

ant.- accept, obey, submit.

Disorder: anarchy, confusion, derangement, chaos, jumble, disarrangement, muddle,

disorganization, disturbance, indisposition, irregularity, tumult.
ant.- order, organization, system, vigour.

Disorderly: chaotic, confused, disheveled, irregular, lawless, tumultuous, unrestrained, unruly.
ant.- disciplined, organised, neat, orderly.

Disparage: asperse, belittle, decry, defame, deprecate, depreciate, derogate, lower, discredit, dishonour, traduce, minimize.
ant.- aggrandize, commend, magnify, praise, sanction, exalt.

Dispatch: communicate, send, consign, convey, direct, remit, forward, transmit.
ant.- hold, retain, slow.

Dispel: banish, dismiss, disperse, dissipate, dissolve, scatter.
ant.- accumulate, amass, assemble, collect, gather.

Dispense: administer, allocate, allot, apportion, assign, distribute, dole out, mete.
ant.- absorb, keep, retain, withhold.

Disperse: diffuse, disseminate, dissipate, distribute, scatter, sow, strew, stud, broadcast, shed, spread, overspread.
ant.- amass, assemble, collect, concentrate, gather.

Displace: crowd out, depose, derange, disarrange, eject, discharge, dislocate, jumble, disestablish, dislodge, dismiss, displant, dispossess, mislay, misplace, mix, remove, shift, unseat, unsettle, uproot.
ant.- arrange, classify, group, sort.

Display: exhibit, expose, flaunt, open, parade, reveal, show, unfold, evince, manifest, array, demonstrate, flourish, layout, manifest.
ant.- conceal, cover, disguise, hide.

Displease: anger, annoy, antagonize, bother, chagrin, disappoint, disgruntle, disgust, dissatisfy, exasperate, gall, harass, irritate, mortify, pester, pique, plague, taunt, tease, trouble, vex, worry.
ant.- delight, gratify, pacify, propitiate, satisfy.

Dispose: adjust, arrange, bestow, classify, conform, give, locate, order, place, regulate, settle.

ant.- disarrange, disorder, displace, retain.

Disposition: arrangement, disposal, classification, distribution, order, state.

ant.- disorder, derangement.

Dispute: altercation, argument, contention, contest, debate, controversy, discord, quarrel, dissension, estrangement, feud, questioning, squabble, variance.

ant.- agreement, concord, harmony, unison.

Disqualify: disable, unfit, invalidate, disenfranchise, incapacitate.

ant.- accept, fit, qualify.

Disregard: contemn, disobey, ignore, neglect, overlook, omit, defy, slight.

ant.- include, notice, regard.

Disrespectful: contemptuous, discourteous, disparaging, flippant, impertinent, impious, impolite, insolent, insulting, derisive, irreverent, uncivil.

ant.- courteous, respectful.

Dissatisfaction: displeasure, disappointment, discontent, disgruntlement, malcontentment.

ant.- contentment, gratification, happiness, satisfaction.

Dissect: anatomize, cut up, analyze, examine.

ant.- assemble, synthesize.

Dissent: censure, condemn, conflict, contend, differ, disagree, disapprove, vary, disclaim, oppose, dissension, dissidence, discordance, discord.

ant.- agree, commend, concur, endorse, sanction.

Dissipate: debauch, diffuse, disperse, lavish, scatter, spread, squander, waste.

ant.- absorb, accumulate, conserve, preserve, save.

Dissolve: disappear, render, disintegrate, liquefy, break up, melt, evanesce, evaporate, fade, thaw, vanish.

ant.- assemble, concentrate, unite.

Distant: afar, apart, far, far off, remote, indistinct, removed, far away, out of the way.

ant.- close, near.

Distasteful: unpleasant, disagreeable, disgusting, displeasing, loathsome, nauseating, objectionable, obnoxious, offensive,

repellent, repugnant, repulsive, unpalatable, unsavoury.
ant.- agreeable, delectable, pleasing, savoury, welcome.

Distend: blow up, dilate, expand, grow, inflate, stretch, swell, tumefy.
ant.- constrict, contract, shrink, narrow.

Distinct: detached, different, discrete, dissimilar, individual, unattached, unconnected, separate.
ant.- indistinct, similar.

Distinction: difference, variety, separateness, variation, disparity, dissimilarity.
ant.- congruity, similarity, uniformity.

Distinguished: brilliant, great, celebrated, conspicuous, well-known, noted, notable, eminent, extraordinary, famous, glorious, illustrious, prominent, renowned.
ant.- common, unknown, unobtrusive.

Distort: bend, contort, deface, deform, disfigure, falsify, gnarl, slant, impair, mangle, misconstrue, misshape, warp, pervert, twist, wrest, writhe, mutilate.
ant.- align, balance, explain, straighten.

Distract: bewilder, confound, confuse, derange, disorder, embarrass, mislead, mystify, daze, perplex.
ant.- allay, assure, mitigate, pacify, reassure.

Distress: adversity, agony, anguish, discomfort, grief, hardship, misadventure, misery, misfortune, pain, sorrow, suffering, torment, trouble, unhappiness, wretchedness.
ant.- comfort, joy, relief, satisfaction.

Distribution: allotment, deal, apportionment, arrangement, classification, dispensation, disposal, division, dole, sharing, partition.
ant.- collection, maintenance, hoard, retention, storage.

Distrust: disbelief, doubt, misgiving, mistrust, skepticism, suspicion, uncertainty.
ant.- belief, certainty, faith, conviction, trust.

Disturb: bother, interrupt, perturb, rouse, trouble, unsettle, disrupt, interfere.
ant.- compose, pacify, quiet, settle, soothe.

Divergent: branching, diverse, contrary, deviating, differing, disagreeing, separation, varying.
ant.- convergent, identical, parallel, similar.

Diverse: contrary, different, dissimilar, distinct, divergent, diversified, heterogeneous, unlike, varied, variant, miscellaneous, numerous, several, sundry, various.
ant.- alike, identical, same, similar.

Divest: deprive, dismantle, disrobe, peel, strip, unclothe, uncover, undress.
ant.- clothe, cover, invest, restore (property).

Divide: detach, disconnect, disengage, disjoin, disunite, partition, separate, sever, allot, split, sunder, apportion, dispense, distribute.
ant.- combine, convene, fasten, join, unite.

Divine: celestial, Godlike, heavenly, sacred, sanctified, spiritual, superhuman, holy, supernatural, transcendent, angelic.
ant.- blasphemous, diabolical, impious, profane, wicked.

Division: allotment, share, compartment, department, detachment, difference, schism, disunion, partition, portion, severance, separation, disjunction, apportionment.
ant.- concord, indivisibility, oneness, union, unity.

Divulge: describe, disclose, discover, expose, impart, inform, let slip, relate, reveal, show, tell, uncover, unveil.
ant.- cloak, conceal, disguise, hide.

Do: accomplish, achieve, complete, effect, conclude, finish, consummate, execute, fulfil, perform, carry on, make, produce, contrive, work, manage.
ant.- evade, shirk.

Docile: amenable, compliant, gentle, manageable, meek, mild, obedient, pliable, pliant, submissive, tame, tractable, teachable, yielding.
ant.- determined, mulish, obstinate, stubborn, unyielding.

Dodge: avoid, elude, duck, escape, equivocate, evade, sidestep.
ant.- approach, confront, encounter, face, meet.

Dogmatic: arrogant, doctrinal, authoritarian, dictatorial, doctrinaire, domineering, imperious, magisterial, opinionated, over-bearing, peremptory, authoritative.
ant.- liberal, generous.

Domestic: homely, gentle, household, internal, native, tame.
ant.- foreign, untamed, wild.

Dominant: authoritative, commanding, controlling, domineering, governing, imperative, imperious, lordly, predominant, prevailing, ruling.
ant.- humble, non-aggressive, obscure, retiring, subordinate.

Dominion: ascendancy, sway, authority, commonwealth, control, government, jurisdiction, country, power, district, empire, region, territory.
ant.- bondage, dependency, inferiority, subjection, submission.

Donation: benefaction, bequest, bounty, charity, contribution, endowment, gift, grant, boon, gratuity, largess, present, provision, subscription.
ant.- deprivation, loss.

Done: achieved, completed, concluded, consummated, ended, executed, finished, over, performed, solved.
ant.- inchoate, incomplete, partial, raw, unfinished.

Dormant: inactive, inert, quiescent, sleeping, unconscious, unoccupied.
ant.- active, alert, awake.

Double: pairs, twice, duplicate, stand-in, bipartite, coupled, dual, binate, duplex, paired, twin, two-fold.
ant.- lone, single, unique.

Doubt: suspect, mistrust, query, misgive, disbelief, distrust, dubiousness, hesitancy, hesitation, incredulity, indecision, irresolution, misgiving, mistrust, perplexity, qualm, quandary, question, scruple, skepticism, suspense, suspicion, unbelief, uncertainty.
ant.- assurance, belief, certainty, conviction, faith.

Draw: drag, haul, pull, tow, tug, extract, remove, take out, unsheathe, depict, sketch, trace, compose, formulate, draft, write, conclude, deduce, derive,

infer, extend, protract, lengthen, prolong, stretch.
ant.- alienate, rebuff, reject, repel, repulse.

Drawback: disadvantage, problem, defect, detriment, flaw, hindrance, injury, rebate.
ant.- advantage, benefit, extra, premium.

Dread: alarm, anxiety, awe, apprehension, consternation, dismay, fear, fright, horror, misgiving, panic, terror, trepidation.
ant.- boldness, bravery, confidence, courage.

Dreadful: appalling, awful, dire, shocking, fearful, formidable, frightful, ghastly, horrible, terrible.
ant.- beautiful, enchanting, enjoyable, lovely.

Dream: chimera, delusion, fallacy, fancy, fantasy, hallucination, illusion, imagination, nightmare, reverie.
ant.- actuality, materiality, reality, solidity, verity.

Dreary: bleak, cheerless, dark, depressing, discouraging, disheartening, dismal, doleful, dull, funereal, gloomy, somber, lonesome, melancholy, sad, wearisome.
ant.- cheerful, joyous, lively.

Dress: apparel, appearance, array, attire, clothing, garb, costume, drapery, frock, robes, garments, gown, habiliments, raiment, uniform, vestments, vesture.
ant.- bareness, disarray, nakedness, nudity, disrobe, strip.

Drive: move, steer, ride, run, actuate, conduct, control, direct, guide.
ant.- drag, tow, tug.

Drop: collapse, decline, fall, decrease, descend, diminish, plunge, sink, subside, stumble, topple, tumble, droop, extend, downward, faint, hang, drip, dribble, trickle, percolate, abandon, dismiss, give up, relinquish, terminate.
ant.- rise, soar, flow, splash, continue, pursue.

Drown: deluge, engulf, sink, immerse, inundate, muffle, overflow, plunge, submerge, swamp.
ant.- extricate, preserve, recover.

Dry: arid, dehydrated, arid, dried, drained, juiceless, moistless, parched, thirsty, watertight, barren.
ant.- damp, moist, fresh.

Dubious: doubtful, equivocal, hesitant, problematical, questionable, reluctant, uncertain, unclear, unreliable, unsettled.
ant.- certain, definite, positive, sure.

Dull: doltish, half-witted, obtuse, senseless, slow, stupid, witless, blunt, dismal, dreary, gloomy, monotonous, prosy, sad, tedious, uninteresting, insensate, unfeeling, dry, lifeless, dark, dim.
ant.- intelligent, sharp.

Dumb: aphonic, mute, speechless, voiceless, wordless, soundless, mum, silent.
ant.- fluent, talkative, voluble.

Duplicate: copy, counterpart, duplication, double, exemplar, facsimile, likeness, replica, reproduction, tracing, copy, transcript, twin, redo, repeat, reproduce, trace.
ant.- original, prototype.

Duplicity: artifice, deceit, guile, dishonesty, fraud.
ant.- guilelessness, honesty, openness, simplicity.

Durable: abiding, changeless, constant, continuing, fixed, enduring, lasting, permanent, remaining, unchangeable.
ant.- ephemeral, temporary, transient, transitory, unstable.

Duty: accountability, allegiance, responsibility, service, business, calling, charge, employment, function, obligation, office.
ant.- betrayal, disloyalty, falsehood, inconstancy, irresponsibility.

Dwindle: abridge, curtail, decline, decrease, diminish, drop, lessen, narrow, reduce, shorten, shrink, wane.
ant.- augment, enlarge, expand, multiply, widen.

Dye: colour, imbue, pigment, stain, tinge, tint.
ant.- bleach, fade.

❑

E

Eager: ambitious, desirous, earnest, fervent, intent, keen, longing, solicitous, fervid, hot-headed.
ant.- apathetic, indifferent, phlegmatic, uninterested.

Earn: achieve, acquire, attain, deserve, gain, get, make, merit, obtain, secure, win.
ant.- forfeit, lose.

Earnest: serious, intent, intense, grave, solemn, sober, determined.
ant.- not firm, tickle, playful.

Earning: emoluments, income, interest, profits, remuneration reward, salary, stipend, wages.
ant.- cost, expense.

Earthly: carnal, earthy, global, material, mundane, profane, temporal, worldly.
ant.- immaterial, incorporeal, spiritual.

Ease: comfort, facilitate, contentment, simplicity, easiness, expertise, facility.
ant.- discomfort, unease, difficulty.

Easy: comfortable, effortless, elementary, facile, light, relaxed, simple, unanxious, uncomplicated, restful, indolent, unconcerned, untroubled.
ant.- difficult, hard, laborious.

Ebb: abate, decay, decline, dwindle, fall, lessen, recede, fall back, outflow, withdraw.
ant.- flow, improve, increase, revive, wax.

Eccentric: erratic, queer, strange, insanity, cranky, wayward.
ant.- common, conventional, familiar, normal, regular.

Economical: frugal, penurious, stingy, careful, parsimonious, provident, saving, sparing, chary, thrifty.
ant.- extravagant, lavish, improvident, munificent.

Ecstasy: gladness, bliss, delight, ebullience, elation, exaltation, glee, glorification, joy, rapture, ravishment.
ant.- depression, despair, doldrums, melancholy.

Eddy: swirl, whirl, vortex, whirlpool, countercurrent.
ant.- calm, still.

Edge: border, boundary, brim, brink, extremity, fringe, tip, margin, periphery, rim, side, verge, brow, curb.

ant.- center, extension, interior, bluntness, dullness.

Education: cultivation, culture, development, discipline, edification, enlightenment, study, instruction, knowledge, training, scholarship, learning, schooling.

ant.- ignorance, illiteracy.

Eerie: weird, frightening, uncanny, strange.

ant.- usual, ordinary.

Efface: annul, blot, cancel, wipe out, expunge, obliterate, erase, delete.

ant.- confirm, keep, renew, retain, strengthen, restore.

Effect: achieve, accomplish, attain, complete, conclude, consummate, do, execute, finish, fulfil, perform, realize, completion, conclusion, consequence, consummation, issue, outcome, result.

ant.- abandon, defeat, fail, neglect, omit, begin, cause, commencement, origin.

Effective: adept, competent, capable, conducive, potent, effectual, efficacious, useful, efficient, fruitful, productive, proficient, serviceable, talented, trenchant.

ant.- fruitless, incompetent, ineffectual, inefficient, non-productive.

Effeminate: feminine, unmanly, unvirile, womanish, womanly, womanlike, poofy.

ant.- manly, masculine, robust, virile, macho.

Effervescent: bubbling, gay, buoyant, frothy, gleeful, volatile.

ant.- flat, sedate, sober, staid.

Efficiency: ability, adeptness, capability, capacity, competency, effectiveness, fitness, suitability, thoroughness, proficiency.

ant.- impotence, inability, inadequacy, incompetency, weakness.

Effort: attempt, endeavour, energy, essay, exertion, trial, work, labour, pains, strain, strife, struggle, toil, trouble.

ant.- ease, failure, neglect.

Egotistic: boastful, bombastic, conceited, egocentric, inflated, narcissistic, ostentatious, self-centered, pretentious, pompous, self-important, showy, vain.

ant.- deferent, humble, modest, reserved, unobtrusive.

Eject: banish, cast out, evict, discard, discharge, dislodge, dismiss, exile, expel, oust, throw, remove, reject, push out, turn out.
ant.- accept, appoint, settle, establish, retain.

Elaborate: expand, develop, embellish, enhance, enlarge, detailed.
ant.- common, ordinary, simple, unrefined, usual.

Elapse: slipaway, expire, glide by, go away, intervene, lapse, pass.
ant.- remain, stand, still, stay.

Elastic: compliant, ductile, extensible, flexible, limber, lithe, pliable, pliant, resilient, rubbery, springy, tensile, buoyant, stretchable, supple, tractable.
ant.- brittle, rigid, stiff, tense, unbending.

Elated: animated, delighted, ecstatic, joyful, joyous, gleeful, cheered, exhilarated, exultant, high-spirited.
ant.- depressed, dispirited, gloomy, sad.

Elect: choose, cull, decide on, pick, fix upon, select.
ant.- cancel, recall, refuse, reject.

Elegant: beautiful, courtly, elaborate, fair, fine, handsome, lovely, luxurious, opulent, polished, pretty, refined, rich, sophisticated, sumptuous, classical, correct, artistic, chaste, pure, appropriate, graceful, felicitous.
ant.- common, repulsive, rustic, unrefined, vulgar.

Elementary: basic, elemental, incipient, fundamental, initial, primary, rudimentary pure, simple, uncompounded, unmixed.
ant.- abstruse, advanced, complex, mixed, intricate, compounded.

Elevate: advance, dignify, lift, erect, exalt, glorify, heighten, hoist, improve, promote, raise, revere, uplift.
ant.- abase, condemn, deprecate, depreciate, depress.

Elicit: bring forth, draw forth, educe, evoke, extort, extract, prompt.
ant.- repress, suppress.

Eliminate: abolish, abrogate, banish, cancel, delete, efface, discharge, dislodge, eject, eradicate, erase, excise, exclude, expel, expunge,

expurgate, exterminate, extirpate, obliterate, oust, pluck, remove.
ant.- accept, admit, include, maintain, preserve.

Elongate: extend, lengthen, prolong, protract, stretch, string out.
ant.- contract, shrink, slacken, shorten.

Elucidate: clarify, decipher, explain, expound, illuminate, illustrate, interpret.
ant.- becloud, confuse, darken, distract, obscure.

Elude: avert, avoid, baffle, foil, dodge, escape, eschew, frustrate, parry, evade.
ant.- attract, confront, encounter, meet, solicit.

Emanate: arise, come, stem, emerge, flow, issue, originate, proceed, radiate.
ant.- return, sink, withdraw.

Emancipate: free, let go, set free, liberate, release, deliver, manumit, enfranchise.
ant.- confine, imprison, subjugate.

Embarrass: abash, annoy, bewilder, bother, complicate, confound, confuse, discomfit, disconcert, distress, rattle, encumber, entangle, fluster, hamper, hinder, mortify, obstruct, perplex, plague, trouble, vex.
ant.- cheer, encourage, help, inspire, relieve.

Embellish: adorn, beautify, deck, decorate, enrich, garnish, ornament.
ant.- debase, defame, strip, obliterate, simplify.

Embezzle: steal, defalcate, defraud, falsify, filch, forge, misapply, misappropriate, pilfer, plunder, purloin, rob, swindle.
ant.- balance, recompense, reimburse, return, satisfy.

Embody: codify, comprise, concentrate, contain, hold, embrace, include, incorporate, integrate, systematize, join, unite, organize, impersonate, personify.
ant.- discharge, disperse, disintegrate, exclude.

Embrace: caress, clasp, hug, encircle, hug, subscribe to, welcome, comprehend, hold, comprise, contain, embody, include, incorporate, clutch, fold.
ant.- exclude, reject, renounce, scorn, spurn.

Emergency: casualty, crisis, dilemma, distress, exigency,

juncture, pressure, quandary, urgency.
ant.- conventionality, routine, regularity, stability, solution.

Emigrate: depart, egress, escape, migrate, move, quit.
ant.- dwell, remain, reside, stay.

Eminent: celebrated, well-known, conspicuous, noted, distinguished, elevated, exalted, famous, outstanding, foremost, glorious, illustrious, prominent, renowned, superior, supreme.
ant.- common, humble, insignificant, ordinary.

Emit: breathe, send, forth, discharge, eject, emanate, exhale, expel, issue.
ant.- contain, retain, stop, suppress.

Emotion: affection, feeling, impression, inspiration, mood, passion, presentiment, sensation, sensibility, sentiment.
ant.- apathy, dispassion, impassivity, indifference, insensibility.

Empathy: affinity, appreciation, commiseration, compassion, insight, sensitivity, understanding.
ant.- insensitivity, unfeelingness.

Emphatic: affecting, pointed, determined, effective, potent, energetic, forceful, forcible, insistent.
ant.- bashful, bland, modest, reserved, weak.

Employment: business, job, calling, career, engagement, occupation, profession, work, service, vocation.
ant.- idleness, inactivity, laziness, leisure.

Empty: vacant, vacuous, void, deplete, exhaust, evacuate, drain, deflate, discharge, unload.
ant.- full, inhabited, occupied, replete.

Enable: allow, authorize, let, empower, permit, sanction, invest, endow.
ant.- disallow, oppose, prevent.

Enchant: bewitch, captivate, charm, enrapture, enthrall, entice, fascinate, ravish.
ant.- disenchant, disgust, offend, repel.

Encompass: beset, enclose, circumscribe, encircle, hem in, enfold, envelop, environ, gird, invest, span, surround.
ant.- free, release, unwrap.

Encounter: assailment, assault, attack, battle, clash, collision, combat, conflict, engagement, fight, invasion, meeting, onslaught, skirmish, struggle.
ant.- avoidance, concord, amity, consonance, harmony, retreat, union.

Encourage: animate, cheer, comfort, embolden, enliven, exhilarate, hearten, impel, incite, inspire, inspirit, instigate, promote, stimulate, spur, support, strengthen, fortify, reassure, rally.
ant.- deject, discourage, deter, dispirit, dissuade.

Encroach: infringe, intrude, invade, poach, transgress, trespass, violate, advance, usurp, overstep.
ant.- abandon, avoid, evacuate, relinquish, shun.

Encumbrance: burden, clog, difficulty, drawback, hindrance, impediment, lien, load, mortgage, obstacle, weight.
ant.- advantage, assistance, incentive, stimulant.

End: cessation, close, completion, conclusion, conclude, consequence, expiration, stop, extremity, finish, termination, terminus, cease, terminate, finish, ending, wind-up, finale, period, stopping.
ant.- beginning, commencement, inception, introduction, inaugurate, start.

Endanger: hazard, imperil, jeopardize, peril, risk.
ant.- guard, protect, secure.

Endeavour: aim, attempt, contend, contest, essay, try, exert, strive, labour, struggle, toil, seek, offer, effort.
ant.- idle, lazy.

Endless: boundless, undying, ceaseless, constant, never-ending, continuous, eternal, everlasting, illimitable, immeasurable, imperishable, incessant, infinite, interminable, perpetual, unbounded, uninterrupted, unlimited, unceasing, unending, continual, indefinite.
ant.- bounded, finite, limited, transient, transitory.

Endorse: assist, attest, back, authorize, confirm, guarantee, corroborate, ratify, secure, recommend, sanction, sign, subscribe, support, approve, second.

ant.- admonish, censure, denounce, oppose, reject.

Endowment: benefaction, benefit, bequest, bounty, donation, gift, grant, property, fund, gratuity, natural gift, provision.
ant.- drawback, harm, injury, loss.

Endurance: diligence, firmness, forbearance, fortitude, long suffering, patience, perseverance, persistence, resignation, submission, tolerance.
ant.- succumbing, surrender, weakness.

Enemy: adversary, antagonist, attacker, calumniator, rival, competitor, defamer, defiler, falsifier, opponent, vilifier.
ant.- accomplice, comrade, ally, confederate, friend.

Energetic: active, animated, brisk, determined, diligent, dynamic, enterprising, forcible, industrious, lively, mighty, potent, powerful, spirited, vigorous.
ant.- idle, lazy, listless, spiritless, vacillating.

Energy: effectiveness, force, efficiency, might, potency, power, puissance, robustness, strength, vigour, vim, vitality, zeal.
ant.- apathy, frailty, impotence, indolence, weakness.

Enervate: attenuate, debilitate, enfeeble, impair, paralyze, reduce, sap, soften, weaken, weary, devitalize, unnerve, emasculate, unman, effeminate.
ant.- animate, energize, invigorate, strengthen.

Enforce: coerce, compel, urge, constrain, drive, force, impel, necessitate, oblige, press.
ant.- dismiss, disregard, give up, leave, omit.

Enfranchise: empower, amality, enable, license, grant, voting, right.
ant.- disenfranchise, disqualify, revoke (license).

Engage: busy, employ, engross, enlist, hire, bind, pledge, obligate, retain, reserve, secure, entangle, interlock.
ant.- dismiss, release, decline, refuse, disengage.

Engender: breed, beget, populate, crop up, create, formulate, generate, incite, originate, procreate, produce, reproduce, make.
ant.- annihilate, demolish, destroy.

Engross: absorb, assimilate, bewitch, captivate, consume, engulf, fascinate, monopolize, swallow up, busy, engage, occupy.
ant.- dissatisfy, neglect, repel.

Engulf: swamp, flood, immerse, engorge, deluge, drown, en-tomb, fill up, inundate, sink, overcome, overflow, overwhelm, swallow up.
ant.- discharge, suspense, emit, expel.

Enhance: advance, augment, exaggerate, elevate, heighten, increase, intensify, magnify, raise, swell.
ant.- assuage, degrade, reduce, diminish.

Enigmatic: cryptic, puzzling, inscrutable, mysterious.
ant.- clear, explicit, obvious, open, plain.

Enjoyment: bliss, comfort, joy, delight, ecstasy, exultation, gladness, gratification, liking, happiness, pleasure, rapture, fun, satisfaction.
ant.- dejection, discomfort, misery, sorrow, unhappiness.

Enlarge: add, amplify, grow, augment, broaden, dilate, distend, expand, extend, heighten, increase, lengthen, magnify, spread, swell.
ant.- abbreviate, abridge, condense, contract, diminish.

Enlighten: brighten, educate, elucidate, illuminate, illumine, illustrate.
ant.- confound, indoctrinate, irradiate, confuse, darken, obfuscate, obscure.

Enlist: engage, employ, enrol, enter, get, hire, incorporate, induce, obtain, procreate, register, reserve, retain, draft, volunteer, sign up, recruit, join, muster, press.
ant.- check, constrain, demobilize, deter, holdback.

Enliven: animate, arouse, brighten, cheer, encourage, exhilarate, quicken, refresh, rouse, stimulate, vivify.
ant.- dampen, debilitate, exhaust, sadden, stultify, deaden.

Enmity: acrimony, animosity, antagonism, antipathy, aversion, detestation, disgust, ill-will, hatred, hostility, malevolence, malice, malignity, rancour, repugnance, spitefulness, opposition, unfriendliness.
ant.- affection, cordiality, friendliness, goodwill, love.

Ennui: boredom, languor, listlessness, dullness, doldrum, tedium.
ant.- buoyancy, enthusiasm, energy, vigour.

Enough: adequate, ample, full, plenty, satisfactory, sufficient, equal, abundant, plenteous.
ant.- deficient, inadequate, lacking, scant.

Enrich: make rich, make wealthy, endow, aggrandize.
ant.- deplete, impoverish, reduce, rob.

Enroll: enlist, enter, inscribe, join, list, record, register, subscribe.
ant.- cancel, deactivate, reject, discard.

Ensue: follow, succeed, come, next, result, supervene, happen.
ant.- forsake, precede, cause.

Enter: penetrate, pierce, come in, perforate, enlist in, enroll, join, register, encroach, start, intrude, begin, introduce.
ant.- depart, exit, vacate, withdraw.

Enterprise: activity, venture, adventure, business, commerce, endeavour, project, engagement, undertaking, work.
ant.- inaction, indolence, passivity, sloth.

Entertainment: amusement, diversion, enjoyment, fun, game, merriment, party, pastime, pleaser, recreation, play, sport.
ant.- boredom, ennui, labour, toil, work.

Enthusiasm: ardour, devotion, eagerness, earnestness, zeal, ecstasy, frenzy, fanaticism, excitement, fervency, fervour, inspiration, intensity, optimism, passion, vehemence, vigour, warmth, fanaticism.
ant.- apathy, calmness, ennui, indifference, lethargy.

Entice: allure, attract, beguile, captivate, charm, draw, enchant, ensnare, fascinate, inveigle, lure, seduce, tempt, wheedle, induce, coax, cajole.
ant.- alienate, disgust, reject, repel, repulse.

Entire: complete, intact, integral, all, perfect, total, unabridged, undivided, unimpaired, whole, unscathed, thorough, absolute, gross.
ant.- defective, deficient, partial, incomplete.

Entrance: entry, doorway, gate, gateway, ingress, opening, inlet, portal, entrée, incoming, ingoing.
ant.- egress, outlet, departure.

Entreat: ask, beg, beseech, implore, plead, request, solicit, supplicate, crave, pray.
ant.- command, compel, demand, force, take.

Envelop: blanket, conceal, cover, embrace, enclose, hide, encompass, enfold, surround, wrap, enshroud.
ant.- open, reveal, uncover, unwrap.

Envious: spiteful, invidious, jealous, malicious, resentful, grudging, jaundiced, green-eyed, begrudging.
ant.- benevolent, charitable, helpful, laudatory, pleased, well-disposed.

Epicurean: gastronomic, luxurious, sensual, sybaritic, voluptuous.
ant.- ascetic, puritanical, self-denying, austere.

Epitome: abridgment, digest, abstract, compendium, brief, summary, syllabus, synopsis, essence, shortness, condensation.
ant.- augmentation, development, expansion, extension, increment.

Equable: constant, equal, even, regular, serene, steady, unchanging, uniform.
ant.- changeable, fluctuating, spasmodic, variable.

Equal: alike, commensurate, equable, equitable, even, equivalent, invariable, same, uniform, unvarying, compare, match, parallel, like.
ant.- different, disparate, disproportionate, dissimilar, unjust, inferior, subordinate.

Equanimity: balance, calmness, composure, evenness, poise, serenity, self-control.
ant.- agitation, anxiety, disturbance, excitation, perturbation.

Equitable: fair, honest, just, impartial, objective, reasonable, unbiased, unprejudiced, ethical.
ant.- biased, dishonourable, fraudulent, inequitable, partial.

Equivalent: alike, identical, like, commensurate, equal, indistinguishable, same, interchangeable, reciprocal, synonymous, tantamount.

ant.- contrary, disparate, dissimilar, opposed, unequal.

Eradicate: abolish, annihilate, destroy, eliminate, erase, expel, exterminate, extirpate, kill, nullify, uproot, weed out.

ant.- establish, fortify, foster, propagate, secure.

Erase: cancel, cross out, rub out, delete, efface, eliminate, expunge, obliterate, wipe out, blot out, scratch out.

ant.- confirm, enact, perpetuate.

Erect: unbent, upright, straight, vertical, standing, stiff.

ant.- bent, cringing, crooked, horizontal.

Erotic: carnal, concupiscent, erogenous, libidinous, lustful, passionate, sensual, sexual.

ant.- celibate, passionless, spiritual.

Erratic: abnormal, eccentric, queer, aberrant, capricious, flighty, odd, peculiar, strange.

ant.- dependable, steady, methodical, regular, reliable.

Erroneous: apocryphal, false, fallacious, faulty, inaccurate, incorrect, mistaken, untrue, wrong.

ant.- correct, right, true.

Error: blunder, fallacy, fault, inaccuracy, indiscretion, misapprehension, misconception, inexactness.

ant.- accuracy, certitude, correction, precision, truth.

Erudite: cultured, educated, enlightened, knowing, wise, learned, scholarly, literate.

ant.- ignorant, illiterate, uneducated, unlettered.

Escape: abscond, break free, elope, decamp, defect, flee, fly, avert, avoid, elude, evade, shun.

ant.- confront, face, invite, meet.

Essential: necessary, requisite, vital, needful, cardinal, indispensable.

ant.- unnecessary, trivial, unimportant.

Establish: found, institute, organize, raise, set up, fix, settle, constitute, create, build.

ant.- abolish, demolish, overthrow, unsettle, upset.

Estate: belongings, domain, effects, goods, holdings, land, possessions, property, fortune, interest.

ant.- destitution, poverty, privation, want.

Esteem: admiration, respect, appreciation, favour, regard, deference, honour, value, veneration, estimation, rate.
ant.- disrespect, dishonour, disgrace, insult.

Estimate: appraise, assess, calculate, compute, count, evaluate, measure, reckon, rate, value, weigh, consider, gauge, judge.
ant.- disregard, guess.

Estrangement: alienation, disaffection, removal, withdrawal, separation.
ant.- affinity, alliance, bond, coalition, union.

Eternal: boundless, ceaseless, deathless, endless, enduring, immortal, imperishable, infinite, never-ending, perpetual, timeless, undying, unending, continual, incessant.
ant.- ephemeral, temporal, mortal, mutable, transient, finite.

Ethical: decent, good, honest, honourable, just, moral, principled, righteous, scrupulous, virtuous.
ant.- amoral, dishonest, corrupt, licentious, unethical.

Eulogize: applaud, celebrate, commend, compliment, extol, praise, glorify, panegyrize, laud.
ant.- condemn, degrade, demean, scorn.

Evacuate: abandon, clear, emit, empty, expel, leave, purge, quit, vacate, eject, discharge, excrete, defecate, void.
ant.- charge, enter, occupy, fill, take-over.

Evade: avoid, shun, dodge, equivocate, quibble, elude, parry.
ant.- confront, face, declare, verify.

Evaluate: appraise, assess, calculate, estimate, judge, rate, value, weigh.
ant.- surmise, supposition, guess.

Evaporate: disappear, dry up, dehydrate, desiccate, dry, vaporize, distill, vapour.
ant.- consolidate, crystallize.

Even: flat, flush, level, plane, parallel, smooth, unbroken, uniform, unvaried, equal.
ant.- jagged, rough, broken, irregular.

Event: affair, episode, issue, happening, incident, result, milestone, occurrence, outcome, occasion.
ant.- antecedent, cause, origin, start.

Everlasting: ceaseless, deathless, endless, eternal, immortal, imperishable, incessant, infinite, interminable, perpetual, timeless, unceasing, undying, unending, never-ending.
ant.- ephemeral, finite, mortal, temporal, transient.

Evict: debar, deprive, discard, dispossess, eject, exclude, expel, oust, remove, put out.
ant.- accept, admit, receive, welcome.

Evidence: confirmation, data, corroboration, demonstration, documentation, proof, facts, grounds, premises, testimony, authentication, verification.
ant.- contradiction, disproof, fallacy, invalidity, refutation.

Evident: apparent, clear, open, conspicuous, discernible, plain, distinct, obvious, perceptible, visible.
ant.- concealed, covert, hidden.

Evil: baseness, calamity,crime, contamination, corruption, depravity, disaster, harm, ill, immorality, iniquity, malignity, mischief, misfortune, offense, profligacy, sin, transgression, ungodliness, vice, viciousness, wickedness, wrong, base, deleterious, immoral, noxious, pernicious, sinful, vicious, wicked.
ant.- goodness, innocence, purity, virtue, honourable, moral, reputable.

Evince: demonstrate, disclose, display, evidence, exhibit, indicate, manifest, prove, show.
ant.- conceal, hide, repress, suppress.

Evoke: call, recall, summon, waken, draw forth, invoke.
ant.- contain, inhibit.

Exact: accurate, correct, definite, literal, precise.
ant.- approximate, erroneous, inaccurate, vague, variable, inaccurate.

Exaggerate: amplify, build up, pile up, hyperbolize, embellish, embroider, enlarge, expand, heighten, magnify, overdo, overstate, stretch.
ant.- depreciate, lessen, minimize, reduce, understate.

Exalt: advance, aggrandize, promote, consecrate, dignify, elevate, ennoble, erect, extol, glorify, hallow, honour, laud, magnify, praise, raise, lift up.
ant.- degrade, dishonour, humble, humiliate, scorn.

Examination: analysis, audit, check-up, exploration, inquiry, inquisition, inspection, interrogation, investigation, probing, query, quest, quiz, questioning, research, trial, scrutiny, search, test, review.
ant.- disregard, inattention, negligence.

Exceed: excel, outdo, outstrip, surmount, transcend, beat, top, surpass.
ant.- fail, fall, behind, lag, tarry.

Excellent: admirable, great, commendable, eminent, estimable, good, exemplary, notable, superb, favourable, meritorious, peerless, prime, proficient, superior, worthy, surpassing, valuable.
ant.- inferior, lesser, poor, negligible.

Except: barring, but, excepting, apart from, besides, omitting, excluding, exempting, saving, rejecting.
ant.- admitting, embracing, including.

Exceptional: unusual, extraordinary, incomparable, marvelous, novel, precious, rare, unique, remarkable, scarce, singular, uncommon, unparalleled, unprecedented, wonderful.
ant.- customary, frequent, ordinary, usual, abundant, numerous, worthless.

Excess: extravagance, plenty, immoderation, intemperance, lavishness, luxuriance, waste, profusion, superabundance, redundance, surplus, superfluity, redundancy.
ant.- dearth, deficiency, lack, paucity, want.

Exchange: barter, change, swap, convert, reciprocate, substitute, switch, transfer, trade.
ant.- preserve, retain.

Excite: agitate, arouse, stir up, awaken, disconcert, disquiet, disturb, goad, incense, incite, induce, inflame, impassion, irritate, kindle, perturb, provoke, rouse, stimulate.
ant.- allay, calm, pacify, quiet, tranquilize.

Exclaim: clamour, call out, cry, ejaculate, shout, vociferate, cry out.
ant.- murmur, mutter, whisper.

Exclude: boycott, debar, omit, except, expel, obviate, shut out, ostracize, reject.

ant.- accept, admit, include, incorporate, allow.

Excruciating: acute, extreme, gruelling, intense, severe, overwhelming, racking, rending.

ant.- comforting, pleasing, mild, soothing.

Excuse: exempt, forgive, free, pardon, release, remit, alibi, apology, overlook, condone.

ant.- convict, prosecute, punish, accusation.

Execrate: abhor, condemn, curse, damn, revile.

ant.- applaud, commend, extol, laud, praise.

Execute: accomplish, perform, administer, complete, do, effect, finish, fulfil, make, enforce.

ant.- abandon, fail, neglect, omit, shelve.

Exempt: absolved, clear, free, excluded, excused, liberated, privileged, unbound, released, unchecked, uncontrolled, undrafted, unrestricted, freed.

ant.- bound, compelled, non-exempt, obliged.

Exercise: act, action, activity, drill, employment, exertion, lesson, practice, operation, performance, task, training, use, calisthenics, gymnastics.

ant.- idleness, indolence, relaxation, repose, rest.

Exertion: attempt, effort, toil, endeavour, labour, strain, struggle, travail.

ant.- idleness, inaction, laziness, lethargy.

Exhausted: consumed, fainted, depleted, drained, fatigued, jaded, tired, wasted, wearied, worn.

ant.- fresh, invigorated, hearty, rested, restored.

Exhibit: demonstrate, disclose, display, evince, expose, flaunt, manifest, parade, reveal, show.

ant.- conceal, cover, disguise, hide.

Exhilarate: elate, enliven, inspirit, invigorate, rejoice, stimulate, thrill, animate, cheer, make merry, gladden.

ant.- deject, discourage, depress, repress, sadden.

Exigency: crisis, difficulty, distress, emergency, need, strait, urgency, want.

ant.- normality, regularity.

Exile: banishment, deportation, expatriation, expulsion, extraction, proscription.

ant.- admittance, welcome.

Existence: animation, being, liveliness, reality, vivacity, entity, subsistence, presence, life, actuality.
ant.- death, demise, languor, lethargy.

Exonerate: absolve, acquit, clear, discharge, exempt, free, justify, release, relieve, restore, vindicate, exculpate.
ant.- accuse, condemn, blame, censure, indict.

Exorbitant: excessive, extravagant, extreme, inordinate, overpriced, unreasonable.
ant.- below cost, inexpensive, fair, moderate, reasonable.

Expand: amplify, augment, develop, dilate, distend, grow, enlarge, extend, increase, swell, magnify, mature, spread, stretch, widen.
ant.- abbreviate, atrophy, contract, diminish, shrink, wane.

Expansion: development, dilation, distention, spreading, enlargement, unfolding, unravelling, growth, maturing, progress.
ant.- abbreviation, compression, curtailment.

Expect: anticipate, await, hope, envision, contemplate, look for, foresee, anticipate, second-guess.
ant.- despair of, doubt, fear.

Expedite: accelerate, speed, advance, dispatch, facilitate, forward, hasten, hurry, quicken, rush, urge.
ant.- binder, impede, slow, obstruct, retard.

Expel: banish, discharge, dismiss, evict, excommunicate, exile, ostracize, oust, proscribe, remove, dislodge, eject, void, eliminate, excrete, extrude, dispel, exclude.
ant.- gain, income, profits, receipts, revenue.

Expensive: costly, dear, high-priced.
ant.- cheap, inexpensive, worthless.

Experience: background, knowledge, practice, feeling, sagacity, seasoning, testing, adventure, occurrence, sensation, wisdom, encounter.
ant.- ignorance, lack of knowledge, inexperience.

Expert: accomplished, adept, apt, clever, competent, master, ingenious, practiced, proficient, skilled, skilful.

ant.- awkward, bungling, incompetent, inexpert, maladroit, unskilful.

Expire: cease, decease, die, end, depart, pass away, sink, perish, vanish.
ant.- commence, survive, live.

Explain: clarify, decipher, elucidate, expand, illustrate, interpret, manifest, resolve, solve, teach, unfold, unravel, expound, fathom, account for.
ant.- confuse, mystify, obscure.

Explicit: clear, definite, plain, determinate, distinct, evident, express, lucid, manifest, open, obvious, unambiguous.
ant.- ambiguous, equivocal, hazy, obscure, vague.

Exploit: adventure, bold, act, achievement, deed, feat.
ant.- neglect, omission.

Exposed: open, disclosed, uncovered, unlocked, clear, unmasked, unveiled, passable, unobstructed.
ant.- concealed, suppressed, hidden.

Expound: analyze, clarify, state, elucidate, explain, express, illuminate, illustrate, interpret, lecture, present, set forth.
ant.- baffle, confuse, darken, obscure.

Express: clear, show, reveal, definitive, represent, denote, explicit, lucid, manifest, positive, specific.
ant.- confined, narrow, restricted.

Exterior: face, front, outside, outward, outer, outermost, outmost, outdoor, round about, extrinsic, external, shell, skin, surface.
ant.- core, inside, interior, internal.

Exterminate: abolish, destroy, annihilate, decimate, kill, eradicate, extirpate, root out.
ant.- cherish, maintain, guard, preserve, protect.

External: exterior, extrinsic, foreign, outer, outside, superficial.
ant.- domestic, inside, internal, intrinsic, within.

Extinguish: douse, blow out, put out, snuff out, quench, smiff.
ant.- animate, ignite, kindle, light.

Extol: celebrate, commend, applaud, eulogize, exalt, glorify, honour, laud, praise.
ant.- disgrace, dishonour, decry, profane.

Extract: derive, distill, tear out, pluck out, educe, elicit, extort, pull.
ant.- insert, instill, introduce.

Extraneous: irrelevant, alien, remote, strange, foreign, unconnected.
ant.- akin, germane, relevant.

Extraordinary: exceptional, rare, marvellous, peculiar, phenomenal, remarkable, singular, special, uncommon, unusual, unwonted, wonderful, abnormal.
ant.- common, customary, ordinary, standard, usual.

Extravagant: spend-thrift, waster, wastrel, excessive, extreme, exuberant, immoderate, improvident, inordinate, lavish, liberal, luxuriant, overflowing, plentiful, prodigal, profuse, wasteful.
ant.- economical, meager, parsimonious, penurious, sparse.

Extreme: maximum, farthest, greatest, outermost, utmost, final, last, terminal, ultimate, intensive.
ant.- minimum, common, mild, average.

Extricate: affranchise, deliver, disengage, disentangle, free, let go, liberate, loose, release, unbind, unchain, unfasten, untie.
ant.- bind, chain, incarcerate, confine, restrain.

Exuberant: abundant, copious, energetic, lavish, luxuriant, overflowing, profuse, prolific.
ant.- austere, barren, depleted.

❑

F

Fabricate: assemble, make, manufacture, build, compose, construct, form, make up, innent, frame.
ant.- demolish, disrupt, ruin, shatter, wreck.

Fabulous: amazing, astounding, extraordinary, fictitious, incredible, astonishing, striking.
ant.- common, credible, usual.

Facade: appearance, face, fore, forepart, forefront, front, ornamentation, veneer.
ant.- character, sincerity, base.

Facile: easy, simple, effortless, smooth, uncomplicated, light, painless.
ant.- awkward, difficult, stern, stiff.

Facilitate: ease, lighten, sooth, mitigate, relieve.
ant.- confound, distress, disturb.

Facility: convenience, amenity, aid, appliance, resource.
ant.- awkwardness, difficulty, discourtesy, ineptitude.

Facsimile: duplicate, pattern, picture, replica, reproduction, copy.
ant.- distinction, opposite, variation.

Fact: actuality, certainty, truth, evidence, reality.
ant.- fiction, supposition, theory, delusion, falsehood.

Faction: block, cabal, clique, combination, denomination, division, party, sect, wing, coterie, splinter, party.
ant.- conformity, entirety, homogeneity, unity.

Factious: contentious, dissident, insubordinate, rebellious, recalcitrant, seditious.
ant.- cooperative, helpful, united.

Factitious: artificial, bogus, sham, counterfeit, fabricated, forced, spurious, synthetic, phony, unnatural.
ant.- authentic, bona fide, genuine, natural, real.

Faculty: ability, aptitude, skill, capability, capacity, knack, power, skill, talent.
ant.- impotence, inability, incapacity, incompetence, ineptness.

Fade: bleach, blur, deteriorate, dim, disappear, dwindle, ebb, pale, taper off, vanish, wane, whiten.

ant.- enhance, improve, recover, strengthen.

Fail: be unsuccessful, not succeed, collapse, decline, defeat, disappoint, miscarry.
ant.- succeed, accomplish, achieve, capture, deliver, recover.

Faint: dim, faded, faltering, fatigued, feeble, languid, listless, pale, powerless, thin, timid, weak, wearied, worn.
ant.- distinct, forceful, intrepid, strong, vigorous.

Fair: bright, clear, light, mild, pleasant, sunny, attractive, blond, comely, lovely, candid, decent, equitable, frank, honest, impartial, just, reasonable, open, unbiased.
ant.- foul, tempestuous, ugly, unattractive, devious, dishonourable, fraudulent.

Faith: assurance, conviction, credence, reliance, trust, belief.
ant.- incredulity, skepticism, mistrust, doubt, infidelity.

Faithful: trustworthy, attached, constant, dependable, trusty, devoted, loyal, staunch, true, steadfast, unswerving, reliable, unwavering.
ant.- disloyal, false, fickle, treacherous, untrustworthy.

Fall: collapse, decline, plunge, decrease, descend, diminish, drop, ebb, lessen, sink, topple, subside, weaken, stumble, tumble.
ant.- arise, ascend, climb.

Fallacy: casuistry, delusion, error, equivocation, flaw, fantasy, subterfuge, misconception, sophistry, illusion, untruth.
ant.- certainty, fact, reality, truth, verity.

False: counterfeit, deceptive, bogus, dishonest, deceitful, erroneous, fabricated, lying, fallacious, illusory, incorrect, mendacious, misleading, mock, pretended, sham, spurious, unreal, untrue, faithless, truthless.
ant.- accurate, confirmed, substantiated, true, valid.

Falter: hesitate, hobble, pause, reel, shrink, slip, stammer, tremble, vacillate.
ant.- continue, endure, preserve.

Familiar: accustomed, versed, acquainted, cognizant, well-known, conversant, informed, knowing, accessible, affable, amicable, approachable, friendly, informal, sociable, unconstrained, unreserved.

ant.- constrained, distant, formal, unfamiliar.

Famous: celebrated, eminent, distinguished, glorious, honourable, illustrious, noted, renowned, well-known, famed.
ant.- ignominious, infamous, obscure, undistinguished, unknown.

Fanatical: biased, bigoted, dogmatic, extreme, illiberal, intolerant, narrow-minded, obsessed, prejudiced, rabid, radical, unreasonable, zealot, enthusiast, dogmatist, fanatic.
ant.- dispassionate, liberal, reasonable, tolerant.

Fancy: conceit, conception, idea, imagination, notion, caprice, fantasy, vagary, whim, fondness, inclination, elaborate, ornamental.
ant.- actuality, reality, plain, precision, stability, aversion, unadorned.

Fantastic: bizarre, grotesque, imaginative, odd, peculiar, vague, quaint, strange, amazing, wonderful, capricious, fanciful, farfetched, imaginary, whimsical, visionary.
ant.- fixed, precise, steady, common, ordinary, usual.

Far: away, distant, remote, afar.
ant.- close, nearby, near.

Farcical: absurd, comic, droll, funny, hilarious, ludicrous, ridiculous.
ant.- sober, tragic.

Far-sighted: clairvoyant, clear-sighted, foresighted, judicious, level-headed, prudent, prepared, hypermetropic, eagle-eyed.
ant.- impractical, imprudent, injudicious, unprepared, rash.

Fascinate: allure, beguile, bewitch, captivate, delight, enamour, enchant, enrapture, enthrall, entrance, ravish.
ant.- agitate, anger, disgust, repel, weary.

Fast: accelerated, brisk, fleet, expeditious, quick, rapid, speedy, swift.
ant.- slow, sluggish, insecure, loose, unstable, unsteady, exemplary, upright, virtuous.

Fasten: affix, attach, bind, lock, secure, make fast, fix, lock up, tie.
ant.- detach, loosen, open, release, untie.

Fastidious: choosy, critical, finicky, fussy, particular, squeamish, crotchety.
ant.- gross, indifferent, tasteless, uncritical.

Fat: beefy, corpulent, fleshy, obese, portly, rotund, stout, swollen, plump, chubby.
ant.- gaunt, lean, slender, slim, thin, indigent.

Fatal: deadly, lethal, mortal, murderous, pernicious.
ant.- animating, enlivening, nourishing, vital.

Fate: fortune, destiny, doom lot, predestination, kismet.
ant.- misfortune, bad luck, ill luck.

Fatigue: exhaustion, languor, lassitude, tiredness, weakness, weariness.
ant.- liveliness, rejuvenation, restoration, vigour, vivacity.

Fault: blemish, defect, detriment, drawback, error, flaw, foible, imperfection, slip, misdeed, mistake, weakness, omission, shortcoming, failing.
ant.- correctness, merit, perfection.

Favourable: advantageous, useful, assisting, auspicious, beneficial, conducive, helpful, propitious, salutary, opportune, commendatory, well-inclined.
ant.- detrimental, harmful, disadvantageous, hindering, opposed.

Fear: alarm, apprehension, dread, fright, horror, panic, phobia, scare, terror, timidity, trepidation, awe, fearfulness.
ant.- boldness, bravery, courage, fearlessness.

Feasible: achievable, suitable, attainable, practicable, workable, possible.
ant.- impractical, inconceivable, unrealistic, visionary.

Feat: accomplishment, gest, adventure, achievement, act, action, attainment, deed, stunt, execution, exploit, performance.
ant.- failure, inactivity, laziness, passivity.

Feeble: debilitated, decrepit, delicate, enervated, forceless, exhausted, faint, impaired, infirm, languid, puny, sickly, frail, weak.
ant.- forceful, hearty, robust, stout, strong, vigorous.

Feeling: consciousness, sense, sensation, sensitivity, passion, affection, emotion, sensibility, sentiment, sentience.

ant.- anesthesia, coldness, unconsciousness, imperturbability, insensibility.

Felicitate: compliment, greet, congratulate, gratulate.
ant.- discourage, dismay, reject.

Felonious: corrupt, criminal, depraved, evil, heinous, injurious, malicious, noxious, perfidious, perverse, vicious.
ant.- commendable, decent, honourable, meritorious, praiseworthy.

Feminine: female, ladylike, maidenly, womanish, woman-like, womanly, matronly, effeminate, maternal, unmanly.
ant.- male, manly, mannish, masculine.

Ferment: agitate, boil, bubble, concoct, embroil, excite, fret, heat, leaven, raise, roil, seethe, stir.
ant.- calm, cool, dampen, quiet, soothe.

Ferocious: barbarous, brutal, brutish, cruel, fearsome, fierce, murderous, violent, wild.
ant.- docile, gentle, harmless, manageable, tame.

Fertile: abundant, bountiful, copious, exuberant, fecund, fruitful, luxuriant, plenteous, plentiful, productive, prolific, rich, teeming.
ant.- barren, chillness, fruitless, sterile, unproductive.

Fervent: animated, ardent, eager, enthusiastic, intense, passionate, zealous, earnest, fervid, vehement, impassioned.
ant.- cool, grudging, hesitant, impassive, phlegmatic.

Fetid: foul-smelling, malodorous, smelly, foul, noisome, putrid, rank, stinking.
ant.- aromatic, fragrant, perfumed, sweet-smelling.

Feudal: dependent, downtrodden, enslaved, servile, vassal, bond man.
ant.- aristocratic, free, independent.

Fever: delirium, excitement, frenzy, heat, mania, temperature.
ant.- calmness, coolness.

Fiasco: debacle, failure, slip, miscarriage, misfire.
ant.- achievement, success, triumph, victory.

Fickle: capricious, changeable, fanciful, fitful, inconstant, irresolute, restless, shifting, unreliable, unstable, variable, volatile, wavering, wayward.
ant.- constant, reliable, stable, steady, trustworthy.

Fiction: allegory, creation, epic, fable, fabrication, falsehood, fancy, figment, imagination, invention, legend, myth, narrative, parable, romance, novel, story, tale, hypothesis.
ant.- fact, history, reality, truth.

Fidelity: adherence, allegiance, constancy, devotion, faithfulness, fealty, integrity, loyalty, obedience, reliability.
ant.- disloyalty, faithlessness, inconstancy, perfidy, treachery.

Fiendish: atrocious, cruel, demoniac, devilish, diabolical, infernal, inhuman, malicious, malignant.
ant.- angelic, benign, kindly.

Fierce: angry, barbarous, brutal, dangerous, enraged, ferocious, fiery, savage, truculent, violent, wild.
ant.- docile, kind, peaceful, placid, tender.

Fight: battle, brawl, combat, conflict, contend, contest, dispute, quarrel, scuffle, skirmish, squabble, strive, struggle, wrangle, affray.
ant.- calmness, quiet.

Figment: fabrication, fiction, falsehood, fantasy, chimera, imagination, invention, pipe dream.
ant.- fact, reality, truth.

Fill: complete, fill up, pack, pervade, distend, feed, gorge, load, permeate, stuff.
ant.- deplete, drain, empty, exhaust, void.

Final: concluding, conclusive, decisive, definitive, ending, extreme, last, terminal, ultimate.
ant.- first, inaugural, original, initial, rudimentary, unending.

Fine: admirable, attractive, choice, clarified, dainty, delicate, elegant, excellent, pure, exquisite, polished, refined, sensitive, smooth, splendid, amercement, nice, charge, forfeiture, penalty.
ant.- blunt, coarse, rough, unpolished, thick, reward, compensation.

Finish: close, complete, fulfil, conclude, consummate, end, execute, get done, perfect, terminate, completion, termination, terminus.
ant.- begin, initiate, start, initiation, origin, source.

Finite: bounded, limited, circumscribed, determinate, measurable, restricted, teminate.
ant.- endless, eternal, infinite, unbounded.

Firm: constant, enduring, fixed, resolute, strong, tenacious, unfaltering, immovable, solid, secure, unyielding.
ant.- disjointed, irresolute, wavering, weak.

First: beginning, earliest, initial, leading, original, premier, primary, prime, primeval, primitive, pristine, foremost.
ant.- hindmost, last, at the end.

Fit: accommodate, adapt, adjust, conform, equip, prepare, suit, adapted, appropriate, proper, becoming, befitting, competent, congruous, pertinent, prepared, qualified, seemly.
ant.- awkward, inadequate, unfit.

Fitful: capricious, changeable, intermittent, off-and-on, recurrent, flickering, fickle, desultory, inconstant, restless, spasmodic, unstable, variable.
ant.- constant, reliable, stable, steady, trustworthy, unfirm.

Fix: affix, attach, bind, fasten, link, glue, stick, tie.
ant.- displace, remove, unfasten, alter, change, disturb, modify.

Flaccid: drooping, flabby, lax, limber, loose, soft, weak, yielding.
ant.- firm, strong, sturdy, tenacious, unyielding.

Flagrant: atrocious, glaring, gross, infamous, monstrous, outrageous, rank, wicked, notorious, shocking.
ant.- mild, unrestrained.

Flame: blaze, burn, flare, fire, ignite.
ant.- extinguish, quench.

Flashy: flamboyant, gaudy, garish, jazzy, meretricious, pretentious, showy.
ant.- simple, sober, subdued.

Flat: even, flush, horizontal, level, smooth, plane.

ant.- irregular, mountainous, hilly, sloping.

Flatter: blandish, blarney, adulate, puff, cajole, coax, court, entice, exalt, extol, fawn, laud, praise, soften, wheedle.

ant.- denounce, insult, mock, ridicule, spurn.

Flaunt: flash, flourish, parade, vaunt.

ant.- cloak, conceal, disguise, hide.

Flavouring: tasty, flavourful, delicious, toothsome, sapid, saporific.

ant.- pungent, acrid.

Flawless: defectless, perfect, faultless, immaculate, impeccable, spotless, unblemished, unmarred, whole.

ant.- defective, damaged, flawed, imperfect, tainted.

Fleeting: brief, ephemeral, evanescent, flitting, fugitive, momentary, passing, short, temporary, transient, transitory.

ant.- enduring, eternal, long-lived, perpetual.

Flexible: bendable, compliant, elastic, limber, lithe, plastic, pliable, pliant, supple, tractable, yielding.

ant.- obstinate, rigid, stiff, unbending.

Flicker: fluctuate, flutter, glint, vibrate, quiver, waver, blink.

ant.- motionless, still.

Flinch: cower, cringe, falter, recoil, retreat, run, shrink, wince, withdraw.

ant.- confront, face, hold, out, sustain.

Fling: cast, chuck, heave, soar, pitch, be wafted, throw, toss, hurl, sling.

ant.- catch, seize, check.

Float: drift, glide, hover, sail.

ant.- dip, drown, sink.

Flourish: increase, prosper, grow, multiply, thrive.

ant.- collapse, decay, fade, diminish, weaken.

Flow: circulate, course, float, glide, gush, move, pass, roll, spout, spurt, stream, run, trickle.

ant.- cease, retard, stagnate, cork, stop.

Fluctuate: change, oscillate, sway, swerve, teeter, totter, undulate, vacillate, vary, veer, vibrate, wander, waver.

ant.- adhere, persist, remain, stick.

Fluent: copious, easy, flowing, liquid, moving, smooth, voluble.

ant.- hesitant, motionless, slow, sluggish, stammering.

Flux: discharge, fluctuation, motion, transition, current, flow, course.
ant.- constancy, inactivity, fixity, stability.

Fly: flit, float, flutter, hover, mount, rise, wing, abscond, decamp, escape, flee, aviate, run away.
ant.- descend, fall, plummet, sink, remain, stay.

Foe: adversary, antagonist, enemy, opponent, rival, vilifier.
ant.- assistant tally, comrade, friend, helper.

Follow: adopt, copy, imitate, mimic, accompany, attend, come next, succeed, comply, conform, heed, obey, observe, practise, chase, pursue, trace, trail, ensue, result.
ant.- precede, guide, lead, avoid, elude, flee, cause.

Follower: adherent, attendant, devotee, disciple, henchman, partisan, pupil, protege, pursuer, servant, successor, supporter, votary.
ant.- adversary, antagonist, objector, oppressor, scorner.

Folly: absurdity, fatuity, foolishness, imbecility, imprudence, indiscretion, madness, silliness, simplicity, weak-mindedness, inanity, idiocy.
ant.- cunning, discernment, judgement, prudence, reasonableness, wisdom.

Fondle: caress, cuddle, nuzzle, pet, stroke, toy, cosset.
ant.- disdain, reject.

Fool: blockhead, dolt, dunce, idiot, imbecile, nincompoop, numbskull, oaf.
ant.- philosopher, scholar.

Foolish: asinine, brainless, witless, fatuous, idiotic, imbecile, irrational, nonsensical, silly, simple.
ant.- astute, judicious, prudent, sagacious, wise.

Forbearance: abstention, fortitude, abstinence, leniency, patience, self-denial, tolerance.
ant.- excess, impatience, haste, intolerance, self-indulgence.

Force: energy, intensity, might, potency, power, strength, vigour, army, battalion, company, division, navy, regiment, troops.
ant.- feebleness, frailty, impotence, weakness, retard, persuasion, hamper, thwart, suppress.

Foreign: alien, distant, far, extraneous, remote, strange, exotic.
ant.- indigenous, local, domestic.

Forever: always, continually, ever, endlessly, eternally, everlastingly, immortally, unremittingly.
ant.- briefly, temporarily, shortly.

Forget: disregard, ignore, neglect, omit, overlook, slight, dismiss.
ant.- recollect, remember, recall, reminisce.

Forgo: abandon, abstain, desist, leave out, quit, relinquish, renounce, resign, waive, give up, do without, pass up.
ant.- accomplish, execute, fulfil, perform, yield.

Form: assemble, build, create, construct, design, erect, fashion, forge, make, mould, produce, shape, compose, constitute, devise, frame, figure, formation, structure, image, likeness.
ant.- destroy, disfigure, dismantle, misshape, wreck.

Formal: ceremonial, ceremonious, decorous, exact, functional, methodical, proper, orderly, precise, punctilious, regular, ritualistic, solemn, stiff, systematic, stylized, conventional, traditional.
ant.- casual, easy, natural, unconstrained, unconventional.

Former: antecedent, anterior, before, foregoing, preceding, previous, prior, erstwhile, whilom, sometime, quondam.
ant.- after, ensuing, later, succeeding, subsequent.

Formulate: devise, concoct, fabricate, formularize, frame.
ant.- fumble, guess, hazard.

Forte: speciality, feature, skill, genius, knack, talent.
ant.- clumsiness, incompetence.

Fortuitous: accidental, casual, chance, contingent, random, incidental.
ant.- arranged, calculated, deliberate, plotted.

Fortunate: opportune, advantageous, auspicious, favoured, fortuitous, lucky, propitious.
ant.- ill-starred, unlucky, unfortunate, ill-fated.

Fortune: predestination, nemesis, chance, destiny, lot, fate, luck.
ant.- misfortune, bad luck, ill luck.

Forward: advance, cultivate, aggrandize, bring forward, elevate, encourage, favour, expedite, impel, dispatch, deliver, further, promote, help.
ant.- hinder, oppose, retard, retreat, withhold.

Foul: dirty, fetid, filthy, grimy, muddy, polluted, putrid, soiled, squalid, tainted, indecent, nasty, obscene, offensive, vulgar, base, contemptible, corrupt, despicable, low, mean, pitiful, shabby, disgusting.
ant.- clean, immaculate, neat, presentable, unblemished, pure, wholesome.

Foundation: base, basis, bottom, footing, ground, groundwork, root, substructure, support, underpinning, understructure.
ant.- arch, crown, peak, top, superstructure.

Fraction: bit, division, part, percentage, piece, portion, section, segment, fragment.
ant.- all, entirety, total, whole.

Fracture: break, crack, cleft, rift, rupture, split.
ant.- conjugation, juncture, union.

Fragile: breakable, brittle, delicate, feeble, frail, infirm, weak.
ant.- durable, enduring, hardy, strong, sturdy, tough.

Frank: candid, honest, ingenuous, sincere, open, straightforward, forthright.
ant.- cunning, deceptive, dishonest, hypocritical, insincere.

Fraud: artifice, chicanery, cheat, deceit, deception, dishonesty, duplicity, guile, forgery, hoax, imposition, imposture, swindle, trick, treachery.
ant.- fairness, honesty, integrity, sincerity, truth.

Free: autonomous, emancipated, exempt, freed, independent, liberated, unconfined, loose, unconstrained, unfettered, unobstructed, unrestricted, clear, open, unfastened.
ant.- confined, restrained, restricted, illiberal.

Freedom: deliverance, liberty, emancipation, exemption, franchise, immunity, liberation, independence, unrestraint.
ant.- bondage, dependence, slavery, constraint, servitude.

Frenzy: agitation, delirium, fury, excitement, madness, mania, rage, wildness.
ant.- calmness, delight, sanity.

Frequent: numerous, often, persistent, recurrent, usual, recurring, regular, repeated everyday, incessant, constant, continual.
ant.- exceptional, infrequent, rare, scanty, sporadic.

Fresh: modern, new, novel, recent, unused, healthy, unfaded, green, natural, refreshing, unjaded, unhackneyed.
ant.- decayed, faded, musty, hackneyed, stagnant, stale.

Fret: agitate, anger, annoy, vex, chafe, gall, irritate.
ant.- calm, placate, please, soften, soothe.

Friction: abrasion, attrition, erosion, grating, rubbing, traction, discord, conflict, disagreement, disharmony.
ant.- lubrication, smoothness, accord, agreement, harmony, unity.

Friend: companion, comrade, confidant, crony, intimate, pal, patron, supporter, ally, associate, colleague.
ant.- adversary, enemy, foe, stranger, rival.

Friendly: affable, affectionate, amicable, brotherly, kindly, companionable, neighbourly, genial, intimate, propitious, sociable, cordial, solicitous, sympathetic.
ant.- unfriendly, antagonistic, cool, distant, hostile, reserved.

Frighten: abash, alarm, appal, browbeat, daunt, discourage, dishearten, dismay, dispirit, hector, horrify, intimidate, startle, terrify, terrorize, scare, threaten.
ant.- embolden, encourage, hearten, gladden, inspire, reassure, soothe.

Frigid: arctic, chilling, cool, icy, frosty, frozen, gelid, dull, formal, inhibited, lifeless, passionless, freezing.
ant.- hot, temperate, warm, amorous, fervid.

Fringe: border, boundary, edge, edging, outskirts, perimeter, trimming.
ant.- center, heart, inside, core, interior.

Front: anterior, facade, face, fore, forefront, forepart, forehead.
ant.- astern, back, posterior, rear.

Frown: glare, glower, lower, scowl, sulk.
ant.- beam, shine, smile.

Frugal: conservative, miserly, economical, moderate, saving, parsimonious, penurious, stingy, provident, sparing, temperate, thrifty.
ant.- extravagant, intemperate, self-indulgent, wasteful.

Fruitful: fertile, productive, profitable, advantageous, beneficial, useful.
ant.- barren, fruitless, sterile, impotent, unproductive.

Frustrate: baffle, balk, bar, circumvent, confound, foil, defeat, counteract, hinder, disappoint, disconcert, nullify, prevent, stop, thwart.
ant.- accomplish, facilitate, fulfil, further, promote.

Fulfil: accomplish, compete, consummate, finish, realize, terminate, perform, comply, fill.
ant.- abandon, disappoint, fail, neglect, withdraw.

Full: crammed, filled, glutted, gorged, packed, replete, sated, satiated, soaked, stocked, surfeited, swollen, complete, plentiful, sufficient, whole, baggy, flowing, loose, voluminous, circumstantial, detailed, exhaustive.
ant.- depleted, devoid, empty, vacant, insufficient, lacking, partial.

Function: business, duty, job, office, position, role, task, do, officiate, operate, perform, preside, serve, work.
ant.- idleness, unemployment, malfunction, mismanagement, ignore.

Fundamental: basic, radical, elemental, essential, intrinsic, primary, principal, underlying, original, rudimentary.
ant.- auxiliary, dispensable, secondary, subordinate, superficial.

Funny: absurd, amusing, bizarre, comic, comical, diverting, droll, farcical, humorous, laughable, ludicrous, ridiculous.
ant.- melancholy, sad, serious, sober, solemn.

Furious: angry, ferocious, wild, frenzied, fuming, inflamed, infuriated, raging, turbulent, fierce, violent, unrestrained.
ant.- calm, peaceful, self-possessed, tranquil.

Furnish: appoint, cater, endow, equip, outfit, provide, purvey, supply, afford, give, produce, fit, yield.
ant.- denude, despoil, divest, strip, withhold.

Further: advance, expedite, promote, support.
ant.- check, delay, hinder, impede.

Furtive: clandestine, covert, secret, sly, stealthy, surreptitious, sneaking, skulking, concealment.
ant.- aboveboard, forthright, open, overt.

Futile: abortive, empty, idle, fruitless, ineffectual, useless, vain, resultless, unsatisfying.
ant.- beneficial, conducive, efficient, profitable, useful.

❑

G

Gain: acquisition, advantage, behalf, benefit, emoluments, favour, good, increase, earn, enhance, increment, interest, procure, accomplish, achieve, acquire, attain, consummate, effect, get, obtain, profit, win.
ant.- decrease, forfeit, lose, damage, injury.

Gamble: bet, chance, hazard, play, risk, speculate, stake, wager.
ant.- insure, invest, plan, safeguard.

Game: amusement, contest, play, diversion, entertainment, fun, festivity, frolic, gaiety, lark, gambol, match, merriment, merrymaking, pastime, sport, recreation.
ant.- business, duty, job.

Garble: corrupt, deface, distort, falsify, misquote, misrepresent, misreport, misstate, mix, muddle, mutilate, pervert, scramble.
ant.- clarify, communicate, correct, edit, unscramble.

Garment: apparel, array, garb, attire, clothes, clothing, robe, drapery, dress, habiliment, raiment, vestment, vesture.
ant.- nakedness, nudity.

Garnish: adorn, array, beautify, bedeck, deck, decorate, embellish, enrich, furnish, grace, ornament, trim.
ant.- debase, defame, expose, strip, uncover.

Garrulous: babbling, verbose, chattering, chatty, loquacious, prattling, prolix, talkative, wordy.
ant.- laconic, reticent, silent, taciturn, uncommunicative.

Gather: accumulate, amass, assemble, collect, congregate, convoke, group, meet, muster, garner, glean, harvest, heap, pile.
ant.- disband, disperse, distribute, scatter, separate.

Gaudy: glaring, flamboyant, gay, flashy, garish, tawdry, showy, cheap, blatant, bright.
ant.- pale, refined, solemn, somber.

Gauge: calculation, caliber, criterion, diameter, evaluation, measure, standard, template, norm.
ant.- estimate, guess, hazard.

Gaunt: attenuated, emaciated, flimsy, haggard, hollow, lank, bony, lean, meager, scraggy, scrawny, skinny,

slender, slight, slim, spare, thin.
ant.- broad, bulky, fat, obese, portly.

Gay: blithe, buoyant, cheerful, convivial, frolicsome, glad, happy, hilarious, jolly, jovial, joyful, light-hearted, lively, merry, sprightly, vivacious.
ant.- depressed, mournful, sad, glum, sullen.

Gaze: behold, discern, glance, eye, gape, look, peer, stare, ogle, pore.
ant.- avert, ignore, overlook, miss.

General: common, ordinary, commonplace, conventional, customary, everyday, familiar, generic, habitual, popular, normal, regular, universal, usual.
ant.- exceptional, singular, rare, particular, specific.

Generally: commonly, usually, ordinarily, regularly, normally.
ant.- especially, occasionally, particularly, rarely.

Generation: age, breed, era, epoch, creation, engendering, family, period, formation, procreation, production, reproduction, span, time.
ant.- breakdown, dissolution, obliteration, wreckage.

Generic: characteristic, ideal, comprehensive, general, representative, typical.
ant.- individual, particular, peculiar, special.

Generosity: altruism, bounty, beneficence, benevolence, bounteousness, charity, kindness, lavishness, liberality, magnanimity, munificence, nobleness, philanthropy, prodigality.
ant.- cruelty, inhumanity, malevolence, selfishness.

Generous: beneficent, bountiful, high-minded, liberal, magnanimous, munificent, open-handed, open-hearted, unselfish, whole-hearted.
ant.- greedy, miserly, selfish, covetous, stingy.

Genial: affable, animated, well-disposed, hearty, brotherly, cheerful, congenial, convivial, cordial, fraternal, hospitable, pleasant, pleasing, warm-hearted, jovial, friendly.
ant.- doleful, inhospitable, moody, petulant, sullen.

Genius: ability, aptitude, brains, brilliance, capacity, creativity, endowment, faculty, gift, intellect, knack, leaning, sagacity, talent, intellectual.

ant.- ineptitude, obtuseness, shallowness, stupidity, dullard, dolt, moron.

Gentle: benign, calm, placid, compliant, docile, genteel, meek, mild, moderate, pacific, peaceful, relaxed, serene, well-bred, soft, high-born, soothing, tame, temperate, tender, tractable, kindly, tolerant, considerate, courteous.

ant.- fierce, harsh, rough, savage, violent.

Genuine: actual, authentic, real, bona fide, exact, frank, honest, legitimate, natural, proven, sincere, tested, true, right, unadulterated, valid, un-alloyed, unmixed, veritable.

ant.- artificial, counterfeit, bogus, false, sham.

Germ: bud, embryo, bug, virus, microbe, microorganism, pathogen, bacterium.

ant.- conclusion, end, fruit, issue, outgrowth.

Germane: allied, appropriate, apropos, congnate, fitting, to the point, pertinent, related, relevant.

ant.- inapplicable, irrelevant, unfitting, unrelated.

Germinate: bud, develop, effloresce, evolve, grow, shoot, sprout, vegetate, impregnate, swell, begin.

ant.- set, fade, die.

Get: achieve, acquire, attain, earn, gain, grasp, obtain, procure, receive, secure.

ant.- abnegate, forfeit, leave, renounce, surrender.

Ghastly: dreadful, frightful, ghostly, hideous, horrible, terrifying, terrible, fearsome, grisly.

ant.- attractive, captivating, healthy, pleasant, rosy.

Ghost: apparition, goblin, spirit, shade, haunt, image, phantom, spectre, sprite, spook, wraith, shadow.

ant.- essence, existence, fact, reality, substance.

Giant: colossal, enormous, vast, huge, gigantic, immense, titan, monstrous, titanic, whopping, jumbo, monster, colossus.

ant.- dwarf, infinitesimal, minute, stunted, tiny.

Gift: present, benefaction, boon, bequest, bestowal,

bounty, charity, donation, endowment, favour, grant, gratuity, largess, legacy, munificence.
ant.- deprivation, forfeiture, indemnity, loss.

Gigantic: colossal, elephantine, enormous, great, extensive, gargantum, huge, immense, mammoth, massive, monstrous, titanic, vast.
ant.- diminutive, little, minute, tiny.

Gird: belt, bind, cloth, encircle, endow, equip, fortify, furnish, girdle, invest, support, strap, surround, secure.
ant.- divest, loosen, release, strip, untie.

Give: bestow, bequeath, grant, confer, contribute, convey, deliver, donate, furnish, yield, impart, present, provide, supply.
ant.- deprive, keep, retain, seize, withdraw.

Glad: blithesome, cheerful, cheering, content, delighted, exulting, gay, gratified, happy, jolly, joyful, joyous, light-hearted, merry, pleased, pleasing.
ant.- dejected, depressed, dispirited, melancholy, sad.

Glamour: allure, aura, charm, bewitchment, enchantment, fascination, magic, spell.
ant.- blandness, dullness, lackluster, obscurity.

Glance: eye, gaze, look, scan, see, view, watch.
ant.- avert, hide, miss, overlook.

Glassy: bright, glazed, glossy, crystalline, lustrous, polished, silken, smooth, transparent, vitreous.
ant.- dim, lustreless, obscure, opaque, tarnished.

Glib: facile, fluent, insincere, vocal, voluble.
ant.- harsh, inarticulate, rough, rugged, stammering.

Gloat: brag, boast, crow, exult, flaunt, rejoice, revel.
ant.- condole, commiserate, sympathize.

Gloomy: cheerless, crestfallen, dejected, depressed, depressing, despondent, disconsolate, discontented, discouraged, dismal, dispirited, doleful, downcast, down-hearted, dull, funereal, glum, heavy, melancholy, miserable, moody, morose, sullen, oppressive, pessimistic,

sad, somber, sorrowful, unhappy, clouded, dark, dim, dusky, shady.
ant.- cheerful, happy, joyous, merry, optimistic.

Glorify: adore, applaud, bless, celebrate, dignify, elevate, enshrine, esteem, exaggerate, exalt, extol, hallow, laud, magnify, revere, sanctify, venerate.
ant.- abase, debase, degrade, dishonour, mock.

Glorious: brilliant, celebrated, elevated, exalted, grand, high, lofty, magnificent, majestic, marvellous, noble, raised, resplendent, shining, splendid, sublime, wondrous.
ant.- atrocious, contemptible, base, ignoble, ridiculous.

Glossy: elegant, glazed, lustrous, polished, refined, reflecting, shining, sleek, smooth, flossy, velvety.
ant.- lustreless, rough, unpolished.

Glow: beam, blaze, burn, flame, flare, flash, flicker, glare, gleam, glimmer, glisten, glitter, light, radiate, scintillate, shimmer, shine, sparkle, twinkle.
ant.- die, fade, wither.

Glum: blue, dejected, dismal, dispirited, gloomy, low, moody, morose, unhappy, sulky, sullen.
ant.- amiable, buoyant, cheerful, joyous, merry.

Glut: excess, abundance, cloy, greatamount, increase, gorge, overfeed, overstock, overeat, oversupply, cram, deluge, sate, flood, satiate, satisfy, stuff, surfeit.
ant.- abstain, curb, deplete, empty, void.

Glutinous: adhesive, cohesive, tenacious, mucilaginous, gluey, gummy, sticky, viscid, viscous.
ant.- clean, dry, glueless, powdery.

Gnarled: contorted, knotted, cross-grained, knotty, rugged, twisted, burred, grained.
ant.- direct, plain, smooth, straight.

Go: abandon, abscond, budge, decamp, depart, desert, disappear, exit, fade, flee, leave, move, pass, proceed, quit, recede, relinquish, retire, retreat, run, step, stir, travel, vanish, walk, withdraw.
ant.- arrive, come, enter, stay, stop.

Goad: prod, prick, stab, spur, prick, poke.
ant.- deter, discourage, dissuade, restrain.

Godly: devotional, devout, divine, Godlike, hallowed, immaculate, incorrupt, inviolate, pious, pure, religious, reverent, sacred, saintly, sinless, stainless.
ant.- corrupt, profane, sacrilegious, unGodly, wicked.

Good: chaste, conscientious, exemplary, honest, incorrupt, moral, pure, reliable, reputable, righteous, sinless, upright, virtuous, worthy, admirable, commendable, real, excellent, genuine, precious, sound, valid, benevolent, bona fide, gracious, humane, kind, agreeable, cheerful, friendly, genial, gratifying, health-giving, invigorating, pleasant, fair, honourable, immaculate, stainless, capable, unspotted, untainted, efficient, auspicious, beneficial, expert, favourable, profitable, skilful, propitious, serviceable, able, suitable, useful, valuable, proficient.
ant.- contemptible, evil, injurious, odious, vile.

Gorge: bolt, cram, fill, glut, gobble, sate, satiate, surfeit, overeat, gormandize, stuff, gulp.
ant.- diet, fast, starve.

Gorgeous: dazzling, glorious, grand, magnificent, majestic, resplendent, splendid, superb, surpassing, beautiful, beauty.
ant.- common, homely, plain, modest, plain.

Govern: administrate, command, conduct, control, dictate, direct, preside, dominate, guide, lead, manage, order, oversee, reign, rule, superintend, supervise.
ant.- acquiesce, assent, obey, submit, surrender.

Graceful: beautiful, becoming, comely, dignified, elegant, flowing, willowy, pleasing, easy, smooth, symmetrical, tasteful.
ant.- awkward, clumsy, unrefined.

Gracious: agreeable, amiable, beneficent, benevolent, compassionate, courteous, engaging, friendly, good-natured, hospitable, kind, merciful, mild, munificent, pleasing, tender.

ant.- acrimonious, churlish, disagreeable, ill-natured, surly, rude, mean.

Grade: brand, category, class, denomination, genre, kind, order, rank, stage, step, level, quality.

ant.- sameness, uniformity, plane.

Gradual: creeping, dawdling, delaying, deliberate, dull, sloping, laggard, leisurely, progressive, sluggish, slow, step-by-step, unintermittent, tired, moderate.

ant.- abrupt, hasty, quick, rapid, swift.

Grandeur: augustness, dignity, greatness, loftiness, magnificence, majesty, splendour, pomp, stateliness.

ant.- humility, lowliness, simplicity.

Grant: allocate, allot, apportion, appropriate, assign, bestow, confer, deal, dispense, give, distribute, divide, mete, allow, present, accede, concur, yield, agree, comply, concede, permit, benefaction, endowment, present, privilege, reward, gift.

ant.- confiscate, damage, refuse, retain, withhold, loss, oppose, decrement, reject, renounce, charge, deduction, forfeiture.

Graphic: clear, definite, vivid, detailed, distinct, explicit, illustrative, pictorial, powerful, striking, telling.

ant.- abstract, ambiguous, obscure, weak.

Grapple: clasp, clinch, clutch, contend, hook, seize, struggle, wrestle, grasp.

ant.- abandon, ignore, loose, release, surrender.

Grasp: apprehend, arrest, capture, catch, clasp, clutch, grapple, grip, lay hold of, retain, seize, snare, trap.

ant.- extricate, liberate, loss, release.

Grate: abrade, grind, pulverize, rasp, scrape, scratch.

ant.- comfort, placate, please, soothe.

Grateful: appreciative, thankfull, beholden, gratified, indebted, obliged, acceptable, agreeable, pleasing.

ant.- thankless, unappreciative, abusive, careless, rude.

Gratification: comfort, ease, consolation, contentment,

delight, enjoyment, fulfillment, happiness, indulgence, self-indulgence, pleasure, solace, satisfaction.
ant.- affliction, discomfort, suffering.

Gratis: free, freely, gratuitous.
ant.- costly.

Gratuitous: groundless, baseless, uncalled for, spontaneous, voluntary, wanton, gratis, unwarranted, complimentary, free, unpaid.
ant.- deserved, earned, merited, warranted.

Grave: critical, heavy, serious, momentous, weighty, demure, dignified, earnest, intense, ponderous, sedate, sober, solemn, staid, thoughtful.
ant.- insignificant, trifling, trivial, airy, buoyant, frivolous, merry.

Great: big, enormous, gigantic, huge, immense, large, vast, celebrated, eminent, famed, famous, illustrious, prominent, renowned.
ant.- diminutive, little, minute, small, common, ordinary, unknown, menial, paltry, servile, shameful.

Greedy: acquisitive, avaricious, covetous, grasping, mercenary, rapacious, gluttonous, ravenous, voracious.
ant.- charitable, generous, munificent, philanthropic, sharing, full, satisfied.

Greet: accost, address, hail, entertain, admit, receive, salute, speak to, wish, welcome.
ant.- avoid, ignore, pass by.

Gregarious: affable, amiable, companionable, convivial, friendly, hospitable, neighbourly, outgoing, sociable.
ant.- antisocial, disagreeable, hermetic, inhospitable, unsociable.

Grief: affliction, anguish, woe, bereavement, sorrow, distress, heartache, lamentation, misery, mourning, sadness, tribulation, dolor.
ant.- comfort, exhilaration, gladness, happiness, joy.

Grievance: affliction, grief, complaint, damage, detriment, hardship, harm, injury, trial, injustice, sorrow, tribulation, wrong, annoyance.
ant.- benefit, happiness, justice, right, victory.

Grieve: bemoan, bewail, weep, deplore, lament, mourn, rue, regret, sorrow, suffer, afflict, distress, pain, wound.
ant.- celebrate, rejoice, heal, revel, console.

Grim: fearful, fierce, stern, forbidding, horrible, severe, sinister, sullen, terrifying, threatening.
ant.- blithe, enlivening, pleasant, serene, wining.

Grip: capture, clasp, clutch, grab, grasp, hold, seize, snare, trap.
ant.- loosen, relax, release, drop.

Grit: courage, endurance, fortitude, mettle, nerve, pluck, stamina, spirit, gravel, sand.
ant.- cowardice, fear, timidity.

Groan: lament, moan, sigh, sob, wail.
ant.- applaud, cheer, laugh, rejoice, sing.

Grope: attempt, finger, fumble, grapple, hunt, search, try.
ant.- comprehend, perceive.

Gross: aggregate, entire, total, all, entirely, totality, whole, enormous, glaring, grievous, manifest, plain, coarse, crass, earthy, rough, rude, vulgar, big, bulky, corpulent, fat, fleshy, great, large, monstrous, obese, thick.
ant.- proper, refined, moral, purified, spiritual, appealing, comely, delicate.

Grotesque: absurd, bizarre, odd, incongruous, misshapen, monstrous, abnormal, strange, unnatural.
ant.- average, customary, usual, normal, typical.

Grouch: complain, grumble, lament, murmur, mutter, mope, protest, remonstrate, repine, sulk, whine.
ant.- applaud, approve, praise, rejoice.

Ground: base, basis, bottom, foundation, groundwork, fix, support, underpinning, settle, postulate, premise, principle, land, locality, property, region, territory, establish, set, train, educate, instruct.
ant.- derivative, demolish, superstructure, trimming.

Grovelling: abject, begging, contemptible, debased, low, crawling, cringing, cowering, crouching, despicable, vile, dishonourable, fawning, ignoble, ignominious, lowly, vulgar, mean, menial, servile, sneaking, snivelling, sordid.

ant.- commanding, controlling, esteemed, exalted, righteous.

Grow: tumefy, breed, cultivate, farm, nurture, plant, raise, sow, germinate, breed, sprout, advance, accumulate, amplify, augment, bud, burgeon, develop, dilate, distend, enlarge, expand, extend, increase, inflate, mature, puff, stretch, swell, thicken.

ant.- atrophy, contract, decay, diminish, shrink, stagnate, destroy, kill.

Growl: grumble, howl, mumble, murmur, mutter, snarl.

ant.- hum, purr, sing.

Growth: advancement, development, elaboration, expansion, extension, increase, unfolding, unravelling, evolution, multiplication, maturing, progress, proliferation.

ant.- abbreviation, compression, curtailment, decline, failure.

Grudge: animosity, aversion, detestation, enmity, grievance, hatred, hostility, ill will, male-volence, malice, malignity, rancour, resentment, resistance, spite.

ant.- affection, kindness, love, sympathy, toleration.

Gruff: abrupt, acrimonious, blunt, brusque, churlish, coarse, curt, harsh, morose, rough, rude, short, snappish, snarling, sour, stern, surly, unceremonious, uncivil, unpolished, bluff.

ant.- soft, affable, complaisant, gracious, polished, serene.

Guarantee: security, surety, warranty, affirm, assert, certify, declare, endorse, insure, guard, support, testify, verify, vouch, warrant.

ant.- deny, disown, ignore, reject, renounce.

Guess: assume, believe, conjecture, estimate, fancy, imagine, opine, reckon, speculate, surmise, predict, suppose.

ant.- ascertain, calculate, know, measure.

Guide: conduct, control, direct, govern, lead, manage, pilot, regulate, shepherd, steer, supervise.

ant.- misguide, mislead.

Guile: artifice, beguilement, cheat, chicanery, cunning, deceit, double-dealing, duplicity, fraud, hypocrisy, imposture, sham, slyness, trick, wiliness, deception, deceitfulness, trickery, craftiness.

ant.- honesty, integrity, openness, truthfulness.

Guilty: blameworthy, corrupt, criminal, culpable, faulty, immoral, liable, wicked, sinful.

ant.- blameless, faultless, innocent, innocuous, spotless.

Gush: burst, flood, flow, issue, pour, emit, effuse, spout, jet, spurt.

ant.- fade, stop, trickle, wane.

❑

H

Habitual: accustomed, often, common, customary, usual, frequent, general, perpetual, persistent, recurrent, regular.
ant.- exceptional, infrequent, rare, uncommon, unique.

Haggard: debilitated, gaunt, emaciated, hollow-eyed, wasted, weak, skeletal.
ant.- powerful, robust.

Hail: acclaim, applaud, call, approach, cheer, greet, herald, honour, salute, welcome.
ant.- avoid, disregard, ignore, scorn, shun.

Hale: chipper, healthy, hearty, lusty, robust, sound, strong, vigorous, well, wholesome.
ant.- delicate, diseased, unwell.

Half-hearted: cool, indifferent, perfunctory, unenthusiastic, dull, uninterested, apathetic.
ant.- ardent, enthusiastic, wholehearted, zealous.

Hallow: bless, consecrate, dignify, ennoble, erect, exalt, extol, glorify, raise, revere, sanctify, venerate, enshrine.
ant.- debase, degrade, curse, dishonour, humble.

Hallucination: chimera, delusion, fantasy, illusion, mirage, phantasm, phantom.
ant.- existence, reality, truth.

Halt: arrest, bar, cease, check, close, cork, desist, discontinue, end, falter, hinder, impede, intermit, interrupt, linger, obstruct, pause, suspend, stop, terminate.
ant.- advance, preserver, proceed, promote, speed.

Hamper: box or paral sent as a gift, encumber, hinder, impede, obstruct, prevent, restrain, restrict, retard, shackle, thwart, trammel.
ant.- assist, ease, facilitate, promote.

Handicap: burden, impediment, disadvantage, encumbrance, limitation, obstruction, penalty, drag, odds.
ant.- advantage, benefit, asset, remuneration.

Handsome: attractive, beateous, beautiful, charming, comely, elegant, fair, fine, good-looking, graceful, lovely, pretty, shapely, personable.
ant.- foul, hideous, homely, repulsive, mean.

Handy: accessible, advantageous, appropriate, available, commodious, convenient, favourable, fitting, helpful, resourceful, suitable, timely, useful, apt, able, adept, adroit, clever, dexterous, ready, skilled, skilful.
ant.- awkward, inconvenient, inopportune, troublesome.

Happiness: beatitude, bliss, blessedness, contentment, delight, ecstasy, exultation, felicity, gladness, merriment, mirth, pleasure, rapture, well-being.
ant.- adversity, catastrophe, despair, grief.

Happy: blessed, blissful, blith, bright, buoyant, cheerful, contented, ecstatic, delighted, delightful, elated, exhilarated, gay, gratified, jocund, jovial, joyful, merry, mirthful, thrilled, pleasing, propitious, spirited, prosperous, rapturous, glad, successful, vivacious.
ant.- depressed, distressed, gloomy, heartstick.

Harass: aggravate, agitate, anger, annoy, badger, bother, chafe, deride, disturb, enrage, exasperate, harry, incense, inflame, infuriate, irritate, nag, provoke, rouse, ruffle, vilify, tantalize, taunt, tease, worry, torment, traduce, twit, vex, distress, trouble, plague, beset, heckle.
ant.- comfort, delight, sooth, encourage, gratify.

Harbour: cherish, contain, cover, foster, guard, nurture, protect, shelter, shield.
ant.- banish, eject, exile, expel.

Hard: compact, concrete, firm, durable, impenetrable, imprevious, rigid, solid, stable, steady, strong, arduous, burdensome, difficult, laborious, onerous, stern, toilsome, tough, intricate, perplexing, puzzling, austere, cruel, harsh, pitiless, rigorous, severe, strict, unfeeling, unforgiving, unrelenting.
ant.- elastic, flabby, fluid, plastic, pliable, soft, easy, effortless, facile, compassionate, gentle, tender.

Harden: anneal, congeal, ossify, thicken, petrify, solidify, stiffen, toughen.
ant.- melt, soften, warm,

coddle, indulge, pamper, spoil.

Hardship: adversity, difficulty, affliction, burden, calamity, catastrophe, disaster, distress, misery, misfortune, oppression, ordeal, privation, suffering, trial, tribulation, trouble.
ant.- assistance, blessing, consolation, profit.

Hardy: brave, courageous, fearless, intrepid, resistant, robust, tenacious, undaunted, unyielding, vigorous, sturdy, tough.
ant.- delicate, feeble, infirm, puny, weak.

Harm: damage, deprivation, evil, deterioration, detriment, hurt, ill, impairment, infliction, injury, loss, mischief, misfortune, mishap.
ant.- advancement, benefit, boon, favour.

Harmful: baneful, damaging, deleterious, detrimental, hurtful, noxious, injurious, ruinous, mischievous, pernicious, prejudicial.
ant.- advantageous, helpful, beneficial, healing, profitable.

Harmless: faultless, incorrupt, innocuous, inoffensive, reliable, protected, pure, safe, secure, trustworthy, undefiled.
ant.- dangerous, hazardous, injurious, perilous, unsafe.

Harmony: agreement, alliance, coincidence, concord, unison, concurrence, consonance, unanimity, understanding, adaptation, concordance, amity, congruity, consistency, agreeableness, compatibility.
ant.- conflict, disagreement, discord, dissension, variance.

Harsh: acrimonious, austere, bitter, blunt, brutal, caustic, coarse, cutting, exacting, grating, gruff, hard, severe, heartless, jarring, overbearing, rigorous, rough, rugged, stern, strict, stringent, ungenial, ungracious, uncivil, unfeeling.
ant.- courteous, melodious, mild, gentle, soft.

Harvest: crop, fruit, proceeds, produce, product, reaping, yield, outcome, issue, gain, garner, gather, glean, reap.
ant.- lose, squander.

Hassle: argument, brawl, fight, scrap, squabble, controversy, disagreement, dispute, melee, quarrel, wrangle.
ant.- agreement, harmony.

Haste: acceleration, briskness, hastiness, celerity, dispatch, expedition, fleetness, flurry, hurry, quickness, rapidity, speed, swiftness, urgency, rush, velocity.
ant.- delay, lingering, slowness, tarrying, decelerate, procrastinate, retard.

Hasten: accelerate, expedite, hurry, hustle, precipitate, quicken, race, run, rush, speed, spur.
ant.- delay, detain, prolong, retard, tarry.

Hasty: brisk, cursory, fast, hurried, lively, precipitate, quick, rapid, rushing, speedy, swift, careless, excitable, fool hardy, impatient, imprudent, impulsive, rash, indiscreet, irascible, reckless, sharp, testy.
ant.- slow, sluggish, cautious, patient, thoughtful.

Hate: abhor, abominate, detest, despise, dislike, execrate, loathe.
ant.- admire, cherish, like, love, revere.

Hatred: abhorrence, acrimony, animosity, antipathy, aversion, bitterness, detestation, dislike, enmity, grudge, hostility, ill will, loathing, malevolence, malice, malignity, odium, repugnance, rancur.
ant.- admiration, affection, friendship, love, reverence.

Haughty: arrogant, disdainful, contemptuous, egotistical, vain, overbearing, proud, supercilious, swaggering.
ant.- humble, overbearing, lordly, meek, mild, modest.

Haul: drag, draw, tug, pull, tow, trail.
ant.- drive, impel, shove, thrust.

Hauteur: arrogance, disdain, pride, haughtiness, loftiness, sauciness, superciliousness, pomp, scorn.
ant.- humility, lowliness, plainness.

Have: hold, obtain, occupy, own, maintain, possess, keep, retain.
ant.- abandon, lack, lose, surrender.

Hazard: chance, danger, risk, gamble, jeopardy, venture, peril.

ant.- immunity, protection, safety, security.

Hazardous: critical, dangerous, fearful, insecure, menacing, perilous, precarious, risky, threatening, unsafe.
ant.- assured, firm, protected, safe, secure.

Hazy: ambiguous, cloudy, dim, smoky, foggy, indefinite, indistinct, murky, misty, nebulous, unclear.
ant.- clear, explicit, lucid, precise, specific.

Heal: cure, soothe, generate, treat, remedy, repair, restore.
ant.- break, damage, wound, harm, injure.

Healthy: hale, hearty, virile, well, invigorating, robust, sound, strong, vigorous, healing, hygienic, nutritious, salubrious, salutary, sanitary, wholesome, sanguine.
ant.- delicate, frail, infirm, injurious, insalubrious, noxious.

Heap: accumulate, add, bank, aggregate, amass, collect, enlarge, expand, gather, hoard, increase, load, stock, store, swell, mound, pile, assemblage.
ant.- diminish, disperse, dissipate, minimize, scatter.

Heart: organ, center, core, focus, hub, kernel, middle, midpoint, midst, nucleus, pith.
ant.- border, exterior, rim, outside, outskirts, periphery.

Heartache: affliction, anguish, distress, grief, heartbreak, lamentation, misery, sorrow, trial, misfortune, mourning, sadness, tribulation, woe.
ant.- blitheness, comfort, happiness, joy, solace.

Heart-broken: desolate, disconsolate, discouraged, disheartened, distressed, forlorn, miserable, pitiable, wretched, anguished.
ant.- consoled, contented, fortunate, happy, joyful.

Hearty: ardent, cheerful, cordial, enthusiastic, friendly, genial, glowing, gracious, sincere, sociable, warm, healthy, robust, sturdy, vigorous.
ant.- cool, reserved, feeble, weak, deceptive, hypocritical, insincere.

Heat: caloric, warmth, torridity, hotness, sultriness, ardour, warmness, temperature, enthusiasm, excitement, fervour, fervency, impetuosity, intensity, vehemence, zeal, passion.

ant.- cold, frigidity, gelidity, apathy, lethargy, stoicism.

Heathen: Godless, heathenish, infidel, irreligious, pagan, paganic, unbelieving, unconverted, unbeliever, idolatrous.

ant.- believer, theist, religious, devart.

Heave: billow, bulge, elevate, hoist, lift, raise, rise, surge, swell, throw, toss.

ant.- ebb, lower, recede.

Heavy: bulky, hefty, portly, dull, massive, ponderous, unwieldy, weighty, burdensome, trying, cumbersome, grievous, grave, onerous, oppressive, severe, troublesome, vexatious, sad, depressed, gloomy, serious, sluggish.

ant.- light, animated, brisk.

Hectic: agitated, excited, animated, busy, frantic, heated, febrile, unsettling, frenetic, turbulent, feverish.

ant.- calm, cool, unhurried, serene.

Heed: alertness, attachment, heedfulness, attention, care, caution, circumspection, consideration, mindfulness, notice, observance, vigilance, watchfulness, mind, notice, regard.

ant.- apathy, indifference, omission, ignore, neglect, overlook.

Height: acme, apex, peak, culmination, summit, zenith, altitude, loftiness, elevation, eminence, prominence.

ant.- base, floor, lowliness.

Heighten: advance, amplify, augment, enhance, improve, increase, intensify, magnify, strengthen.

ant.- decrease, diminish, lessen, reduce.

Help: aid, assist, benefit, serve, befriend, cooperate, foster, encourage, nourish, succour, support, sustain, uphold, facilitate, promote, mitigate, relieve, remedy.

ant.- discourage, impede, thwart, arrest, counteract, hinder, afflict, injure.

Herald: announce, declare, inform, introduce, precede, proclaim, publish.

ant.- silence, stifle, suppress.

Hereditary: ancestral, genetic, inherent, inherited, innate, patrimonial, transmitted.

ant.- acquired, bought, earned.

Heretic: apostate, dissenter, non-conformist, renegade, schismatic, sectarian, sectary, separatist, unbeliever.
ant.- believer, loyalist.

Heroic: audacious, bold, brave, chivalrous, courageous, fearless, dauntless, gallant, intrepid, majestic, noble, valiant, undaunted, valorous.
ant.- cowardly, cringing, fearful, spiritless, timid.

Hesitate: demur, falter, fluctuate, question, scruple, stammer, stutter, vacillate, waiver, shrink.
ant.- continue, decide, persevere, proceed, resolve.

Heterogeneous: dissimilar, conglomerate, different, diverse, mingled, mixed, non-homogeneous, unlike, varied, variant, various.
ant.- homogeneous, same, identical, uniform, unvarying.

Hidden: abstruse, concealed, covert, esoteric, latent, masked, quiescent, recondite, secret, unrevealed, unseen.
ant. conspicuous, evident, explicit, exposed, visible.

Hide: bury, camouflage, cloak, conceal, cover, curtain, disguise, dissemble, mask, screen, secrete, shroud, veil, suppress.
ant.- disclose, divulge, exhibit, expose, reveal.

Hideous: awful, disgusting, dreadful, frightful, ghastly, grim, grisly, horrible, loathsome, monstrous, repellent, repulsive, revolting, shocking, terrifying.
ant.- alluring, captivating, delightful, soothing, splendid.

High: elevated, lofty, raised, tall, soaring, steep, towering, eminent, exalted, arrogant, boastful, haughty, bumptious, conceited, ostentatious.
ant.- short, stunted, tiny, low base, mean, humble, meek.

Hilarious: blithe, gay, gleeful, jocund, jolly, joyful, merry, mirthful.
ant.- glum, morose, sad, somber.

Hinder: block, check, impede, encumber, hamper, inhibit, interupt, obstruct, postpone, prevent, resist, restrain, stop, retard, thwart.
ant.- assist, expedite, hasten, facilitate, promote.

Hint: allusion, implication, inkling, intimation, innuendo, insinuation, sign, reminder.
ant.- affirmation, declaration, statement, conceal, suppress, withhold.

Hire: charge, cost, fee, price, rent, rental.
ant.- buy, purchase.

History: account, monuments, archives, past, autobiography, biography, chronicle, events, memorial, annals, narration, narrative, recital, record, saga story.
ant.- fable, fiction, legend, myth, romance.

Hoard: accumulate, amass, collect, garner, gather, heap, increase, pile, preserve, retain, save, stock, store, treasure.
ant.- diminish, disperse, dissipate, scatter, waste.

Hoax: artifice, canard, cheat, dupe, deceive, fool, fakery, fraud, guile, humbug, ruse, imposture, spoof, subterfuge, ploy, swindle, trick, wile.
ant.- candour, honesty, openness, sincerity.

Hobble: falter, limp, stagger, totter, bind, fetter, handicap, hold, impede, limit, restrain.

Hobby: amusement, avocation, diversion, enjoyment, game, interest, pastime, recreation, fad, whim.

Hold: clasp, clutch, grasp, grip, have, keep, maintain, occupy, own, possess, retain, support.
ant.- abandon, relinquish, renounce, surrender, vacate.

Hole: aperture, cavity, chasm, fissure, gap, gulf, perforation, pit, rent, opening, pore.
ant.- closure, imperforation.

Hollow: empty, unfilled, vacant, void, artificial, faithless, false, hypocritical, insincere.
ant.- solid, sound, genuine, full, sincere, convex, raised.

Holy: pious, pure, sacred, Godly, blessed, consecrated, devout, devoted, dedicated, divine, devotional, hallowed, immaculate, incorrupt, religious, reverent, righteous, saintly, spiritual, uncorrupt, virtuous.
ant.- diabolical, profane, sacrilegious, secular.

Homely: common, ordinary, plain, unadorned, uncomely, unattractive, inelegant, rustic.
ant.- attractive, beautiful, fair, handsome, pretty,

charming, dignified, polished, suave.

Homogeneous: alike, similar, consonant, harmonious, uniform, same, identical.
ant.- hetrogeneous, mixed, miscellaneous, variegated.

Hone: file, grind, sharpen, strop, whet.
ant.- dull, roughen.

Honest: candid, genuine, conscientious, fair, frank, honourable, ingenuous, just, principled, reliable, reputable, scrupulous, sincere, trustworthy, truthful.
ant.- fraudulent, lying, tricky, adulterated.

Honesty: candor, fairness, integrity, faithfulness, frankness, honour, justice, openness, responsibility, probity, rectitude, sincerity, trustworthiness, uprightness, veracity.
ant.- cheating, dishonesty, deceit, fraud, perfidy.

Honour: admiration, adoration, commendation, dignity, esteem, fame, glory, praise, renown, respect, reverence, worship, confidence, faith, reliance, trust, revere, value, venerate, dignify.
ant.- contempt, derision, disgrace, reproach, abuse, despise, disdain, neglect, scorn.

Honorary: emeritus, gratuitous, titular, nominal, in name only.
ant.- complete, full, true.

Hope: anticipation, aspiration, assurance, belief, desire, expectancy, expectation, confidence, faith, optimism, prospect, trust.
ant.- despair, despondency, fear, gloom, pessimism.

Hopeless: broken-hearted, dejected, forlorn, desperate, despodent, despairing, immitigable, irredeemable.
ant.- cheering, encouraging, promising, reassuring.

Horde: assemblage, gang, mob, bevy, crew, multitude, crowd, crush, host, mass, populace, rabble, swarm, pack, throng, group.
ant.- deserted, desolate.

Horizontal: even, level, linear, parallel, plane, straight, prone, supine.
ant.- hilly, inclined, sloping, erect, upright, vertical.

Horrible: appalling, awful, dire, dreadful, fearful,

frightful, ghastly, grim, heinous, hideous, horrid, shocking, terrible, alarming, horrifying.
ant.- beautiful, enchanting, enjoyable, fascinating, lovely.

Horror: alarm, apprehension, awe, consternation, disgust, dismay, dread, fear, fright, panic, terror.
ant.- assurance, comfort, delight, confidence, consolation.

Hospitable: companionable, convivial, cordial, friendly, kind, neighbourly, receptive, sociable.
ant.- grudging, inhospitable, reserved, solitary, unsociable.

Host: entertainer, hostess, boniface, innkeeper, landlord, army, legion, horde, multitude, throng.
ant.- boarder, caller, guest, patron, visitor.

Hostile: adverse, antagonistic, antipathetic, belligerent, contrary, inimical, malevolent, opposed, rancorous, repugnant, unfriendly, warlike.
ant.- amicable, cordial, favourable, neutral, uncommitted.

Hot: blazing, burning, flaming, heated, scalding, scorching, searing, torrid, warm, ardent, eager, excited, fervent, fervid, fiery, hot-blooded, intense, passionate.
ant.- cold, cool, freezing, frigid, apathetic, impassive, indifferent, passionless.

Hug: caress, clasp, coddle, hold, cuddle, embrace, enfold, fondle, press, squeeze.
ant.- annoy, buffet, spurn.

Huge: capacious, colossal, enormous, extensive, giant, gigantic, great, immense, monstrous, tremendous, vast, gargantuan.
ant.- diminutive, miniature, little, small, tiny.

Humane: benevolent, benign, benignant, charitable, civilized, element, compassionate, kind, forebearing, forgiving, gracious, lenient, merciful, sympathetic, tender, tolerant.
ant.- brutal, cruel, merciless, pitiless.

Humble: compliant, lowly, meek, modest, simple, submissive, unassuming, unobtrusive, unostentatious, unpretentious, plain, abase,

degrade, humiliate, mortify, shame, subdue.
ant.- arrogant, boastful, haughty, proud, vain.

Humbug: cheat, counterfeit, deception, dodge, fake, falseness, feign, fraud, hoax, hypocrisy, imposition, pretense, sham, trick.
ant.- honesty, truthfulness.

Humdrum: boring, everday, dull, commonplace, monotonous, ordinary, prosaic, routine, tedious, tiresome, usual.
ant.- exciting, stimulating, lively.

Humiliation: abashment, shame, chagrin, mortification, odium, abasement, scandal, disgrace, dishonour, disrepute, ignominy, opprobrium, humbleness.
ant.- dignity, glory, honour, praise, renown.

Humour: fun, jest, caprice, chaff, comicality, drollery, facetiousness, fancy, jesting, clowning, jape, jocosity, jocularity, joke, waggery, wit.
ant.- depression, gloom, sorrow.

Hunger: appetite, craving, desire, eagerness, inclination, longing, passion, relish, starvation.
ant.- disgust, distaste, renunciation, repugnance, satiety.

Hungry: famished, starved, empty, famishing, hollow, greedy, ravenous, starving, thirsting, voracious.
ant.- replete, sated, satisfied.

Hunt: hound, chase, ferret, pursue, stalk, follow, trace, run, trail.
ant.- abandonment, cession, resignation, desert, forsake, quit, relinquish, surrender.

Hurry: accelerate, expedite, hasten, precipitate, quicken, rush, scurry, speed.
ant.- dawdle, delay, detain, hinder, impede, procrastinate, retard, tarry.

Hurt: damage, harm, impair, injure, insult, maltreat, mar, outrage, pain, spoil, victimize, wound, ache, throb.
ant.- defend, ameliorate, benefit, compliment, help, preserve.

Hush: calm, muffle, quiet, relieve, silence, stifle, still.

ant.- amplify, encourage, excite, incite.

Hustle: bustle, dash, expedite, jostle, push, rush, jolt, poke. *ant.*- dawdle, procrastinate, delay, slow.

Hybrid: crossbred, half-bred, half-blooded, mixture, mixed, mongrel.

ant.- purebred, thoroughbred, unmixed.

Hygienic: healthy, salubrious, salutary, sanitary, sterile, uncontaminated, wholesome, cleanly.

ant.- contagious, infection, contaminated, diseased, foul, noxious, unsanitary.

Hypnotic: irresistible, lethargic, magnetic, mesmeric, fascinating, narcotic, quieting, soporific.

ant.- disturbing, reviving, stimulating.

Hypocritical: canting, deceiving, deceptive, deluding, dishonest, dissembling, disimulating, double-dealing, false, feigning, pharisee, pretending, pretentious, sanctimonious.

ant.- candid, ingenuous, honest, principled, sincere.

Hypothesis: assumption, thesis, conjecture, inference, postulate, presumption, supposition, theory, condition.

ant.- certainty, confirmation, demonstration, fact, proof.

❑

I

Icy: chilled, chilling, cold, frigid, frosty, frozen, cool.
ant.- fiery, hot, torrid, tropical, warm.

Idea: abstraction, concept, conception, fancy, image, impression, notion, opinion, thought.
ant.- actuality, entity, matter, reality, substance.

Ideal: model, paragon, archetype, criterion, epitome, nonparail, paradigm, pattern, perfection, prototype.
ant.- deficiant, flawed, imperfect.

Identical: alike, coalesce, coincide, similar, tantamount, analogous, duplicate, equal, equivalent, indistinguishable, same, synonymous, uniform.
ant.- contrary, disparate, dissimilar, distinct, opposite.

Identify: determine, distinguish, name, point out, recognize, note, perceive, know.
ant.- confuse, misinterpret, misname, mistake, mix up.

Idiomatic: colloquial, dialectal, peculiar, regional, special, standard, stylized, vernacular.
ant.- classic, cultured.

Idle: dormant, inactive, indolent, inert, lazy, shiftless, slothful, unemployed.
ant.- employed, industrious, fruitful, active, occupied.

Idolize: idolatrize, dore, deify, glorify, revere, venerate, worship.
ant.- abase, desecrate, hate, defile, profane.

Ignoble: abject, base, coarse, contemptible, debased, lowly, degraded, menial, depraved, despicable, dishonourable, grovelling, ignominious, low, mean, scandalous, scurrilous, servile, shameful, humble, lowborn.
ant.- esteemed, exalted, honoured, lofty, noble, righteous.

Ignorant: incognizant, illiterate, unacquainted, uncultivated, unaware, uninformed, unknowing, unlearned, unlettered, untaught.
ant.- cultured, educated, erudite, literate, wise.

Ignore: disregard, forget, neglect, overlook, reject, pass over, pay no attention, pass by.
ant.- acknowledge, heed, notice, recognize, regard.

Ill: afflicted, ailing, diseased, sick, distempered, feeble, impaired, indisposed, infirm, morbid, unhealthy, unwell.
ant.- healthy, robust, well, vigorous.

Illegal: contraband, criminal, illegitimate, illicit, outlawed, prohibited, unauthorized, unlawful, unlicensed, actionable, unsanctioned, unconstitutional, not allowed, unchartered.
ant.- authorized, judicial, lawful, legal, permissible.

Illogical: fallacious, spurious, incoherent, inconsistent, specious, absurd, unsound, unreasoned.
ant.- logical, reasoned, sound, sensible.

Illuminate: brighten, clarify, demonstrate, elucidate, illumine, enlighten, explain, illustrate, irradiate, lighten, reveal.
ant.- complicate, confuse, darken, obfuscate, obscure, puzzle.

Illusion: apparition, chimera, delusion, dream, fallacy, fancy, fantasy, hallucination, mirage, phantom, vision, bubble, figment.
ant.- actuality, certainty, happening, reality, substance.

Illustrious: acclaimed, celebrated, distinguished, eminent, famed, famous, meek, renowned, lonely.
ant.- disgraceful, notorious, contemptible.

Imagination: conceit, concept, conception, creation, fancy, fantasy, idea, impression, notion.
ant.- actuality, existence, materiality, realism, substance.

Imaginative: artistic, creative, fanciful, inventive, poetical, visionary.
ant.- factual, methodical, literal.

Imbecile: blockhead, dolt, oaf, dunce, fool, nitwit, idiot, ignoramus, moron, simpleton, nincompoop.
ant.- genius, intellectual, scholar.

Imitate: ape, copy, counterfeit, duplicate, falsify, follow, impersonate, mimic, mock,

personage, parody, represent, reproduce, simulate, transcribe.
ant.- alter, distort, diverge, oppose, vary.

Immanent: all-pervading, everywhere, worldwide, global, universal.
ant.- acquired, external, extrinsic, objective.

Immaterial: disembodied, ethereal, spiritual, ghostly, metaphysical, unembodied, incorporeal, unsubstantial.
ant.- essential, important, relevant, corporeal, material, substantial.

Immature: callow, childish, crude, embryonic, green, juvenile, premature, raw, undeveloped, unready, unripe, young, hebetic, half-grown.
ant.- adult, aged, grown, mature, ripe.

Immeasurable: limitless, abysmal, boundless, endless, eternal, illimitable, infinite, inexhaustible, interminable, measureless, unbounded, unfathomable, unlimited.
ant.- bounded, circumscribed, finite, limited, measurable.

Immediately: at once, directly, forthwith, instantaneously, instantly, now, presently, promptly, right away, speedily, straightaway.
ant.- after a while, by and by, distantly, hereafter, later.

Immemorial: ancient, dateless, early, immemorable, old, prehistoric, timeless.
ant.- memorable, new, recent, young.

Immense: colossal, elephantine, enormous, huge, gargantuan, gigantic, great, large, mighty, monstrous, prodigious, titanic, stupendous, tremendous, vast, infinite.
ant.- diminutive, dwarfish, microscopic, minute, tiny.

Immerse: bathe, dip, douse, duck, engulf, flood, inundate, plunge, sink, submerge, baptize, absorb, engage, engross, overwhelm.
ant.- elevate, recover, uplift, retrieve.

Imminent: approaching, close, impending, near, nigh.
ant.- passing, momentary, afar, distant, remote.

Immoderation: unrestrained, unreasonable, uncontrolled, undue, unjustified, superfluity, unwarranted, wanton, surplus, excess, exorbitance, extravagance, extremism, inordinateness, intemperance, profusion, superabundance.
ant.- controlled, moderate, reasonable.

Immoral: bad, evil, corrupt, depraved, dissolute, indecent, lecherous, licentious, loose, profligate, unprincipled, vicious, wicked.
ant.- chaste, high-minded, noble, pure, virtuous.

Immortal: abiding, ceaseless, deathless, endless, eternal, everlasting, imperishable, infinite, permanent, perpetual, timeless, undying.
ant.- mortal, ephemeral, finite, temporal, transitory.

Immovable: anchored, firm, cemented, constant, fixed, immobile, rooted, stable, steadfast.
ant.- mobile, notable, plastic, wavering, yielding.

Immutable: abiding, constant, continual, enduring, fixed, invariant, permanent, stable, perpetual, persistent, unalterable, unchanging, unwavering.
ant.- fluctuating, mutable, vacillating, variable,

Impair: adulterate, blemish, blight, corrode, corrupt, spoil, cripple, damage, deface, mar, degrade, deteriorate, harm, hurt, injure, taint, weaken.
ant.- ameliorate, benefit, enhance, mend, repair.

Impart: bestow, confer, give, grant, inform, instruct, notify, relate, reveal, tell, transmit.
ant.- conceal, hide, puzzle, suppress, withhold.

Impartial: disinterested, honest, dispassionate, fair, indifferent, just, neutral, reasonable, non-partisan, unconcerned, non-sectarian, unprejudiced.
ant.- biased, fraudulent, unfair, partial.

Impasse: bar, deadlock, stand-still, stand off, obstacle.
ant.- clearance, opening, solution.

Impatient: eager, impetuous, fidgety, nervous, restless, hurried, restive, intolerant, anxious, uneasy.

ant.- controlled, forbearing, calm, patient, tolerant.

Impeccable: faultless, innocent, immaculate, incorrupt, flawless, irreproachable, spotless.

ant.- defective, corrupt, sinful, stained, faulty, sullied.

Impede: arrest, bar, block, check, clog, counteract, delay, encumber, hamper, hinder, interrupt, obstruct, oppose, prevent, repress, restrain, retard, stop, thwart.

ant.- advance, assist, help, promote.

Impediment: barrier, block, difficulty, hindrance, disability, encumbrance, inhibition, obstacle, obstruction, restriction.

ant.- assistance, collaboration, aid, help, support.

Impel: actuate, coerce, goad, compel, constrain, force, incite, induce, influence, instigate, move, oblige, prod, push, stimulate, urge.

ant.- delay, prevent, repress, repulse, suppress, discoverage, check.

Impenetrable: compact, firm, dense, hard, impassable, impermeable, impervious, rigid, solid, arduous, burdensome, difficult, onerous, tough, abstruse, esoteric, intricate, perplexing, puzzling, adamant, rigorous, cruel, harsh, obtuse, severe, stern, stolid, strict, unfeeling.

ant.- brittle, elastic, flabby, penetrable, plastic, soft, easy.

Imperceptible: invisible, undiscernible, unseen, slight, unapparent, non-apparent, indiscernible, inconspicuous, indistinct, indistinguishable, insignificant.

ant.- visual, perceivable, seeable, perceptible, visible.

Imperfection: defect, frailty, deficiency, drawback, error, failure, flaw, imperfectness, incompleteness, faultiness, inadequacy, wrong, infirmity, shortcoming, transgression, mistake.

ant.- completeness, correctness, purity, faultlessness, perfection.

Imperil: endanger, hazard, jeopardize, risk, threaten.

ant.- defend, safeguard, guard, secure, shield.

Impersonate: ape, duplicate, copy, feign, imitate, mimic, mock.

ant.- alter, distort, diverge, invent.

Impertinent: arrogant, bold, audacious, brazen, impudent, insolent, intrusive, meddling, offensive, officious, rude, absurd, inane, inapplicable, irrelevant, trivial.
ant.- considerate, courteous, polite, respectful.

Impetuous: careless, hasty, heedless, impulsive, incautious, headlong, reckless, rash, ungovernable, unruly.
ant.- cautious, composed, reasoning, retiring, tranquil.

Impinge: clash, collide, dash, infringe, hit, strike, trespass, violate.
ant.- avoid, defer, misspass, respect.

Implant: embed, engraff, fix, graft, inculcate, infuse, insert, instill, plant, set in, sow.
ant.- eliminate, remove, uproot.

Implement: accomplish, do, enact, effect, fulfil, execute, perform, effectuate, realize.
ant.- cancel, defer, hinder, restict.

Implicate: charge, embroil, enfold, entangle, imply, impute, incriminate, inculpate, involve, link, trap.
ant.- absolve, acquit, defend, exonerate, support.

Implicit: not explicit, unclear, blurry, indistinct.
ant.- declared, explicit, specific, expressed.

Imply: connote, hint, infer, insinuate, signify, suggest.
ant.- assert, define, describe, express, state.

Import: import, convey, land, introduce, transport.
ant.- triviality, export, send out, ship out.

Important: consequential, great, essential, imposing, influential, leading, material, momentous, paramount, powerful, pressing, principal, prominent, relevant, serious, significant.
ant.- irrelevant, unimportant, petty, trivial.

Imposing: august, eminent, grand, grandiose, illustrious, imperial, lofty, magnificent, high, majestic, noble, stately, striking, sublime, towering, dignified, awe-inspiring.
ant.- common, insignificant, humble, ordinary, undignified.

Impractical: impracticable, inexpedient, unachievable, unattainable, unfeasible,

unrealistic, unworkable, visionary.
ant.- feasible, possible, workable, practical, reasonable.

Impressive: absorbing, vital, notable, affecting, arresting, awesome, commanding, considerable, imposing, majestic, moving, momentous, stirring, penetrating, profound, thrilling, prominent, striking, weighty, remarkable, touching.
ant.- commonplace, ordinary, shallow, trivial, unimpressive.

Imprison: confine, constrain, detain, incarcerate, hold, jail, lock up.
ant.- acquit, discharge, extricate, free, release.

Impromptu: impulsive, adlib, extemporaneous, improvised, off-hand, spontaneous, unrehearsed, unready, unplanned, unprepared, untutored, undrilled.
ant.- deliberate, prepared, planned, premeditated, rehearsed.

Improper: incorrect, indecent, indelicate, lewd, risque, inapt, offensive, wrong, unsuitable, unbecoming, unfitting, misplaced, bawdy.
ant.- considerate, correct, fitting, proper, seemly.

Imprudent: careless, unwise, heedless, incautious, indiscreet, reckless, thoughtless, unforeseeing, injudicious, ill-advised.
ant.- careful, circumspect, meticulous, prudent, cautious.

Impudence: arrogance, gall, cheek, audacity, boldness, crudity, discourtesy, disrespect, effrontery, impertinence, incivility, insolence, presumption, rudeness, sauciness.
ant.- courtesy, diffidence, gentility, polotense, respect.

Impulsive: excitable, fiery, foolhardy, forcible, hasty, headstrong, heedless, impatient, impetuous, indiscreet, quick, rash, reckless, uninhibited.
ant.- cautious, reasoning, restrained.

Impure: adulterated, defiled, foul, contaminated, corrupt, indecent, mingled, mixed, putrid, spoiled, smutty, tainted, obscene, polluted.

ant.- clean, immaculate, pure, spotless.

Impute: allege, ascribe, blame, attribute, charge, implicate, brand, inculpate, indict, trace (to).

ant.- defend, exculpate, endorse, vindicate, exonerate.

Inactive: dormant, idle, lazy, inanimate, indolent, inert, motionless, passive, quiescent, resting, sedentary, torpid, unemployed, unoccupied.

ant.- active, dynamic, industrious, occupied, working.

Inadequate: deficient, partial, incompetent, incomplete, insufficient, lacking, scanty, short, wanting.

ant.- adequate, ample, enough, sufficient.

Inadvertent: careless, heedless, negligent, thoughtless, unconscious, unobservant.

ant.- attentive, careful, intentional, planned.

Inane: absurd, banal, foolish, meaningless, senseless, silly, stupid, idiotic, frivolous, trite, insipid, pointless, vapid.

ant.- expressive, important, meaningful, salient, sensible, preformed.

Inappropriate: discordent, inapt, improper, incongruous, infelicitius, tasteless, unfitted, unsuitable, unbecoming.

ant.- appropriate, apt, fitting, becoming, proper.

Inaugurate: arise, begin, open, commence, found, initiate, install, induct, institute, start, introduce, originate, launch.

ant.- adjourn, complete, close, finish, terminate.

Inception: beginning, birth, commencement, founding, inauguration, initiation, start, opening, origin, onset, outset, incipience.

ant.- close, completion, end, consummation, termination.

Incessant: ceaseless, constant, continual, continuous, endless, everlasting, interminable, perennial, perpetual, persistent, unceasing, uninterrupted, unremitting.

ant.- interrupted, occasional, periodic, rare, sporadic.

Incidental: accidental, casual, contingent, fortuitous, minor, non-essential, occasional,

subordinate, secondary, undesigned, unintended.
ant.- cardinal, elementary, essential, fundamental, vital.

Incise: cut, gash, notch, chisel, carve, engrave.
ant.- lengthy, prolix.

Incite: actuate, animate, fire, arouse, encourage, enrage, excite, foment, goad, impel, induce, inflame, instigate, prompt, provoke, stimulate, rouse, stir up, urge.
ant.- deter, pacify, quiet, restrain, soothe.

Inclination: bending, gradient, predisposition, bent, leaning bias, slope, affection, allurement, attachment, attraction, disposition, fancy, liking, partiality, penchant, predilection, proneness, propensity, tendency.
ant.- apathy, aversion, distaste, non-chalance, repugnance.

Include: comprise, consist of, contain, embody, embrace, encompass, admit, subsume, comprehend, take up, hold, incorporate, involve, take in, surround.
ant.- eliminate, exclude, omit, preclude, reject.

Income: annuity, dividends, earnings, emoluments, gain, interest, profits, receipts, rents, revenue, salary, wages, stipend, winnings.
ant.- charge, cost, expense, loss, outgo.

Incompetent: clumsy, unfit, floundering, heavyhanded, inadequate, incapable, inept, ineffectual, inefficient, inexpert, maladroit, stumbling, unable, unqualified, unskilled, unsuitable, untalented.
ant.- competent, deft, expert, proficient, skilful.

Incongruous: conflicting, contradictory, contrary, discrepant, disparate, divergent, illogical, incompatible, inconsistent, inharmonious, irreconcilable, mismatched, paradoxical.
ant.- compatible, congruous, consistent, correspondent, harmonious, homologous.

Inconsiderate: careless, unfeeling, heedless, selfish, undiscerning, tasteless, thoughtless, unsympathetic, neglectful.
ant.- attentive, considerate, careful.

Inconsistent: conflicting, discordant, contradictory, discrepant, incoherent, incompatible, incongruous.
ant.- constant, stable, steady, unchanging, uniform.

Incorporate: amalgamate, blend, consolidate, embody, establish, form, merge, mix, unite, federate, join.
ant.- disperse, dissolve, divide, remove, separate.

Increase: accelerate, advance, amplify, augment, develop, dilate, distend, enhance, enlarge, expand, extend, grow, heighten, inflate, intensify, magnify, multiply, raise, spread, swell, wax, add to.
ant.- atrophy, contract, decrease, diminish, reduce.

Incredible: farfetched, suspicious, implausible, unbelievable, inconceivable.
ant.- believable, credible, creditable, plausible, realistic.

Increment: accretion, raise, addition, enlargement, growth, increase.
ant.- decline, decrease, loss, diminution.

Incriminate: accuse, arraign, blame, censure, charge, implicate, impute, indict, inculpate, impeach.
ant.- absolve, acquit, exonerate, release, vindicate.

Incumbent: binding, coercive, imperative, necessary, peremptory, pressing, stringent, urgent, occupant, inescapable, office-holder.
ant.- absolved, exempt, free, liberated, released.

Indebted: appreciative, bound, beholden, grateful, thankful, liable, obligated, owing, unpaid.
ant.- thankless, unappreciative.

Indecent: coarse, dirty, lewd, disgusting, filthy, immodest, immoral, improper, impure, indelicate, salacious, obscene, offensive, pornographic, smutty, shameless, unbecoming.
ant.- decent, modest, pure, refined, virtuous.

Indefinite: ambiguous, hazy, confused, equivocal, inconclusive, indeterminate, inexact, uncertain, unclear, undefined, unfixed, unlimited, unsettled, blurred, vague, unspecified.
ant.- absolute, certain, evident, positive, unquestionable.

Independent: absolute, self-reliant, autonomous, exempt, free, liberated, sovereign, self-governing.
ant.- contingent, dependent, enslaved, subordinate.

Indicate: connote, denote, betoken, designate, differentiate, hint, imply, intimate, manifest, mark, point out, signal, signify, specify.
ant.- conceal, distract, divert, falsify, mislead.

Indict: accuse, arraign, blame, censure, charge, impeach, incriminate.
ant.- acquit, exonerate, release, vindicate.

Indifference: apathy, carelessness, coldness, detachment, disinterest, disinterestedness, impartiality, inattention, insensibility, insouciance, insusceptibility, neutrality, non-chalance, supineness, unconcern.
ant.- affection, ardour, fervour, passion, vivacity.

Indigence: destitution, distress, necessity, need, pauperism, penury, poverty, privation, want.
ant.- abundance, affluence, plenty, riches, wealth.

Indigenous: domestic, inborn, endemic, inherent, innate, countryman, citizen, native, natural.
ant.- alien, foreign, imported.

Indignation: acrimony, agitation, anger, exasperation, fury, huff, irascibility, ire, passion, petulance, pique, rage, resentment, scorn, temper, wrath.
ant.- forbearance, equanimity, patience, self-control, tranquillity.

Indignity: affront, discourtesy, dishonour, disparagement, disrespect, humiliation, ignominy, insult, irreverence, mockery, opprobrium, scurrility, slight, taunt, vituperation.
ant.- courtesy, dignity, praise, reverence.

Indirect: circuitous, crooked, erratic, implied, inferred, devious, oblique, roundabout, swerving, wandering, tricky, winding, cunning.
ant.- direct, straight, candid, unswerving, blunt, explicit, straightforward.

Indiscreet: foolhardy, foolish, heedless, imprudent, reckless, thoughtless, unwise.
ant.- discreet, prudent, wise, sensible.

Indiscriminate: desultory, random, unplanned, unwise.
ant.- chosen, homogeneous, critical, selective.

Indispensable: essential, vital, imperative, necessary, needful, needed, required, requisite.
ant.- dispensable, optional, peripheral, superfluous.

Individual: characteristic, distinct, distinctive, idiosyncratic, particular, peculiar, personal, separate, singular, special, specific, unique, single.
ant.- common, conventional, general, ordinary, universal.

Indoctrinate: discipline, initiate, instruct, teach, train.
ant.- confuse, misguide, mislead, neglect.

Indolent: dull, idle, inactive, inert, lackadaisical, languid, lazy, lethargic, listless, slack, slothful, sluggish, supine, torpid.
ant.- active, alert, assiduous, diligent, industrious.

Indomitable: firm, impregnable, insurmountable, invincible, invulnerable, unassailable, unconquerable, untamable, unyielding.
ant.- feeble, powerless, weak, yielding.

Induce: bring about, cause, spur, create, effect, encourage, urge, evoke, impel, incite, influence, instigate, motivate, originate, persuade, prompt, stimulate.
ant.- discourage, dissuade, hamper, repel, repress.

Induct: initiate, install, introduce, conclude, generalized, lead into, infer.
ant.- expel, lead away, reject, end, withdraw.

Industrious: active, assiduous, busy, diligent, hard-working, indefatigable, persevering, persistent, sedulous.
ant.- inactive, indolent, lack-adaisical, laggard, lethargic.

Inebriated: drunk, drunken, highly intoxicated, tight, tipsy.
ant.- abstinent, temperate, sober, calm, unmoved.

Ineffective: feeble, frail, futile, impotent, inadequate, weak, ineffectual, inefficacious, unavailing, unfruitful,

useless, unproductive,vain, vulnerable.
ant.- strong, effective, efficacious, potent, powerful, successful.

Inept: incompetent, unskilled, all thumbs, awkward, clumsy, foolish, fumbling, inappropriate, incapable, maladroit, unfit, unhandy, unskilful.
ant.- able, adroit, competent, apt, skilful.

Inert: dead, dilatory, dormant, idle, impassive, impotent, inactive, indolent, lazy, lifeless, powerless, quiescent, slothful, sluggish, torpid.
ant.- active, industrious, moving, operational, working.

Inevitable: assured, avoidless, certain, definite, imminent, indubitable, ineluctable, inescapable, necessary, positive, predestined, sure, unavoidable, undeniable, unquestionable.
ant.- avoidable, doubtful, indeterminate, questionable, internment, uncertain.

Inexhaustible: illimitable, indefatigable, infinite, limitless, unlimited, never-ending, untiring, unwearied, endless, unfailing.
ant.- ending, finite, limited, short-lived, wearying.

Inexpensive: cheap, low-cost, low-priced, reasonable, economical.
ant.- costly, dear, expensive, high-priced, valuable.

Infantile: babyish, childish, immature, juvenile, naive, puerile, young.
ant.- adult, mature, grown up, developed.

Infatuated: beguiled, captivated, charmed, deluded, enamoured, enthralled, fascinated.
ant.- disgusted, disillusioned, fancy-free, prudent, sensible.

Infectious: catching, communicable, contagious, contaminating, defiling, epidemic, pestiferous, pestilential, polluting, sickening, virulent, vitiating.
ant.- antiseptic, harmless, healthful, hygienic, sanitary.

Inference: answer, conclusion, consequence, corollary, deduction, illation, judgement, result, solution.
ant.- assumption, foreboding, foresight, preconception.

Inferior: low-grade, second-class, second-grade, lesser, lower, minor, poorer, shoddy, secondary, subordinate, substandard.
ant.- better, foremost, prime, first class, superior.

Infinite: boundless, continual, continuing, countless, endless, eternal, everlasting, ill-imitable, innumerable, interminable, perpetual, unbounded, unlimited, timeless.
ant.- bounded, circumscribed, finite, limited, restricted.

Infirm: ailing, debilitated, decrepit, doddering, drooping, enervated, enfeebled, frail, exhausted, faint, feeble, forceless, impaired, languid, powerless, sickly, unhealthy, weak.
ant.- forceful, hale, robust, sturdy, vigorous.

Inflate: bloat, blow up, dilate, distend, enlarge, exaggerate, expand, fill, aerate, swell.
ant.- compress, condense, deflate, shrink, trim.

Inflexible: hard, hardened, inelastic, non-flexible, taut, determined, firm, headstrong, immovable, inexorable, rigid, intractable, obdurate, strict, obstinate, stiff, unbending, steadfast, grim, stern.
ant.- compliant, elastic, flexible, pliable, yielding.

Influence: attraction, authority, effect, importance, pressure, magnetism, patronage, rule, predominance, prerogative, prominence, reputation, outweigh, predominate.
ant.- impotence, inferiority, subjection, subserviency, weakness.

Inform: accquaint, advise, apprise, enlighten, impart, instruct, notify, relate, teach, tell, warn.
ant.- conceal, delude, distract, mislead.

Informal: casual, conventional, customary, easy, familiar, natural, offhand, regular, simple, unceremonious, unconstrained, unconventional, unofficial.
ant.- ceremonious, formal, official, perfunctory, rigid.

Information: facts, instruction, intelligence, knowledge, news.
ant.- conjecture, guesswork, ignorance, rumour.

Infrequent: occasional, rare, scarce, sporadic, strange, unusual, few, uncommon.
ant.- customary, frequent, ordinary, scheduled, usual.

Infuse: animate, liven, enliven, enspirit, implant, inoculate, inspire.
ant.- kill, deaden.

Ingenious: able, adroit, bright, brilliant, capable, clever, competent, creative, deft, dexterous, expert, inventive, imaginative, novel, original, productive, proficient, quick-witted, qualified, sagacious, sharp, skilful, talented.
ant.- unskilful, uninventive, ineptitude, unqualified.

Ingenuous: aboveboard, fair, artless, candid, frank, plain, guileless, honest, open, truthful, simple, sincere, unsophisticated, naive.
ant.- artificial, cunning, deceptive, designing.

Ingratitude: thanklessness, unappreciativeness, ungratefulness, ingratitude, unthankfulness.
ant.- appreciation, gratitude, gratefulness, thankfulness.

Inhabit: abide, dwell, live, residence, lodge, be present, nestle, occupy, reside, room, settle, sojourn, stay, tenant.
ant.- abandon, exit, retreat, vacate, withdraw.

Inherent: congenital, genetic, inborn, inbred, innate, intrinsic, native, natural.
ant.- alien, extraneous, extrinsic, supplementary.

Inhibit: arrest, bar, constrain, block, bridle, check, cramp, curb, disallow, hinder, impede, interdict, obstruct, obtrude, oppose, prevent, prohibit, proscribe, repress, restrain, restrict, stop, suppress, forbid, suspend, hamper, thwart, circumscribe.
ant.- aid, encourage, liberate, free.

Inhuman: barbarous, bestial, bloodthirsty, brutal, diabolical, coldblooded, cruel, ferocious, fiendish, pitiless, rancorous, remorseless, ruthless, savage, truculent, unfeeling, venomous.
ant.- benevolent, charitable, compassionate, humane, merciful.

Iniquitous: base, criminal, evil, diabolical, dissolute, fiendish, foul, immoral, infamous, lawless, nefarious, noxious, profligate, reprobate, sinful, transgressing, unjust, unrighteous, villainous, wicked.

ant.- exemplary, honorable, good, moral, reputable.

Initial: antecedent, beginning, earliest, elementary, first, fundamental, original, prime, primary, primeval, primitive, pristine, rudimentary, foremost, introductory.

ant.- inmost, last, latest, least, subordinate.

Initiate: begin, commence, enter, establish, inaugurate, originate, indoctrinate, institute, open, introduce, invest, start.

ant.- close, complete, finish, terminate.

Initiative: beginning, incipient, commencement, inception, opening, outset.

ant.- closing, completion, end, termination.

Injurious: damaging, hurtful, defamatory, deleterious, harmful, destructive, detrimental, disadvantageous, libelous, mischievous, pernicious, prejudicial, wrongful.

ant.- advantageous, beneficial, helpful, profitable, salutory.

Injury: damage, detriment, grievance, harm, hurt, loss, impairment, mischief, wound.

ant.- benefit, blessing, relief, emolument, remedy.

Injustice: bias, favouritism, wrong, grievance, illegality, inequality, inequity, infringement, unfairness, unjustness.

ant.- equity, fairness, justice, lawfulness, righteousness.

Innocent: artless, blameless, clean, exemplary, faultless, harmless, guiltless, sinless, impeccable, irreproachable, lawful, pure, righteous, spotless, stainless, uninvolved, upright, viriginal, virtuous, not guilty, unguilty, bloodless, immaculate, unspotted, unblemished, unerring.

ant.- corrupt, culpable, guilty, lascivious, sinful.

Innocuous: gentle, harmless, inoffensive, mild, safe, uninjurious.

ant.- blighting, destructive, detrimental, injurious, pestilential.

Innovation: alteration, change, introduction, invention, modification, newness, novelty, remodelling, variation.
ant.- custom, habit, way, old, tradition.

Inquire: examine, explore, interrogate, meddle, probe, pursue, query, question, scan, reconnoiter, scout, scrutinize, seek, ask, claim, demand, request, solicit.
ant.- abandon, neglect, reply, shelve, answer, contradict.

Inquisitive: curious, inquiring, interrogative, meddlesome, meddling, nosy, peeping, busy, peering, prying, scrutinizing, searching, snoopy, questioning, bodyish.
ant.- apathetic, indifferent, lack-adaisical, unconcerned, negligent.

Insane: aberrant, crazy, daft, delirious, demented, deranged, fanatical, foolish, frenetic, frenzied, idiotic, imbecilic, irrational, lunatic, maniacal, maniac, paranoiac, unsound, psychopathic, psychotic, mad, rabid, raging, unbalanced.
ant.- rational, reasonable, lucid, sane, stable.

Insecure: dangerous, exposed, endangered, hazardous, ill-protected, imperilled, rickety, precarious, risky, shaky, unguarded, unsafe, apprehensive, concerned, fearful, trouble, uncertain, worried.
ant.- safe, secure, fortified, strong, assured, certain, confident, serene.

Insensitive: callous, cold, dull, hard, impenitent, indurate, insensible, obdurate, obtuse, phlegmatic, remote, thick-skinned, tough, unaffected, unemotional, heartless, unfeeling, unimpressionable, unresponsive.
ant.- compassionate, sensitive, empathetic, responsive, tender.

Insertion: implantation, inlay, inclusion, injection, inoculation, installation, interpolation, introduction, addition, interment.
ant.- extraction, removal, transfer, withdrawal.

Insight: acumen, comprehension, discernment, intuition, judgement, penetration, perception, perspicacity, perspicuity, understanding.

ant.- confusion, ignorance, obtuseness, perplexity, shallowness.

Insignificant: cheap, frivolous, inconsequential, meaningless, paltry, petty, small, trifling, trivial, unimportant, valueless, worthless.

ant.- important, momentous, significant, valuable, weighty.

Insinuate: connote, hint, imply, indicate, infer, ingratiate, intimate, purport, signify, suggest.

ant.- assert, express, state, conceal, disguise, suppress, veil.

Insipid: dull, flat, flavourless, inanimate, lifeless, mawkish, stale, tasteless, unimaginative, uninteresting, unsavory, vapid, savourless, unseasoned, zestless.

ant.- appetizing, exhilarating, racy, savoury, tasty.

Insistent: dogged, demanding, exigent, imperative, urgent, importunate, pressing.

ant.- acquiescent, agreeable, indifferent, lenient, tolerant.

Insolent: arrogant, blustering, brazen, haughty, bumptious, contemptuous, contumelious, defiant, disdainful, disrespectful, domineering, rude, imperious, impertinent, impudent, insulting, offensive, overbearing, presumptuous, high-handed, unmannerly, high and mighty, stuck-up, cocky, uppity.

ant.- considerate, courteous, humble, polite, respectful, abased, cowardly, grovelling, parasitic, sniveling.

Inspiration: animation, notion, arousal, whim, brainstorm, brainwave, spur, enthusiasm, exaltation, fancy, incitement, predilection, revelation, stimulation, impulse, incentive, inhalation, influence, stimulus.

ant.- habitude, lethargy, apathy, aversion, exhalation.

Instantaneous: abrupt, at once, direct, hasty, immediate, prompt, sudden, unexpected, momentary, right off, right away, then and there, rapid, here and now.

ant.- anticipated, delayed, gradual, late, slow.

Instantly: abruptly, directly, forthwith, immediately, now, instantaneously, presently, promptly, straightaway, delay, suddenly, urgently, without.
ant.- distantly, hereafter, in a while, later, sometime.

Instinctive: automatic, inborn, congential, constitutional fundamental, habitual, impulsive, ingrained, inherent, innate, intrinsic, involuntry, typical, mechanical, natural, offhand, reflexive, spontaneous, usual.
ant.- acquired, deliberate, learned, meditated, voluntary, willed.

Institute: begin, build, enact, commence, erect, establish, fix, form, found, initiate, introduce, invent, ordain, organize, originate, raise, sanction, settle, commence. start.
ant.- end, stop, close, annul, finish, abolish, terminate.

Instruct: admonish, advise, coach, counsel, direct, discipline, educate, enlighten, exhort, expound, guide, train, school, impart, inculcate, indoctrinate, inform, instill, prime, promulgate, teach, tutor.
ant.- misguide, misinform, delude, falsify, misinterpret.

Instrumental: accessory, assisting, auxiliary, conducive, contributory, expeditious, helpful, promoting, serviceable, serving, subsidiary.
ant.- detrimental, hindering, impeding, injurious, obstructive.

Insubordination: defiance, disobedience, intractability, mutiny, perversity, rebellion, refractoriness, stubbornness, revolt.
ant.- loyalty, obedience, submission, tractability.

Insufficient: deficient, imperfect, inadequate, incompetent, incomplete, lacking, limited, meager, rare, scant, scarce, short, slack, sparse.
ant.- abundant, ample, copious, rich, sufficient.

Insulate: alienate, detach, disconnect, disengage, isolate, part, seclude, segregate, separate, sequester, sunder, withdraw.
ant.- associate, connect, integrate, mingle, unite.

Insult: abuse, affront, disrespect, indignity, insolence, libel, offend, rudeness, slight, slap, snub, dishonour.
ant.- courtesy, salutation, defer, praise, respect, revere.

Integration: alliance, amalgamation, blending, combination, consolidation, fusion, joining, merger, mingling, mixture, unification, union.
ant.- isolation, segregation, seclusion, separation.

Integrity: completeness, integer, embodiment, integration, unity, collectiveness, indivisibility, totality, ensemble, totalness, entirety, wholeness, oneness, candour, constancy, fairness, faithless, loyalty, honesty, incorruptibility, morality, virtue, openness, probity, purity, rectitude, responsibility, trustworthiness, uprightness, righteousness, sincerity.
ant.- division, disunity, discord.

Intelligence: acumen, grasp, aptitude, apprehension, mind, astuteness, comprehension, discernment, insight, intellect, knowledge, mental ability, penetration, perspicacity, reason, sense, understanding, wit.
ant.- dullness, ignorance, stupidity.

Intelligent: apt, astute, bright, brilliant, capable, clever, discerning, keen, knowing, perceptive, quick, sensible, sharp, smart, enlightened, intellectual, knowledgeable, well-informed, brainy, acute, alive, awake, sagacious.
ant.- dull, insipid, obtuse, shallow, stupid.

Intensity: acuteness, ardour, concentration, fervour, depth, eagerness, earnest-ness, force, emphasis, magnitude, might, potency, power, pressure, strain, strength, tension, toughness, vehemence.
ant.- feebleness, lassitude, lethargy, passivity, weakness.

Intentional: calculated, meant, contemplated, deliberate, designed, determined, wilful, intended, planned, premeditated, projected, purposed, studied, voluntary.
ant.- accidental, fortuitous, haphazard, random, unforeseen.

Intercept: arrest, avert, block, catch, check, cut off, hinder, interpose, interrupt, obstruct, prevent, stop, nab, seize.
ant.- aid, boost, forward, succor, uphold.

Interest: attention, behalf, benefit, charm, claim, concern, curiosity, fascination, gain, touch, inquisitiveness, portion, premium, profit, right, share, stake, title, absorb, amuse, cheer, appeal to, beguile, concern, delight, divert, enliven, enthrall, fascinate, gratify, hold attention, intrigue, occupy, please, affect, engross.
ant.- apathy, indifference, insolvency, bore, displease, stupefy, tire, vex.

Interfere: interpose, interrupt, butt in, intrude, meddle, mediate, clash, stall, collide, hamper, hinder, impede, inconvenience, obstruct, obtrude, oppose, tamper, thwart.
ant.- abet, aid, clear, help, stand, aside.

Interior: inmost, inner, inside, internal, inward, middle, bowels, core, enclosure, hinterlands, inland.
ant.- boundary, coast, exterior, external, periphery.

Interminable: boundless, continuous, endless, eternal, everlasting, illimitable, immeasurable, incessant, infinite, limitless, unbounded, unlimited.
ant.- confined, finite, intermittent, periodic.

Intermittent: broken, fitful, discontinuous, flickering, infrequent, periodic, fluttering, interrupted, occasional, recurrent, remittent, spasmodic.
ant.- constant, continual, regular, incessant, perpetual.

Internal: enclosed, inherent, innate, inner, inside, interior, intrinsic, inward.
ant.- alien, external, foreign, outer.

Interpose: inject, insert, intercalated, interject, interpolate, intrude, introduce, intercede, intercept, interfere, interrupt, intersperse, intervene.
ant.- extract, omit, withdraw, avoid, overlook, shun.

Interpret: clarify, construe, decipher, decode, define, describe, elucidate, explain, explicate, expound, illuminate, manifest, paraphrase, render, reveal,

translate, unravel, unfold, solve.
ant.- confuse, misconstrue, distort, misinterpret, mystify.

Interrogation: inquiry, cross-examination, inquisition, investigation, probe, query, test, questioning.
ant.- acknowledgement, answer, rejoinder, reply, repose.

Interrupt: arrest, adjourn, break, check, short, defer, cut, discontinue, disturb, hinder, interfere, obstruct, postpone, stay, stop, suspend.
ant.- continue, maintain, persist, prolong, sustain.

Intervene: arbitrate, intercede, interpose, mediate, step in, intrude, happen, occur, interfere, interrupt.
ant.- ignore, stand aside, assist, assemble, convene, help.

Intimate: affectionate, close, confidential, familiar, friendly, internal, loving, personal, private, secret, special, trusted.
ant.- ceremonious, distant, formal, remote.

Intolerable: insufferable, insupportable, unbearable, painful, unendurable.
ant.- bearable, endurable, passable, satisfying, tolerable.

Intolerant: biased, bigoted, discriminatory, dogmatic, fanatical, illiberal, narrow-minded, prejudiced, unyielding.
ant.- impartial, lenient, non-discriminatory, open-minded, unbiased.

Intrepid: adventurous, brave, audacious, bold, courageous, daring, dauntless, fearless, lion-hearted, unafraid, valiant, valorous, undaunted.
ant.- cowardly, afraid, faint-hearted, flinching, timid, trembling, weak.

Intricate: complex, complicated, compound, convoluted, difficult, disarranged, inextricable, involved, irregular, knotted, labyrinthine, mixed, perplexing, raveled, tangled.
ant.- arranged, clear, plain, simple, uncompounded.

Intrinsic: congenital, essential, fundamental, genuine, inborn, inbred, indigenous, ingrained, inherent, innate, native, real, natural, true.

ant.- external, extraneous, extrinsic, incidental.

Introduction: beginning, prelude, commencement, forward, inception, initiation, interjection, interpolation, meeting, overture, preamble, preface, start, presentation, prologue.

ant.- conclusion, end, epilogue, finale, postlude.

Intrusive: encroaching, snooping, infringing, inquisitive, interfering, invading, meddlesome, obtrusive, trespassing.

ant.- unintrusive, unobtrusive, retiring.

Intuitive: impulsive, instinctive, involuntary, unreasoning, unreflective, discerning, insightful, knowing, perceptive.

ant.- calculated, planned, reasoned, obtuse.

Invalidate: abrogate, annul, cancel, counteract, negate, null, nullify, quash, recall, stop, revoke, void.

ant.- endorse, establish, promote, sustain, validate.

Invaluable: dear, expensive, inestimable, precious, priceless, valuable.

ant.- nugatory, useless, cheap, worthless.

Invasion: aggression, assault, attack, foray, incursion, ingress, ingression, inroad.

ant.- defense, fortification, protection, safeguard.

Invective: abuse, aspersion, blasphemy, censure, condemnation, contumely, defamation, denouncement, denunciation, deprecation, disapprobation, disapproval, disparagement, insult, obloquy, opprobrium, raillery, reproach, reprimand, reprehension, sarcasm, scurrility, upbraiding, vituperation.

ant.- approval, commendation, laudation, plaudit, sanction.

Invent: make, create, coin, conceive, concoct, conjure, contrive, design, devise, draft, fabricate, fashion, frame, imagine, form, improvise, manufacture, originate.

ant.- imitate, reproduce, copy, disabuse.

Investigation: examination, exploration, enquiry, inquisition, interrogation, pursuit, query, quest,

question, research, probe, review, search, scrutiny.
ant.- disregard, inactivity, inattention, overlooking, neglect.

Invincible: formidable, impregnable, incontestable, indomitable, inseparable, insuperable, insurmountable, invulnerable, irresistible, mighty, overpowering, resistless, sovereign, unassailable, unconquerable, unvanquishable, unyielding.
ant.- beatable, conquerable, impotent, powerless, vulnerable, weak.

Invisible: imperceptible, indistinguishable, intangible, undiscernible, microscopic, unseen, occult, undisclosed, unreal, non-apparent, vapourous, unapparent.
ant.- evident, perceptible, real, substantial, visible.

Involve: comprehend, contain, cover, denote, embarrass, entail, entangle, envelop, enwrap, implicate, imply, include, overwhelm, signify.
ant.- disconnect, disengage, extricate, separate, unravel.

Irate: angry, enraged, ferocious, incensed, rabid, infuriated, irritated, nettled, piqued, provoked, raging, stormy, wrathful.
ant.- appeased, calm, quiet, pleased, restrained.

Irk: annoy, bother, chafe, fret, discompose, inconvenience, irritate, perturb, pester, tease, harass, trouble, upset, disturb, vex.
ant.- console, delight, gladden, please, soothe.

Irony: banter, criticism, quip, derision, mockery, paradox, raillery, reproach, ridicule, sarcasm, satire, twist.
ant.- approval, courtesy, deference, esteem, respect.

Irrational: absurd, crazed, daft, crazy, demented, queer, fatuous, feebleminded, inconsistent, injudicious, foolish, illogical, nonsensical, preposterous, ridiculous, silly, self-contradictory, strange, stupid, unreasonable, odd, unsound, vacuous, insensible, weak-minded, brainless.
ant.- logical, lucid, rational, reasonable, sound.

Irreconcilable: divergent, incompatible, incongruous, inconsequent, inexorable, inconsistent, incoherent,

inharmonious, quarrelsome, unappeasable.
ant.- appeasable, compatible, congruous, reconcilable, solvable.

Irregularity: abnormality, caprice, anomaly, asymmetry, deviation, disorderliness, fitfulness, eccentricity, inordinateness, inconstancy, intermittence, tardiness, unruliness, variability, unpunctuality.
ant.- method, order, regularity, stability, system.

Irrelevant: extraneous, immaterial, inapplicable, inapposite, inappropriate, inconsequent, unconnected, unessential, unrelated, unfitting, inconsistent.
ant.- apt, fitting, germane, pertinent, relevant.

Irremediable: beyond help, hopeless, incurable, irrecoverable, unhealable, irreparable, irretrievable, irrevocable.
ant.- curable, recoverable, reparable.

Irresolute: doubting, drifting, fickle, fluctuating, hesitant, half-hearted, hesitating, in-effective, shaky, uncertain, irresponsible, unstable, frail, unsteady, vacillating, wavering, bending, fragile, yielding, wobbling.
ant.- enduring, powerful, potent, relentless, tenacious.

Irresponsible: arbitrary, giddy, capricious, careless, faltering, flighty, fluctuating, foolish, heedless, immature, rash, reckless, thoughtless, remiss, unaccountable, negligent, un-answerable.
ant.- accountable, dependable, reliable, trustworthy, steady.

Irritate: aggravate, agitate, anger, annoy, bother, chafe, enrage, ruffle, exacerbate, exasperate, fluster, foment, inflame, infuriate, tease, irk, provoke, sting, taunt, trouble, vex, nettle.
ant.- accommodate, console, gratify, moderate.

Isolate: alienate, disconnect, cut off, retire, dissociate, detach, seclude, exclude, insulate, withdraw, quarantine, segregate, separate, sequester.
ant.- associate, integrate, join, mingle, unite.

❑

J

Jagged: notched, serrated, indented, denticulated, sharp, rough, pointed, zigzag, snaggy.
ant.- glassy, smooth.

Jam: block, bruise, cram, crowd, crush, impede, improvise, interfere, mass, pack, press, push, tamp, wedge.
ant.- expand, free, diffuse, disperse, separate.

Jealous: covetous, distrustful, doubtful, envious, invidious, jaundiced, mistrustful, resentful, suspicious, solicitous, vigilant, watchful.
ant.- content, indifferent, lenient, serene, trusting.

Jeer: deride, fleer, flout, gibe, hoot, mock, ridicule, scoff, sneer, taunt.
ant.- compliment, flatter, honour, laud, praise.

Jeopardize: chance, expose, conjecture, peril, endanger, hazard, imperil, menace, risk, threaten, venture.
ant.- guard, insure, protect, shield.

Jocular: comical, droll, merry, facetious, funny, humorous, joking, pleasant, sportive, waggish, witty.
ant.- dull, grave, morose, serious.

Join: accompany, add, adjoin, affiliate, associate, attach, bind, cement, link, combine, conjoin, connect, consolidate, federate, couple, marry, tie, unify, unite.
ant.- detach, disconnect, leave, sever, sunder.

Joint: articulation, combination, collaboration, connection, junction, juncture, link, union, welding, shared, associated, combined, united.
ant.- separate.

Jolly: blithe, gay, cheerful, congenial, happy, convivial, frolicsome, humorous, jocose, jocular, jocund, jovial, joyous, merry, playful, witty, springhty, vivacious, mirthful, bouyant, elated.
ant.- depressed, melancholy, mournful, sullen.

Journey: cruise, excursion, expedition, jaunt, passage, peregrination, pilgrimage, tour, travel, trek, trip, voyage.
ant.- stay, stop.

Joy: bliss, cheer, delight, ecstasy, elation, exultation,

felicity, gaiety, gladness, glee, mirth, happiness, merriment, rapture, pleasure, transport, rejoicing.
ant.- affliction, depression, despair, grief, wretchedness.

Judgement: award, decision, decree, injunction, wisdom, adjudication, arbitration, determination, settlement, opinion, verdict.
ant.- arbitrariness, senselessness, stupidity, thoughtlessness.

Jumble: confuse, disarrange, mess, mingle, mix up, muddle, shuffle.
ant.- arrange, classify, file, rectify, systematize.

Just: blameless, conscientious, earned, equitable, honest, honourable, impartial, candid, innocent, judicious, lawful, legal, legitimate, merited, fair, precise, rightful, scrupulous, sincere, unbiased, upright.
ant.- corrupt, deceitful, lying, dishonest, fraudulent.

Justice: equity, fairness, fair play, fair trial, impartiality, justness, lawfulness, legality, propriety, reasonableness, rectitude, righteousness, uprightness, right.
ant.- corruption, dishonour, favoritism, unlawfulness, inequity.

❑

Keen: acute, ardent, discerning, fervid, incisive, intense, lively, perspicacious, shrewd, quick, sagacious, vivid, wily, witty, zealous, eager, enthusiastic.

ant.- apathetic, blunt, dull, lethargic, sluggish.

Keep: conserve, defend, maintain, preserve, protect, save, secure, support, sustain, tend, uphold, hold, reserve, retain, adhere, possess, concubine, have.

ant.- destroy, discard, reject, dismiss.

Kill: assassinate, butcher, immolate, murder, annihilate, massacre, slaughter, slay.

ant.- animate, resuscitate, safeguard, vivify.

Kind: brand, breed, category, character, class, family, genus, nature, sort, type, species, variety, affectionate, accommodating, affable, amiable, beneficent, benevolent, benign, caring, charitable, compassionate, considerate, cordial, forbearing, gentle, good, gracious, humane, indulgent, kind-hearted, kindly, loving, merciful, obliging, sympathetic, tender, thoughtful.

ant.- inhuman, merciless, cruel, ruthless, vicious.

Kindred: affinity, family, consanguinity, kin, kinsfolk, kinsmen, relations, relationship, relatives, analogous, congenial.

ant.- foreigners, strangers, dissimilar, unrelated, foreign, heterogeneous, unlike.

Knack: ability, adeptness, adroitness, aptitude, deftness, dexterity, talent, expertness, proficiency, readiness, skill, skillfulness, trick, handiness.

ant.- awkwardness, clumsiness, incompetence, ineptitude.

Knit: crochet, interlace, web, intermingle, intertwine, twine, entwine, weave.

ant.- divide, separate, untie, unravel.

Know: appreciate, apprehend, ascertain, conceive, cognize, comprehend, hold, discern, distinguish, fathom, interpret, perceive, think,

recognize, remember, understand.
ant.- doubt, misapprehend, forget, misconstrue.

Knowledge: acquaintance, lore, appreciation, wisdom, apprehension, cognition, light, cognizance, comprehension, education, enlightenment, erudition, familiarity, information, learning, perception, recognition, ken, scholarship, understanding, privity.
ant.- ignorance, illiteracy, stupidity.

❑

L

Labour: drudgery, effort, toil, endeavour, exertion, industry, pains, painstaking, plodding, striving, struggle, task, travail, work.

ant.- idleness, inertia, rest, repose, lethargy, relaxation, sloth.

Lack: dearth, deficiency, demerit, depletion, inadequacy, insufficiency, scantiness, scarcity, shortage, need, want.

ant.- abundance, excess, profusion, sufficiency, surplus.

Lag: dally, dawdle, delay, fall behind, falter, idle, linger, loiter, plod, retard, saunter, slacken, stagger, tarry, drag, trudge, hang back.

ant.- accelerate, advance, forward, speed up.

Lame: crippled, defective, halt deformed, disabled.

ant.- agile, robust, solid, vigorous.

Lament: bemoan, bewail, cry, commiserate, deplore, fret, grieve, mourn, wail, weep, rue.

ant.- celebrate, cheer, delight in, exult, rejoice.

Languid: apathetic, debilitated, drooping, drowsy, dull, faint, feeble, flagging, heartless, irresolute, torpid, laggard, languorous, slack, leisurely, lethargic, listless, pensive, pining, sickly, slow, sluggish, weak, wearied, spiritless.

ant.- animated, enthusiastic, brisk, spirited, vigorous.

Lanky: bony, gangling, gaunt, lank, lean, overgrown, raw-boned, slim, spare, wiry.

ant.- brawny, burly, husky, portly, sturdy.

Lapse: blunder, boner, error, oversight, peccadillo, fault, flaw, mistake.

ant.- accuracy, correctness.

Larceny: misappropriation, burglary, embezzlement, peculation, pilfering, pillage, plunder, purloinment, robbery, shoplifting, theft, stealing.

ant.- compensation, recoupment, repayment, restoration, return.

Large: big, broad, bulky, colossal, capacious, commodious, giant, enormous, extensive, gigantic, great, immense, monstrous, long, roomy, sizable, towering, huge, vast, wide.

ant.- infinitesimal, microscopic, minute, paltry, puny.

Last: closing, concluding, final, conclusive, finishing, hindmost, latest, least, supreme, terminal, ultimate, utmost.

ant.- commencing, first, foremost, leading, primary.

Latent: concealed, dormant, hidden, implicit, implied, inherent, invisible, lurking, potential, quiescent, recondite, undeveloped, unobserved, unperceived, unseen, secret.

ant.- apparent, conspicuous, prominent, unmistakable, visible.

Latitude: breadth, compass, extent, freedom, length, range, scope, space, width.

ant.- narrowness, smallness.

Laudable: admirable, creditable, commendable, honourable, meritorious, praiseworthy.

ant.- corrupt, damnable, degraded, iniquitous, odious.

Laughable: absurd, amusing, comic, comical, droll, funny, facetious, jocose, ludicrous, ridiculous, humorous.

ant.- depressive, funereal, melancholy, morbid, painful.

Launch: begin, commence, float, inaugurate, initiate, open, start, get going.

ant.- close, end, finish.

Lavish: abundant, excessive, bountiful, exhaustive, exorbitant, exuberant, generous, inordinate, liberal, luxuriant, prodigal, profligate, profuse, replete, superabundant.

ant.- deficient, inadequate, meager, scanty, curtail, economize, skimp.

Law: act, code, commandment, constitution, covenant, decree, edict, enactment, command, jurisprudence, legality, order, legislation, mandate, precept, ordinance, principle, regulation, rule, statute, maxim, axiom.

ant.- felony, illegality, lawlessness, outlawry, transgression.

Lawful: admitted, allowable, approved, authorized, judicial, constitutional, legitimate, legal, legislative, permissible, recognized, valid, rightful, sanctioned, warranted.

ant.- arbitrary, criminal, prohibited, unauthorized, illegal.

Lax: careless, derelict, desultory, flaccid, neglectful, negligent, remiss, limp, unconscientious, undutiful, unobservant.

ant.- determined, faithful, honourable, meticulous.

Lay: lie down, recline, couch repose, rest, incline, fall.

ant.- rise, stand up, ascend, mount, get up.

Lazy: idle, inactive, indolent, inert, lackadaisical, laggard, lethargic, negligent, shiftless, sleepy, slothful, sluggish, supine, torpid, weak, worn, slow.

ant.- assiduous, industrious, diligent, active, perservering.

Lead: conduct, direct, escort, guide, pilot, steer, command, control, govern, manage, regulate, superintend, precede, supervise, pioneer.

ant.- perform, acquiesce, comply, obey, submit, follow.

Leader: captain, chief, chieftain, bellwether, commander, conductor, director, guide, head, master, principal, ruler, superior, vanguard.

ant.- adherent, devotee, disciple, follower, henchman.

Lean: bend, cant, careen, crook, decline, deflect, dip, heel, incline, list, sag, slant, slope, tend, tilt, tip.

ant.- erect, raise, straighten, rise.

Learned: academic, sagacious, accomplished, discerning, educated, enlightened, erudite, intelligent, knowing, lettered, literate, philosophic, profound, scholarly, well-informed, wise, cultured, knowledgeable, schooled, well-read.

ant.- dull, ignorant, illiterate, uncultured.

Leave: absence, concession, freedom, furlough, holiday, liberty, license, permission, vacation, withdrawal, allow, decamp, depart, go, desert, forsake, give up, let, permit, quit, relinquish, renounce, retire, vacate, withdraw.

ant.- confinement, hindrance, prohibition, restriction.

Legal: admitted, allowable, allowed, lawful, authorized, constitutional, legitimate, permissible, rightful, sanctioned, valid, warranted, vested, permitted, chartered, legalized, statutory.

ant.- criminal, illegal, illicit, prohibited, unconstitutional.

Legendary: fabulous, fanciful, fictitious, mythical, romantic, traditional, historical, mythological, historical.

ant.- actual, factual, real, true.

Legitimate: correct, genuine, justifiable, lawful, legal, logical, real, sanctioned, true, valid, warranted, proper.

ant.- illegal, illegitimate, invalid.

Leisure: ease, quiet, relaxation, repose, rest, freedom, idle hours, free time, time off, leave, liberty, pause, holiday, retirement, respite, spare time, vacation.

ant.- drudgery, duty, toil, travail, work.

Lengthen: dilate, draw out, elongate, extend, increase, prolong, protract, stretch, string out, produce, let out, spin out.

ant.- abbreviate, curtail, cut, shorten.

Lenient: charitable, clement, compassionate, forbearing, forgiving, humane, indulgent, kind, merciful, tender.

ant.- brutal, cruel, pitiless, tyrannical, unfeeling.

Lessen: abate, abridge, pare, contract, curtail, decrease, deduct, diminish, narrow, reduce, shrink, shorten, subtract, trim, mitigate.

ant.- amplify, enlarge, expand, increase, strengthen.

Let: allow, authorize, bear, rent concede, empower, grant, permit, sanction, suffer, tolerate, warrant, yield, lease.

ant.- defeat, halt, inhibit, obstruct, prevent.

Lethargy: apathy, drowsiness, languor, lassitude, listlessness, passivity, stupefaction, stupor, sluggishness, indifference.

ant.- activity, alertness, energy, liveliness, vitality.

Level: balanced, equal, even, flat, flush, horizontal, plain, plane, smooth.

ant.- hilly, irregular, uneven, lumpy, rugged.

Lewd: lecherous, pornographic, lustful, obscene, lascivious, smutty, prurient, salacious, unchaste.
ant.- chaste, decent, modest, pure, refined.

Liable: accountable, amenable, answerable, apt to, chargeable, exposed to, responsible, subject to, in danger, open to, dependent on, incurring.
ant.- absolved, except, free, immune, unlikely.

Libel: asperse, defame, detract, injure, vilify, lampoon, satirize, slander, aspersion, backbiting, calumny, defamation, slander, vilification.
ant.- defend, elevate, help, justify, applause, commendation, defense, flattery, praise.

Liberal: bountiful, broad-minded, lenient, charitable, beneficent, free, extensive, extravagant, left, generous, lavish, magnanimous, munificent, prodigal, noble-mided, tolerant, unselfish.
ant.- confined, conservative, greedy, penurious, narrow, restricted.

Liberate: absolve, discharge, acquit, deliver, emancipate, set-free, extricate, ransom, free, loose, pardon, redeem, release, rescue, unchain, save, unshackle.
ant.- confine, imprison, oppress, prohibit, restrict.

Liberty: autonomy, emancipation, freedom, sovereignty, independence, liberation, exemption, immunity, leisure, release, permission.
ant.- bondage, captivity, imprisonment, slavery, duress, confinement, constant, detention, obligation.

License: allow, commission, approve, authorize, endorse, permit, sanction, warrant, familiarity, liberty, privilege.
ant.- ban, check, forbid, limits, withhold.

Lie: deceive, exaggerate, fib, falsify, stretch, misinform, misrepresent.
ant.- be honest, declare (truth).

Life: animation, being, buoyancy, existence, liveliness, spirit, vigour, vitality, vivacity, duration, longevity, survival, living, vital force.

ant.- cessation, death, demise.

Lifeless: deceased, defunct, dead, demised, departed, extinct, inactive, inanimate, insensible, spiritless, stagnant, unconscious, inert, sluggish.
ant.- alive, animate, brisk, living, vigorous, vital.

Lift: boost, elevate, erect, exalt, heave, heighten, raise, uplift, jack up, pick up, get up.
ant.- abase, depreciate, depress, destroy, lower.

Light: beam, blaze, brightness, ray, brilliancy, dawn, flame, gleam, glow, illumination, incandescence, luminosity, luster, radiance, scintillation, shimmer, sparkle, shine, lamp, enlightenment, insight.
ant.- darkness, gloom, cloud, shadow, dusk, shade.

Likable: agreeable, amiable, companionable, good-natured, enjoyable, friendly, pleasant.
ant.- disagreeable, offensive, unattractive, unpleasant, unlikable.

Like: akin, allied, analogous, cognate, equal, equivalent, identical, indistinguishable, parallel, related, resembling, same, similar, characteristic.
ant.- contrary, disparate, dissimilar, distinct, opposed.

Likeness: analogy, similarity, correspondence, counterpart, equivalence, parity, facsimile, similitude, resemblance, copy.
ant.- difference, distinction, variation.

Limit: border, borderline, end, boundary, frontier, limitation, line.
ant.- boundlessness, endlessness, extension, infinity.

Limpid: bright, clear, crystal, crystalline, glassy, pellucid, translucent, transparent, pure, lucid.
ant.- cloudy, dark, muddy, opaque, turbid.

Linger: abide, bide, dawdle, delay, falter, hesitate, lag, loiter, lumber, remain, rest, stay, tarry, wait, dally, poke.
ant.- bustle, dash, dart, hurry, speed.

Link: associate, attach, bind, bond, conjoin, connect, unite, couple, fasten, join, pin, tie.
ant.- detach, divide, separate, cut, sever.

Liquid: dissolved, flowing, fluent, fluid, juicy, liquefied, melted, molten, sappy, solvent, succulent, watery.
ant.- congealed, dense, solid, undissolved.

Listen: attend to, audit, hear, harken, heed, list, monitor, overhear, follow, grant, obey, observe.
ant.- disregard, ignore, reject, scorn.

Little: diminutive, dwarfish, elfin, infinitesimal, miniature, minute, petite, petty, puny, small, tiny, microscopic, wee, dwarfed, exiguous, pygmy, undersized.
ant.- colossal, enormous, immense, mighty, titanic.

Lively: active, animated, blithe, brisk bustling, ebullient, energetic, exhilarated, frolicsome, intense, rapid, spirited, sprightly, supple, vigorous, vivacious, bright, clear, fresh, glowing, sparking, vivid.
ant.- dull, insipid, listless, stale, vapid.

Load: burden, encumber, cargo, lading, shipment.
ant.- alleviate, console, ease, lighten, mitigate.

Loathe: abhor, abominate, condemn, denounce, despise, detest, dislike, hate.
ant.- admire, approve, cherish, love, respect.

Lofty: high, towering, raised, sky-high, soaring, elevated, tall, pompous, proud, stately, sublime, arrogant, conceited, haughty, pretentious, vain.
ant.- little, short, small, low, common, humble, lowly, modest, ordinary, plebeian.

Logical: cogent, convincing, dialectical, discriminating, effective, efficacious, rational, reasonable, sound, strong, valid, coherent, weightily.
ant.- illogical, irrational, weak, unreasonable, incoherent, incongruous.

Lone: deserted, desolate, only, isolated, lonely, lonesome, secluded, alone, single, sole, solitary.
ant.- accompanied, attended, jointed, group, surrounded, together.

Lonely: alone, desolate, lone isolated, lonesome, secluded, sequestered, solitary, lonesome.
ant.- befriended, together, accompanied, crowded.

Long: drawn out, elongated, extended, interminable, lasting, lengthy, lingering, prolix, prolonged, protracted, tedious, distant, faraway, far-off, remote.
ant.- abridged, brief, concise, short, terse, accessible.

Look: behold, contemplate, discern, distinguish, eye, gaze, glance, glimpse, perceive, scan, see, stare, watch, appear, seem, examine, inspect, investigate, observe.
ant.- avert, hide, ignore, miss, overlook.

Loose: disengaged, flowing, free, indefinite, lax, limp, relaxed, slack, unbound, unconfined, unfastened, untied, vague, careless, dissolute, heedless.
ant.- bound, curbed, fast, taut, tied, tight.

Lose: drop, fail, falter, flounder, flunk, fold, forfeit, fumble, miscarry, mislay, miss, squander, stumble, waste.
ant.- accomplish, improve, overcome, regain.

Loss: casualty, damage, decline, deficiency, lack, deprivation, deterioration, detriment, disadvantage, impairment, retardation, failure.
ant.- achievement, finding, acquisition, advancement, gain, improvement.

Lot: accumulation, pile, abundance, hoard, mass, lump, luck, destiny, predestination, chance.
ant.- empty, blank, vacant, void.

Loud: blaring, blatant, shrill, clamorous, deafening, noisy, piercing, resonant, resounding, sonorous, stentorian, vociferous.
ant.- dulcet, faint, inaudible, quiet, soft, subdued.

Love: adoration, affection, desire, attachment, charity, devotion, endearment, favour, fondness, intimacy, liking, passion, respect, sentiment.
ant.- aversion, dislike, enmity, hatred, indifference, scorn.

Lovely: adorable, attractive, beauteous, beautiful, captivating, charming, fine, comely, delightful, enticing, elegant, enchanting, fair, graceful, handsome, lovable, pretty, sweet, winsome.

ant.- foul, hideous, homely, repulsive, repugnant.

Low: abject, contemptible, debased, degraded, despicable, disgraceful, dishonourable, grovelling, ignoble, ignominious, lowly, mean, menial, servile, shameless, sordid, vile, vulgar.

ant.- esteemed, exalted, honoured, lofty, noble.

Lower: inferior, junior, lesser, low level, smaller, minor, poorer, adulterate, secondary, subordinate, abase, corrupt, debase, degrade, deprave, defile, depress, humiliate.

ant.- better, greater, higher, superior, enhance, improve, raise, restore, vitalize.

Loyal: constant, dedicated, true, devoted, earnest, faithful, patriotic, steadfast, trustworthy, unfailing, unswerving.

ant.- disloyal, faithless, false, seditious, treacherous.

Lucid: bright, clear, diaphanous, glossy, limpid, luminous, radiant, serene, transparent, explicit, manifest, obvious, understandable, visible, unmistakable.

ant.- dark, gloomy, murky, nebulous.

Lucky: advantageous, benign, successful, auspicious, happy, conquering, favoured, felicitous, flourishing, fortuitous, fortunate, thriving, propitious, prosperous, triumphant, victorious, opportune.

ant.- cheerless, defeated, ill-fated, persecuted, down-trodden.

Lucrative: advantageous, gainful, profitable, remunerative, self-sustaining, worthwhile, well-paying, money-making, productive.

ant.- costly, failing, losing, troublesome, wasteful.

Ludicrous: absurd, bizarre, incongruous, comical, farcical, funny, laughable, outlandish, ridiculous.

ant.- logical, normal, reasonable, serious, solemn.

Luminous: bright, brilliant, clear, gleaming, glowing, incandescent, lucid, lustrous, radiant, shining, luminary, lighted.

ant.- dim, murky, obscure, dull, unclear.

Lunacy: aberration, craziness, feeblemindedness, dementia, derangement, idiocy, frenzy, imbalance, insanity, madness, mania, psychosis. *ant.*- balance, prudence, sanity, normality, rationality, stability.

Lure: allure, attract, bewitch, charm, coax, decoy, ensure, bait, entangle, entice, entrap, fascinate, induce, inveigle, mesmerize, tempt, wheedle. *ant.*- alienate, antagonize, discourage, repel, revolt.

Lust: avarice, carnality, desire, concupiscence, craving, urge, cupidity, greed, hankering, hungering, longing, yearning, wantonness. *ant.*- chastity, purity, restraint, abomination, aversion, distaste, loathing.

Lustre: brightness, brilliance, brilliancy, effulgence, glossiness, luminosity, radiance, sheen, shimmer, splendour, distinction, fame, renown, repute. *ant.*- cloudiness, darkness, drabness, murkiness, shade, baseness, shame, dishonour, disrepute, reproach.

Luxurious: elegant, epicurean, opulent, ornate, pampered, rich, self-indulgent, sensuous, splendid, sumptuous. *ant.*- ascetic, bare, monastic, drab, spartan.

❑

M

Mad: crazy, daft, delirious, demented, deranged, insane, lunatic, maniacal, paranoid, psychotic, scatterbrained, unbalanced, unhinged.
ant.- serene, balanced, sane, rational, reasonable, sensible, sound.

Magnanimous: beneficent, bountiful, charitable, unselfish, chivalrous, generous, giving, great-hearted, heroic, liberal, high-minded, munificent, great-souled, openhanded.
ant.- covetous, egotistical, greedy, miserly, selfish.

Magnificent: elegant, excellent, glorious, gorgeous, grand, kingly, majestic, radiant, rich, spectacular, splendid, stately, sublime, sumptuous, superb.
ant.- common, humble, modest, ordinary, plebeian.

Magnify: aggrandize, amplify, augment, embroider, enhance, enlarge, exaggerate, expand, heighten, hyperbolize, stretch, increase, overstate.
ant.- decrease, depreciate, diminish, minimize, understate.

Magnitude: amplitude, bigness, brightness, bulk, dimensions, expanse, extension, extent, girth, greatness, immensity, highness, largeness, vastness.
ant.- dimness, insignificance, smallness, triviality, paucity.

Main: cardinal, central, chief, essential, first, foremost, prime, highest, leading, paramount, predominant.
ant.- auxiliary, unessential, minor, secondary, subordinate.

Maintain: continue, keep, claim, preserve, retain, sustain, support, uphold, affirm, allege, assert, confirm, contend, declare, defend, hold, justify, prove, vindicate.
ant.- abandon, discontinue, desert, forsake, condemn, quit, deny, oppose, reject, resist.

Majestic: august, dignified, distinguished, eminent, stately, exalted, grand, grandiose, illustrious, imperial, imposing, impressive, lofty, magnificent, noble, pompous, prominent, splendid, sublime, towering.

ant.- humble, insignificant, low, ordinary, shabby.

Make: assemble, build, carve, complete, create, compose, construct, do, drive, establish, execute, fabricate, fashion, forge, form, frame, generate, invent, manufacture, mold, produce, shape.

ant.- annihilate, demolish, break, destroy, mutilate.

Makeshift: alternative, stop-gap, expedient, momentary, provisional, substitute, short-term, temporary.

ant.- abiding, permanent, fixed.

Malady: affliction, ailment, disease, disorder, illness, indisposition, infirmity, sickness.

ant.- health, soundness, well-being, vigour.

Malevolence: animosity, enmity, evil, grudge, hate, hostility, ill will, malice, malignancy, malignity, rancour, recrimination, spite, treachery.

ant.- affection, charity, love, sympathy, toleration.

Malign: asperse, besmirch, calumniate, defame, detract, discredit, disparage, libel, revile, scandalize, slander, vilify, traduce.

ant.- acclaim, celebrate, extol, praise, respect.

Malignant: deadly, evil, fatal, hostile, malevolent, malign, mischievous, pernicious, spiteful, virulent.

ant.- benign, good, helpful, peaceful.

Malleable: changeable, ductile, flexible, impressionable, mouldable, plastic, pliant, supple, yielding.

ant.- fixed, indomitable, resolute, rigid, unyielding.

Manage: administer, watch, command, conduct, control, direct, rule, dominate, govern, guide, run, head, officiate, oversee, regulate, steer, bridle, superintend, supervise.

ant.- abandon, maladminister, misconduct, mismanage, bungle, spoil.

Manifest: clear, fair, sunny, cloudless, limpid, defined, transparent, apparent, conspicuous, definite, distinct, evident, explicit, lucid, plain, obvious, patent, unmistakable, unveiled, visible, open, unobstructed, disclose, show, exhibit, reveal.

ant.- cloudy, foul, overcast, ambiguous, complex, vague, obscure, unclear, buried, concealed, covered, hidden, conceal.

Manoeuvre: artifice, design, feint, plan, plot, ruse, scheme, stratagem, tactic, wile.

ant.- cessation, inaction, inactivity, rest.

Many: countless, innumerable, diverse, manifold, multifarious, multitudinous, myriad, numerous, several, sundry, various.

ant.- infrequent, meager, few, scanty, scarce.

Mar: damage, deface, deform, distort, harm, hurt, impair, injure, mutilate, scar, spoil, stain, twist, warp, waste, disfigure, blemish, scratch.

ant.- adorn, beautify, better, embellish.

Margin: bank, border, brim, brink, boundary, fence, fringe, leeway, limit, rim, shore, edge, verge.

ant.- center, extension, heart, interior, surface.

Marine: aquatic, hydrographic, maritime, natatorial, nautical, naval, ocean, going, oceanic, oceanographic, pelagic, seafaring, seagoing.

ant.- alluvial, ashore, earthly, geodetic, terrestrial.

Marriage: conjugality, union, espousal, matrimony, nuptials, wedding, wedlock.

ant.- celibacy, divorce, virginity, separation, singleness.

Massacre: slaughter, butchery, murder, killing, carnage.

ant.- animation, preservation, protection, resuscitation.

Massive: colossal, heavy, huge, large, ponderous, grievous, trying, unwieldy, gloomy, grave, serious, sluggish, bulky.

ant.- airy, delicate, light, small.

Master: captain, champion, chief, commander, conqueror, director, employer, governor, head, lord, manager, mentor, overseer, potentate, principal, ruler, superior, teacher, victor, owner, proprietor, expert.

ant.- apprentice, dependent, follower, pupil, amateur, beginner, greenhorn, novice, neophyte.

Mastery: ability, deftness, skill, dexterity, expertise, skillfulness, expertness.

ant.- defeat, failure, impotence, inferiority, subjugation.

Material: body, cloth, fabric, matter, stuff, substance, thing, bodily, concrete, corporeal, physical, ponderable, sensible, solid, somatic, substantial, tangible, temporal.

ant.- nothingness, airy, bodiless, ethereal, spiritual.

Mature: adult, aged, complete, consummate, developed, experienced, full-grown, matured, mellow, pubescent, ready, ripe, seasoned.

ant.- immature, juvenile, premature, raw, undeveloped.

Mean: abject, contemptible, debased, base, degraded, low, despicable, ignoble, obscure, plebeian, sordid, vile, vulgar, bad-tempered, malicious, offensive, stingy, mercenary, miserly, selfish, parsimonious, nasty, penurious.

ant.- admirable, high, liberal, distinguished, extraordinary, superior, benevolent, charitable, generous, indulgent, philanthropic, profuse.

Mechanical: automated, rote, automatic, routine, impulsive, instinctive, powerdriven, involuntary, machinelike, autonomic, unreasoned, powered, perfunctory.

ant.- manual.

Meddle: impede, interfere, interpose, interrupt, intervene, intrude, obtrude.

ant.- aid, encourage, support.

Mediocre: average, medium, mean, median, intermediate, commonplace, fair, middling, moderate, ordinary, passable, normal, medium, medial.

ant.- exceptional, superior, extraordinary, outstanding, unusual.

Meditate: cogitate, consider, contemplate, deliberate, study, muse, ponder, reason, reflect, speculate, remember, think, imagine.

ant.- dismiss, disregard, divert, neglect, overlook.

Meek: compliant, demure, mild, docile, domestic, gentle, humble, modest, obedient, pacific, patient, peaceful, subdued, submissive, tame, tolerant.
ant.- arrogant, obstinate, pompous, savage, animated, exciting, lively, spirited, fierce.

Meet: assemble, connect, find, converge, encounter, engage, greet, intersect, join, touch, answer, fulfil, gratify.
ant.- avoid, cleave, disperse, miss, separate.

Melancholy: dejected, glum, depressed, despondent, sad, disconsolate, dismal, moody, dispirited, doleful, forlorn, funereal, gloomy, joyless, mournful, sorrowful, sulky, wistful, pensive, somber.
ant.- cheerful, happy, jubilant, spirited, vivacious.

Mellow: full-flavoured, mature, perfected, sweet, delicate, pleasing, refined, relaxed, subdued, sweet-sounding, ripe, soft, rich.
ant.- dull, hard, immature, sour, stale, callous, crude.

Memory: recollection, remembrance, reminiscence, retention, retrospection, retentiveness, recognition, recurrence, retrospect, afterthought.
ant.- amnesia, effacement, forgetfulness, oblivion, unconsciousness.

Mend: fix, patch, repair, sew, restore, touch up, ameliorate, better, correct, improve, heal, rectify, refine, reform, well, refresh, remedy, renew, get, revive, recover.
ant.- damage, deform, impair, mar, wound, deteriorate, fall, ill, wane, weaken.

Mendicant: beggar, pauper, ragamuffin, poverty-stricken, starveling, tatterdemalion.
ant.- benefactor, contributor, donor, giver.

Menial: abject, degrading, base, humble, ignoble, lowly, mean, servile.
ant.- elevated, expert, noble, professional, uplifting.

Mentality: consciousness, brain, intellect, intelligence, judgment, mind, perception, intention, psyche, thought, understanding, wisdom, will, disposition, inclination, wish.
ant.- corporeality, materiality, matter.

Mentor: advisor, counsellor, coach, guide, instructor, leader, monitor, teacher.
ant.- disciple, follower, pupil, student.

Mercenary: avaricious, venal, greedy, grasping, selfish, sordid, calculating.
ant.- generous, honourable, liberal, unselfish.

Merciful: beneficent, kind, benignant, compassionate, clement, forbearing, forgiving, gracious, humane, pitying, philanthropic, soft-hearted, sympathetic, tender, lenient, tolerant.
ant.- barbarous, cruel, pitiless, ruthless, tyrannical.

Mercy: benevolence, benignity, charity, clemency, leniency, compassion, forbearing, pity, forgiveness, grace, kindness, mildness, tolerance.
ant.- banishment, inhumanity, oppression, punishment, vengeance.

Merge: amalgamate, blend, coalesce, combine, commingle, conjoin, consolidate, fuse, integrate, join, mingle, mix, unify, unite, absorb.
ant.- decompose, divest, divide, separate.

Merit: excellence, goodness, quality, talent, regard, value, virtue, worth, worthiness, effectiveness, efficacy, force, power, strength.
ant.- weakness, unworthiness.

Merry: animated, blithe, gay, buoyant, cheerful, ebullient, elated, exhilarated, exuberant, gleeful, hilarious, jocular, jolly, jovial, joyous, jubilant, light-hearted, lively, mirthful, rollicking, spirited, sprightly, vivacious.
ant.- gloomy, melancholy, morose, pessimistic, wretched.

Mess: confusion, dilemma, conglomeration, disorder, disorganization, hodgepodge, jumble, litter, medley, melange, mixture, potpourri, difficulty, plight, predicament, problem.
ant.- arrangement, method, order, system, tidiness.

Method: arrangement, design, fashion, form, manner, mode, order, plan, procedure, process, scheme, system, technique, vogue, way, schematic, style, stylistic, modal, procedural, planned, arranged.

ant.- chaos, confusion, disarrangement, disorder, muddle, irregularity.

Meticulous: cautious, heedful, regardful, scrupulous, careful, thorough.

ant.- careless, disheveled, cursory, sloppy, unkempt.

Methodical: orderly, stylistic, systematic, schematic, well-regulated, planned, arranged, routine.

ant.- careless, disordered, disorderly, informal, loose, rough, vague.

Microscopic: diminutive, fine, imperceptible, tiny, invisible, infinitesimal, minute.

ant.- enormous, huge, large.

Middle: axis, center, midpoint, focus, heart, mean, midst, nucleus, middle, medium, pivot, axial, central, halfway, interjacent, intermediate, core, mediocre, pivotal.

ant.- border, boundary, rim, outskirts, periphery.

Might: energy, force, potency, power, puissance, strength, sturdiness, sway, tenacity, vigour, vitality.

ant.- frailty, impotence, inability, vulnerability, weakness.

Mighty: doughty, forceful, hale, energetic, forcible, husky, manful, momentous, robust, muscular, overpowering, potent, powerful, puissant, healthy, sound, stalwart, strapping, strong, sturdy, vigorous.

ant.- delicate, enervated, feeble, flaccid, weak.

Mild: calm, genial, gentle, humane, kind, meek, mellow, moderate, pacific, patient, peaceful, placid, quiet, soft, smooth, soothing, temperate, tender, tranquil, savoury, bland, sweet.

ant.- bitter, pacifist, fierce, harsh, irritating, uncouth, acid, biting, bitter, sour, stringent.

Militant: aggressive, armed, belligerent, combative, contentious, fighting, hostile, pugnacious, warring, belicose, war-like.

ant.- amenable, pacific, pacifist, peaceful, submissive.

Mimic: ape, caricature, copy, duplicate, parody, imitate, impersonate, repeat, echo, reproduce, simulate, mime.

ant.- create, design, discover, invent.

Mingle: amalgamate, blend, associate, conjoin, combine, commingle, join, compound, confound, merge, mix, unite, intermingle.

ant.- disjoin, separate, sort.

Miniature: abridged, small, diminutive, little, minuscule, minute, reduced, tiny, petite, minikin, dwarf, pygmy.

ant.- fullsize, large, normal, regular.

Minimize: belittle, curtail, deduct, detract, diminish, disparage, lessen, reduce, shorten, subtract.

ant.- amplify, enlarge, exalt, expand, magnify.

Minister: ambassador, cleric, churchman, clergyman, diplomat, consul, curate, delegate, divine, ecclesiastic, envoy, official, padre, parson, pastor, preacher, priest, rector, representative, revered, legate.

ant.- apostate, disciple, follower, layman, juvenile.

Minor: youthful, immature, underage, teenage, younger, adolescent, child.

ant.- adult, of age.

Minute: diminutive, exiguous, fine, infinitesimal, insignificant, little, microscopic, miniature, minuscule, molecular, petty, precise, puny, small, tiny.

ant.- colossal, comprehensive, enormous, extensive.

Miraculous: amazing, astounding, astonishing, awesome, extraordinary, incredible, inexplicable, marvelous, unearthly, metaphysical, preternatural, spectacular, supernatural, prodigious, wondrous.

ant.- commonplace, customary, insignificant, natural, ordinary.

Mirage: apparition, delusion, fantasy, figment, hallucination, illusion, phantasm.

ant.- actuality, substance, reality.

Miscarriage: defeat, failure, mischance, misadventure, fiasco, abortion.

ant.- achievement, success, victory.

Miscellaneous: assorted, dissimilar, diverse, diversified, heterogeneous, indiscriminate, motley, promiscuous, sundry, variant, varied, many-sided, various.

ant.- classified, homogeneous, ordered, same, sorted.

Mischief: naughtiness, pranks, roguery, roguishness, shenanigans.

ant.- betterment, favour, kindness, support, vindication.

Miserable: afflicted, crushed, comfortless, disconsolate, discontented, dismal, sickly, distressed, suffering wretched, forlorn, heartbroken, pained, pitiable, sorrowful, despicable, contemptible, insufficient, low, lamentable, mean, abject, meager, paltry, poor, scanty, small, stingy.

ant.- contented, happy, lively, rejoicing, noble, respectable, fortunate, prosperous, significant.

Miser: avaricious, close-fisted, niggard, parsimonious, tight-fisted, penurious, stingy, hoard, money-grubber, skinflint.

ant.- altruistic, extravagant, generous, liberal, bountiful, munificent.

Misery: agony, anguish, anxiety, desolation, despair, disaster, despondency, distress, grief, heartache, mortification, pain, sorrow, suffering, torment, trial, tribulation, woe, wretchedness, affliction, calamity, misfortune, trouble, doleful, poverty.

ant.- bliss, delight, ecstasy, element, fortune, peace, health, salubrity, vigour.

Misfortune: accident, injury, calamity, adversity, affliction, bereavement, casualty, catastrophe, disaster, distress, hardship, loss, misadventure, mishap, privation, setback, tribulation.

ant.- advantage, blessing, contentment, prosperity, success, well-being.

Misgiving: distrust, doubt, hesitation, mistrust, suspicion, uncertainty, apprehension, premonition.

ant.- certainty, security, sureness, trust.

Misinterpret: distort, falsify, misconceive, misconstrue, misunderstand, misjudge, misrepresent, pervert.

ant.- comprehend, perceive, understand.

Misleading: deceitful, illusive, deceptive, delusive, delusory, fallacious, specious.
ant.- authentic, forthright, genuine, straightforward, direct, truthful.

Misrepresent: misreport, misinterpret, misconstrue, misquote, garble, dissemble, distort, falsify, mislead, belie, misstate, pervert, simulate.
ant.- delineate, depict, represent.

Miss: fail, default, lack, lose, miscarry, omit, overlook, skip.
ant.- achieve, attain, have, succeed, catch, grab, hold.

Mistake: blunder, error, failure, fallacy, fault, flaw, inaccuracy, misapprehension, slip, misconception.
ant.- accuracy, correctness, perfection, precision, truth, veracity.

Misunderstanding: confusion, difference, disagreement, dissension, misapprehension, misconception, discord, misinterpretation.
ant.- understanding.

Misuse: abuse, asperse, defame, desecrate, disparage, harm, ill-use, injure, malign, maltreat, maul, mishandle, pervert, revile, scandalize, traduce, vilify, wrong, consume, dissipate, misemploy, misappropriate, misapply.
ant.- succour, accumulate, conserve, economize, retain, preserve.

Mitigate: abate, allay, alleviate, ameliorate, assuage, palliate, decrease, dilute, diminish, extenuate, lessen, lighten, moderate, modify, mollify, relieve, soften, solace, soothe, subdue, temper, weaken.
ant.- aggravate, deepen, increase, inflate, intensify, provoke.

Mix: adulterate, alloy, blend, commix, merge, combine, commingle, compound, join, mingle, concoct, crossbreed, homogenize, incorporate, intermingle, intermix, fuse, coalesce, jumble, integrate, confound, mix up, tangle, associate, consort, join, unite.

ant.- detach, disperse, divide, separate, sort, segregate.

Mixture: assortment, hotchpotch, jumble, medley, alloy, association, amalgam, amalgamation, combination, union, junction, concoction, conglomeration, composite, blend, compound, fusion.
ant.- isolation, separation, purity, simplicity, pedigree, purebred.

Mob: assemblage, bevy, crowd, crush, drove, flock, gang, gathering, herd, horde, host, multitude, populace, press, concourse, rabble, riffraff, swarm, throng.
ant.- recluded, lonely.

Mock: deride, fleer, flout, gibe, jeer, mimic, practice, ridicule, satirize, tantalize, scoff, sneer at, taunt.
ant.- compliment, flatter, honour, praise, support.

Mode: condition, course, way, custom, design, fashion, manner, method, practice, procedure, scheme, state, system, usage, vogue, style.
ant.- confusion, disorder.

Moderate: abate, allay, assuage, decrease, diminish, lessen, lower, palliate, quell, reduce, subdue, suppress, temper, weaken.
ant.- excessive, extravagant, liberal, radical.

Modern: contemporary, current, fresh, latest, novel, present, new, recent, renovated.
ant.- ancient, antiquated, bygone, primitive, obsolete, outmoded.

Modest: bashful, diffident, humble, meek, reserved, retiring, shy, timid, unassuming, unpretentious.
ant.- arrogant, bold, conceited, egotistical, ostentatious, immodest.

Modification: adaptation, alteration, change, limitation, modulation, mutation, variety, substitution, transformation, variation, vicissitude.
ant.- monotony, stability, uniformity.

Modify: adapt, alter, change, convert, reform, recast, redo, refashion, reshape, remodel, transfigure, transform, vary.
ant.- spoil, corrupt.

Moist: aqueous, damp, dank, dewy, dripping, humid, juicy, muggy, saturated, sloppy, soaked, swampy, vapourous, sodden, watery, clammy, wet, soppy.

ant.- arid, barren, parched, dehydrated, dry, waterless.

Molest: annoy, bother, disturb, harass, irritate, maltreat, oppress, persecute, pester, plague, tease, trouble, vex.
ant.- aid, comfort, defend, encourage, protect, soothe.

Momentous: consequential, far-reaching, important, notable, great, influential, material, memorable, salient, pressing, prominent, relevant, significant, solemn, vital, weighty.
ant.- boring, commonplace, immaterial, insignificant, trivial.

Monotonous: boring, dreary, depressive, dry, dull, flat, humdrum, prosy, repetitious, sluggish, tedious, tiresome, uninteresting, unvaried, tardy, wearisome.
ant.- appealing, entertaining, exciting, refreshing, varied, versatile.

Moral: chaste, decent, ethical, good, honest, honourable, just, noble, pure, right, righteous, scrupulous, upright, virtuous.
ant.- amoral, dishonourable, evil, immoral, unethical.

Morose: cantankerous, dour, churlish, crabbed, depressed, fretful, gloomy, grouchy, gruff, petulant, splenetic, sulky, sullen, unamiable, glum, surly.
ant.- buoyant, cheerful, exhilarated, good natured, pleasant.

Mortal: deadly, destructive, fatal, lethal, poisonous, serious, ephemeral, passing, temporal, transient.
ant.- curative, life-giving, reviving, strengthening, vivifying, trifling, trivial, everlasting, immortal, perpetual.

Mortification: abasement, annoyance, dissatisfaction, embarrassment, humiliation, chagrin, shame, vexation.
ant.- elevation, happiness, praise, satisfaction, success.

Motion: action, activity, change, mobility, move, movement, passage, revolution, movableness.
ant.- halt, immobility, inaction, repose, stillness.

Motley: assorted, composite, diverse, heterogeneous, incongruous, indiscriminate, mixed, miscellaneous, mottled, sundry, speckled,

variegated, jumbled, kaleidoscopic, crazy-quilt.
ant.- homogeneous, like, pure, similar, unvaried.

Mount: arise, ascend, aspire, climb, grow, increase, rise, scale, scramble, soar, surge, swell, tower, go up.
ant.- collapse, decline, drop, descend, diminish, slump.

Mourn: agonize, bewail, cry, bemoan, bewail, deplore, droop, fret, rue, grieve, groan, languish, wail, lament, miss, pray, regret, repine, sigh, sing, sorrow, suffer, whimper, yearn.
ant.- celebrate, exult, laugh, rejoice.

Move: actuate, advance, agitate, arouse, convey, drive, excite, impel, incite, induce, influence, instigate, operate, persuade, proceed, propel, run, propose, push, rouse, shift, start, simulate, stir, transfer, transport, travel, urge.
ant.- cease, deter, dissuade, halt, pacify, rest, suppress.

Muddled: addled, befuddled, bewildered, chaotic, messy, confounded, confused, mixed up, deranged, disarrayed, disconcerted, disordered, disorganized, indistinct, jumbled.
ant.- orderly, exact, precise, clear, organized.

Multiply: augment, enlarge, generate, grow, increase, propagate, reproduce, proliferate, accrue, outnumber.
ant.- lessen, reduce, precise.

Multitude: aggregation, host, assemblage, congregation, crowd, glassy, gathering, horde, legion, numerousness, multiplicity, profusion, mob, populace, swarm, throng.
ant.- fraction, handful, nobody, paucity, scarcity.

Mundane: carnal, earthly, mortal, profane, secular, temporal, terrestrial, worldly.
ant.- celestial, heavenly, unearthly, eternal, paradisaic, spiritual.

Munificent: altruistic, free-handed, beneficent, liberal, benevolent, charitable, generous, hospitable, philanthropic, princely, unselfish, lavish, bounteous, bountiful, open-handed.
ant.- miserly, avaricious, selfish, covetous, grasping.

Murder: annihilate, assassinate, butcher, execute, immolate, kill, massacre, poison, slaughter, shoot, slay, stab, victimize.
ant.- animate, propagate, nurse, refresh, restore, vitalize.

Murmur: babble, growl, purr, grouse, grumble, hum, mumble, mutter.
ant.- silent, quiet, noiseless, soundless.

Muscular: athletic, brawny, forceful, husky, powerful, sinewy, stalwart, strong, sturdy, vigorous.
ant.- feeble, flabby, infirm, weak.

Musical: assonant, choral, euphonic, lyrical, euphonious, harmonious, melodic, tuneful, melodious, symphonic, tonal, orchestral.
ant.- clashing, discordant, dissonant, grating, harsh.

Muster: accumulate, amass, assemble, collect, congregate, convene, mobilize, convoke, gather, organize, summon up, garner, harvest, pick.
ant.- disjoin, disperse, divert, scatter, separate.

Mute: aphasia, aphasic, mum, aphonic, unspoken, dumb, tonguetied, tongueless, still, gagged, hushed, inarticulate, inaudible, noiseless, quiet, silent, soundless, speechless, taciturn, voiceless.
ant.- articulate, garrulous, loquacious, loud, raucous, talkative, vocal.

Mutual: analogous, common, correlative, reciprocal, joint, correspondent, equivalent, like, interchangeable, shared, similar.
ant.- dissociated, separate, unlike, divergent, unshared.

Mysterious: abstruse, arcane, baffling, covert, cryptic, dark, enigmatical, impenetrable, incomprehensible, inexplicable, inscrutable, hidden, mystical, mystifying, obscure, occult.
ant.- apparent, distinct, explicit, lucid, obvious.

Mystery: cabala, conundrum, enigma, problem, puzzle, riddle, secret.
ant.- answer, key, solution.

Myth: allegory, chronicle, fable, phantasy, fiction, folk-tale, legend, lore, saga, tale.
ant.- fact, history.

Mythical: allegorical, apocryphal, fabricated, fabulous, fanciful, fantastic, fictitious, imaginary, mythological, legendary, visionary.
ant.- actual, factual, real, true, historical.

❑

N

Nag: aggravate, annoy, badger, bother, discompose, disturb, goad, harass, harry, heckle, irritate, exacerbate, molest, pester, plague, provoke, vex, scold, tease, torment, worry.
ant.- comfort, delight, mollify, please, soothe.

Naive: guileless, inexperienced, ingenuous, innocent, plain, unaffected, unsophisticated, unworldly.
ant.- cunning, experienced, crafty, sophisticated, wise.

Naked: bare, nude, stripped, unclad, unclothed, uncovered, undressed, unappareled.
ant.- covered, wrapped up, attired, clothed, dressed.

Name: appellation, cognomen, denomination, designation, epithet, surname, character, reputation, repute, distinction, title, eminence, fame, renown.
ant.- anonymity, namelessness.

Narrate: declaim, describe, detail, disclose, enumerate, mention, portray, proclaim, recite, recapitulate, recount, tell, rehearse, relate, repeat, report, reveal, state, unfold.
ant.- conceal, disguise, stifle, repress, withhold.

Narrow: confined, contracted, cramped, limited, restricted, scrawny, slender, spindling, thread like, bigoted, dogmatic, fanatical, illiberal, intolerant, narrow-minded, prejudiced.
ant.- broad, expanded, fleshy, extended, wide, corpulent, fat, stout.

Nasty: dirty, foul, polluted, squalid, indecent, obscene, smutty, disgusting, nauseating, lewd, filthy.
ant.- clean, spotless, unsullied, decent, attractive, delightful, pleasant, sweet, clear, sunny.

Native: citizen, resident, aboriginal, congenital, local, domestic, endemic, inborn, indigenous, inherent, innate, natal, natural, original, pristine, regional, vernacular.
ant.- alien, artificial, extrinsic, foreign, imported, unnatural.

Natural: fundamental, genetic, inherent, innate, intrinsic, native, original, normal, regular, artless, genuine, ingenuous, legitimate, real, simple, spontaneous, unaffected, unsophisticated.

ant.- abnormal, artificial, unnatural contingent, external, extrinsic, objective, irregular.

Nauseous: abhorrent, nasty, abominable, despicable, detestable, disgusting, loathsome, repulsive, sickening, unpalatable.

ant.- ambrosial, delectable, delicious, desirable, savory.

Near: abutting, adjacent, close, alongside, nearby, adjoining, contiguous, neighbouring, proximate, touching, nigh, approaching, expected, coming, imminent, impending.

ant.- far, remote, deferred, expired, distant, remote.

Neat: clear, correct, exact, finished, orderly, precise, proportioned, shapely, spotless, spruce, suitable, symmetrical, tidy, trim, well-done, well-ordered.

ant.- awkward, disordered, irregular, lax, slipshod.

Necessary: compulsory, essential, expedient, imperative, indispensable, inevitable, inexorable, irrevocable, needful, obligatory, pressing, required, requisite, unavoidable, undeniable, urgent, in demand.

ant.- extravagant, optional, superfluous, unnecessary.

Need: necessity, needfulness, essentiality, indispensability, exigency, urgency, obligation, requirement, require, want, wish.

ant.- comfort, luxury, plenty, fullness.

Neglect: apathy, carelessness, default, evasion, deferment, dereliction, failure, disregard, disrespect, heedlessness, negligence, nonchalance, procrastination, recklessness, scorn, slight, thoughtlessness, delinquency, omission.

ant.- attention, care, diligence, surveillance.

Neutral: disinterested, impartial, indeterminate, indifferent, non-partisan, unallied, unconcerned, undecided, irresolute.

ant.- biased, decided, involved, positive, predisposed.

New: advanced, current, fresh, latest, modern, novel, original, recent, unfamiliar, untried, up-to-date.
ant.- ancient, archaic, obsolete, outmoded.

Nimble: active, agile, alert, brisk, fast, lively, prompt, quick, rapid, speedy, sprightly, spry, supple, swift, acute.
ant.- clumsy, dull, inert, lumbering, slow.

Noble: aristocratic, august, dignified, distinguished, elevated, eminent, exalted, genteel, grand, honourable, illustrious, imperial, lordly, loyal, majestic, princely, regal, stately, sublime, superior.
ant.- abject, base, ignoble, low, plebeian servile.

Noise: babel, blare, clamour, clatter, cry, din, hubbub, pandemonium, racket, row, sound, tumult, uproar.
ant.- calm, hush, quiet, silence, tranquillity.

Nonchalant: inconsiderate, indifferent, negligent, cool, unconcerned, careless, imperturbable, casual, unruffled, composed.
ant.- attentive, considerate, concerned, vigilant, active, agitated, eager, enthusiastic, careful, excitable, fervid, zealous.

Nonsense: absurdity, babble, drivel, foolishness, gibberish, imbecility, inanity, jargon, rigmarole, senselessness, silliness, trash.
ant.- accuracy, common sense, clarify, substance, wisdom.

Normal: average, common, conventional, general, natural, ordinary, reasonable, regular, standard, typical, uniform, sane, usual.
ant.- abnormal, exceptional, irregular, peculiar, strange.

Nosey: curious, inquiring, prying, inquisitive, interrogative, intrusive, meddlesome, snoopy, searching.
ant.- decorous, incurious, indifferent, restrained, unconcerned.

Noted: celebrated, distinguished, eminent, exalted, exceptional, extraordinary, famous, glorious, illustrious, imposing, memorable, outstanding, prominent, remarkable, renowned, well-known, significant.

ant.- infamous, undistinguished, insignificant, unknown.

Notice: intimation, information, announcement, attention, bulletin, civility, cognizance, comment, consideration, heed, mention, note, observation, placard, poster, recognition, regard, respect, warning, attend to, behold, detect, discern, discover, see, distinguish, examine, mark, observe, heed, perceive, recognize, regard, remark.

ant.- avoid, disregard, ignore, overlook, shun, evation, forgetfulness, laxity.

Notify: acquaint, advise, alert, apprise, call, communicate, convey, express, impart, indicate, inform, instruct, intimate, signify, specify, teach, tell, warn.

ant.- conceal, deceive, delude, mystify, suppress.

Novel: fiction, narrative, epic, romance, story, tale, fresh, modern, new, original, unique, unprecedented.

ant.- fact, history, reality, truth.

Novice: amateur, apprentice, beginner, greenhorn, learner, neophyte, newcomer, recruit, postulant, probationer, tyro, tenderfoot.

ant.- expert, master, mentor, professional.

Nude: naked, stripped, bare, unclad, unclothed, exposed, disrobed, undressed.

ant.- attired, clothed, covered, dressed.

Nullify: cancel, countermand, cross out, delete, destroy, discard, eliminate, erase, expunge, negate, obliterate, suppress, void, abolish, abrogate, annual, invalidate, quash, repeal, rescind, revoke, abjure, reverse, retract, recall, overrule, override, set aside, dissolve, disestablish, disendow, veto, deconsecrate.

ant.- confirm, enact, enforce, execute, ratify, support.

Number: aggregate, total, amount, digit, figure, list, score, quantity, sum, volume, calculate, compute, count, enumerate.

ant.- nothing, nothingness, zero, estimate, guess.

Numerous: many, myriad, multitudinous, plentiful, numberless, various, several.
ant.- few, not many, little, rare.

Nurture: cherish, feed, foster, nourish, nurse, rear, support, sustain, tend.
ant.- dislike, disregard, ignore, neglect, abandon, deprive, reject.

Nutriment: diet, meal, edibles, food, nourishment, nutrition, provision, rations, sustenance, viands, victuals.
ant.- decayed, decaying, rotten, decomposed.

❑

O

Obdurate: adamant, callous, dogged, hard-head hearted, hardoned, harsh, impenitent indurate, inflexible, mulish, obstinate, tenacious, tough, unbending, unfeeling, flinty, stubborn, unyielding.
ant.- compassionate, soft-hearted, amenable, sensitive, tender, submissive, tractable.

Obedient: acquiescent, dutiful, compliant, conformable, loyal, deferential, faithful, law-abiding, submissive, tractable, yielding, observant, complying, devoted.
ant.- defiant, insubordinate, disobedient, intractable, lawless, obstinate.

Obese: corpulent, fat, fleshy, portly, stout, swollen, thickset, overweight, plump, bulky.
ant.- emaciated, gaunt, lean, skeletal, slender, thin.

Objection: counter, argument, censure, protest, criticism, disagreement, disapproval, dissent, opposition, rejection, remonstrance, variance.
ant.- acceptance, accord, agreement, approval, compliance.

Objective: aim, ambition, aspiration, design, desire, destination, end, goal, motive, object, purpose, scheme, target.
ant.- biased, emotional, partial, personal, subjective.

Obligation: accountability, bond, contract, engagement, liability, onus, pledge, duty, promise, requirement, responsibility, stipulation.
ant.- choice, exemption.

Oblige: bind,, coerce, compel, constrain, enforce, force, help, hinder, impel, insist, necessitate, benefit, restrain, accommodate, favour, gratify, please.
ant.- absolve, discharge, exempt, free, realize, spare, unshackle.

Obliterate: annihilate, cancel, dele, wipe out, wash out, delete, demolish, destroy, devastate, expunge, efface, eradicate, erase, nullify, ravage, raze, ruin, wreck.
ant.- build, construct, create, establish, make.

Obscene: bawdy, coarse, foul, defiled, dirty, disgusting, filthy, gross, indecent, lascivious, licentious, pornographic, lewd, smutty, vulgar, wanton.
ant.- chaste, immaculate, innocent, modest, virtuous, pure.

Obscure: abstruse, unlighted, unilluminated, cloud, rayless, darksome, muddy, muzzy, ambiguous, blurred, concealed, cryptic, dark, dim, dusky, hazy, incomprehensible, indistinct, nebulous, shadowy, veiled.
ant.- apparent, clear, explicit, lucid, visible.

Observant: alert, attentive, aware, careful, considerate, heedful, mindful, perceptive, wary, watchful, submissive, vigilant.
ant.- careless, inattentive, lax, indifferent, non-observant.

Observe: behold, comprehend, detect, discover, examine, eye, heed, inspect, mark, note, perceive, regard, see, view, watch, commemorate, keep, celebrate.
ant.- disregard, ignore, neglect, overlook.

Obsolete: past, ancient, archaic, antiquated, disused, extinct, obsolescent, old, old-fashioned, outdated, outmoded, out of date, outworn, primitive.
ant.- current, modern, new, novel, recent, up-to-date.

Obstacle: bar, barrier, block, check, difficulty, hindrance, impediment, interruption, obstruction, snag, stumbling, block, barrage, baffle.
ant.- aid, blessing, boost, clearance, encouragement, help.

Obstinate: contumacious, firm, determined, dogged, fixed, head-strong, immovable, indomitable, inflexible, intractable, mulish, obdurate, persistent, pertinacious, recalcitrant, resolute, stubborn, uncompromising, unflinching, unyielding, wilful, tenacious, persistent, persevering.
ant.- amenable, compliant, docile, pliable.

Obstruct: barricade, block, clog, choke, close, curb, hamper, dam, hinder, impede, inhibit, interfere,

oppose, prevent, restrain, retard, stop, thwart.
ant.- assist, facilitate, forward, promote, support.

Obtain: achieve, acquire, earn, attain, gain, gather, procure, get, recover, secure.
ant.- forfeit, forsake, loss, miss, sacrifice.

Obtuse: slow-witted, bovine, dullard, imbecile, blunt, dull, impassive, dulled, rounded, pointless, unsharpened, edgeless.
ant.- acute, pointed, keen, quick, sharp.

Obvious: apparent, clear, plain, definite, distinct, evident, explicit, manifest, palpable, patent, precise, self-evident, unmistakable, visible.
ant.- ambiguous, confused, esoteric, obscure, puzzling.

Occupy: absorb, busy, have, fill, engage, engross, hold, keep, monopolize, capture, invade, seize, inhabit, possess, tenant, use.
ant.- relinquish, surrender, empty, leave, vacate, abandon.

Odd: abnormal, bizarre, curious, eccentric, exceptional, negative, queer, extraordinary, peculiar, quaint, singular, strange, unnatural, unusual, weird, lone, single, uneven, unmatched.
ant.- common, familiar, natural, normal, ordinary, matched, even.

Odious: abhorrent, detestable, disgusting, hateful, hideous, horrible, loathsome, repellent, obnoxious, foul, offensive, repugnant, vile, odorousness, repulsive, revolting, effluvium.
ant.- delightful, inviting, lovable, pleasant, refreshing, upright, wholesome.

Offense: crime, fault, felony, sin, injustice, scandal, misdeed, misdemeanour, transgression, trespass, wrong, wrongdoing.
ant.- gentleness, support, justice, morality, right.

Offer: overture, proposal, bid, proposition, exhibit, present, suggestion, proffer, propose, submit, suggest, volunteer, tender.
ant.- denial, rejection, reject, withdraw, withhold.

Often: commonly, frequently, generally, of times, recurrently, repeatedly.

ant.- infrequently, rarely, seldom, sporadically.

Old: older, oldest, aged, ancient, antediluvian, antiquated, antique, archaic, immemorial, obsolete, hoary, old-fashioned, patriarchal, prehistoric.

ant.- new, novel, recent, up-to-date, contemporary, current, fresh, modern.

Omen: augury, auspice, foreboding, foreshadow, gesture, harbinger, indication, mark, note, portent, precursor, prediction, presage, signal, symbol, symptom, token, sign, forerunner, warning.

ant.- ill-omen.

Omit: cancel, delete, discard, disregard, drop, eliminate, skip, evade, except, exclude, forget, ignore, miss, neglect, overlook, preclude, reject, repudiate, remove.

ant.- add, enroll, enter, include, insert, introduce.

Onerous: arduous, difficult, hard, burdensome, heavy, laborious, oppressive, exacting, intricate, ponderous, puzzling, perplexing, troublesome.

ant.- easy, effortless, facile, clear, simple.

Opaque: cloudy, dark, dim, dull, dusky, filmy, gloomy, misty, murky, non-transparent, obfuscated, shadowy, shady, smoky, unilluminated.

ant.- bright, glassy, lustrous, clear, pellucid, transparent.

Open: agape, ajar, expanded, extended, clear, unfastened, unfolded, gaping, unbarred, unclosed, artless, uncovered, unlocked, passable, sincere, disengaged, free, unoccupied, exposed, candid, explicit, frank, honest, overt, unreserved.

ant.- blocked, closed, locked, impassable, obstructed, busy, engaged, occupied, concealed.

Operate: act, conduct, direct, execute, function, manage, perform, react, run, go work.

ant.- breakdown, cutout, halt.

Operation: action, execution, instrumentality, maneuver, manipulation, performance, procedure, proceeding, process, transaction, working.

ant.- dormant, inactive, still, inefficient, quiet.

Opinion: belief, conclusion, consensus, conviction, feeling, idea, impression, judgment, notion, persuasion, sentiment, theory, thought, verdict, view.

ant.- fact, knowledge.

Opponent: adversary, antagonist, assailant, challenger, competitor, contestant, dissentient, opposer, disputant, enemy, foe, rival.

ant.- ally, colleague, comrade, consort, partner.

Opportunity: advantage, chance, contingency, scope, occasion, opening, possibility, time.

ant.- blockage, deterrent, disadvantage, hindrance, obstacle.

Oppose: bar, check, combat, confront, contradict, contrast, contravene, counter, cross, defy, deny, hinder, impede, interfere, obstruct, protest, rebuff, resist, restrain, retaliate, thwart, withstand, refute, repel.

ant.- approve, endorse, fraternize, defend, promote, help, sanction, support.

Opposite: antithesis, anonymous, contradictory, contrary, inverse, reverse, opponent, foeman, archenemy, nemesis.

ant.- compatible, identical, like, same.

Oppress: afflict, burden, crush, harass, harry, hound, grieve, maltreat, plague, overbear, persecute, suppress, torture, depress, subjugate, torment, tyrannize, vex, load.

ant.- aid, assist, comfort, relieve, support.

Optimistic: assured, confident, bright, buoyant, heerful, encouraged, positive, sanguine, encouraging, enthusiastic, expectant, hopeful, trusting.

ant.- despairing, doubtful, gloomy, hopeless.

Opulent: affluent, lavish, luxurious, moneyed, well-to-do, prosperous, well-heeled, well-off, rich, sumptuous, wealthy.

ant.- destitute, indigent, poor, scarce.

Oral: articulate, said, spoken, uttered, verbal, viva voce, vocal, unwritten.

ant.- printed, recorded, written.

Ordain: command, control, lead, govern, rule, manage, supervise, direct, decree, dictate, order.
ant.- appeal, ask, beg.

Ordeal: assay, judgment, strain, suffering, test, trial, tribulation.
ant.- alleviation, comfort, joy, pleasure.

Order: arrangement, class, method, rank, regularity, sequence, series, succession, symmetry, decree, system, command, dictate, directive, injunction, instruction, law, mandate, precept, prescription, regulation, requirement, rule.
ant.- disorder, irregularity, muddle.

Ordinary: average, common, conventional, customary, familiar, habitual, medium, natural, normal, regular, typical, unremarkable, usual, inferior, low, plain, trite.
ant.- bizarre, eccentric, irregular, strange, exceptional, exclusive, extraordinary, unconventional, wonderful.

Organic: animate, biological, biotic, live, living, natural, vital.
ant.- inorganic, artificial, man-made.

Organize: adjust, arrange, assort, classify, constitute, coordinate, frame, dispose, establish, form, institute, plan, prepare, regulate, shape, systematize.
ant.- disband, disorganize, disperse, divide, scatter.

Origin: base, basis, beginning, birth, cause, commencement, derivation, foundation, inception, root, source, descent, fountainhead, ancestry.
ant.- conclusion, consequence, finality, result, termination.

Original: archetypal, casual, first, formative, inceptive, initial, primary, rudimentary, fresh, inventive, model, new, novel.
ant.- terminal, banal, copied, imitated, plagiarized.

Oscillate: change, fluctuate, swing, liberate, reciprocate, vacillate, vary, vibrate, waver.
ant.- halt, persist, remain, resolve, stay.

Ostentation: boasting, flourish, exhibition, glitter, pageantry, parade, frippery,

pomp, display, ostentatiousness, tawdriness, gaudiness, show, pomposity, pretension, tinsel.
ant.- humility, modesty, reserve, restraint, timidity.

Ostracize: banish, blackball, bar, deport, exclude, exile, expel.
ant.- accept, admit, embrace, include, welcome.

Oust: banish, deport, depose, discharge, dislodge, dismiss, dispel, eject, evict, exclude, exile, expatriate, expel, ostracize, remove.
ant.- admit, appoint, retain, shelter, empower.

Outrageous: atrocious, fierce, flagrant, furious, heinous, monstrous, nefarious, violent, scandalous, villainous.
ant.- calm, dispassionate, favourable, peccable, tranquil, soothing.

Outspoken: bluff, blunt, candid, direct, forthright, frank, open, plainspoken, unceremonious, unreserved, loud.
ant.- reserved, sincere, taciturn, suave.

Outstanding: conspicuous, distinguished, dominant, salient, eminent, exceptional, important, notable, noticeable, preeminent, remarkable.
ant.- average, commonplace, inconspicuous, ordinary, usual.

Overcome: beat, conquer, defeat, master, overpower, overthrow, crush, subdue, subjugate, surmount.
ant.- fail, lose, succumb, surrender.

Overflowing: super, bountiful, copious, plenteous, plentiful, profuse, abundant, teeming, abounding, unlimited.
ant.- deficient, insufficient, poor, scanty, scarce.

Overlook: disregard, drop, eliminate, exclude, forget, ignore, miss, neglect, omit, skip, slight.
ant.- note, observe, regard, see, watch.

Oversee: administer, guide, command, direct, engineer, maintain, manage, order, superintend, supervise.
ant.- obey, follow, take, orders.

Oversight: blunder, error, failure, fault, inlapse, mistake, neglect, omission, slip, charge, control, direction, guidance, inspection, management, regulation superintendence, supervision, surveillance, watchfulness.
ant.- attention, diligence, care.

Overt: apparent, manifest, plain, obvious, open, patent, public, visible, unconcealed, undisguised.
ant.- concealed, covert, hidden, latent, private, secret.

Overthrow: abolish, conquer, crush, defeat, demolish, overcome, overpower, overturn, subjugate, subvert, supplant, upset, vanquish, confute.
ant.- develop, maintain, assist, preserve, restore, support.

Own: admit, allow, avow, concede, confess, hold, have, possess, acknowledge.
ant.- deny, disavow.

❑

P

Pacific: calm, composed, cool, peaceful, placid, quiet, serene, smooth, tranquil, undisturbed, unruffled.
ant.- belligerent, combative, stormy, tempestuous, turbulent.

Pacify: allay, alleviate, appease, calm, compose, lull, placate, quell, quiet, reconcile, relieve, soothe, still, tranquillize.
ant.- anger, antagonize, excite, incense, rile, roil.

Pack: bale, stow, packet, bag, bundle, collection, gathering, group, load, luggage, kit, kitbag, truss, package, parcel, trunk.
ant.- allocate, distribute, dispose, loosen, scatter.

Pain: affliction, agony, anguish, discomfort, distress, grief, misery, suffering, torment, torture, woe, ache, pang.
ant.- happiness, pleasure, solace, well-being.

Painful: aching, agonizing, distressing, excruciating, grievous, hurting, hurtful, poignant, saddening.
ant.- delightful, enjoyable, pleasant.

Palpable: apparent, evident, discernible, manifest, clear, unquestionable, obvious, patent, plain, unmistakable, visible, definite, distinct.
ant.- concealed, doubtful, mysterious, obscure.

Paltry: abject, contemptible, despicable, insignificant, low, mean, meagre, petty, picayune, pitiful, poor, puny, worthless, trifling, trivial, inconsequential.
ant.- important, momentous, large, rich, significant.

Panic: alarm, apprehension consternation, dismay, dread, fright, horror, perturbation, terror, trepidation, fear.
ant.- calm, placidity, repose, serenity.

Parallel: akin, alike, analogous, comparable, concurrent, congruous, correlative, corresponding, like, similar, uniform.
ant.- different, divergent, incongruous, opposed.

Paralyse: cripple, daze, lame, deaden, disable, debilitate,

incapacitate, maim, mutilate, unnerve.
ant.- excite, revive, stimulate, vitalize.

Pardon: absolve, acquit, condone, efface, exculpate, forgive, excuse, exonerate, liberate, overlook, quash, remit, amnesty, parole, deliverance, discharge, forgiveness, freedom, release, remission.
ant.- banish, castigate, chastise, condemn, punish.

Parsimonious: avaricious, frugal, miserly, penurious, scrimping, sparing, stingy, tight, mean, shabby, piddling, pennywise, niggardly.
ant.- altruistic, generous, lavish, liberal, prodigal.

Part: apportionment, bit, chip, chunk, division, fragment, lump, morsel, piece, portion, scrap, section, segment, share, slice, component, element, ingredient, member, concern, faction, constituent, party, side, fraction, item, particular.
ant.- aggregate, entirety, sum, whole, combine, gather.

Partiality: bias, bigotry, liking, favouritism, preconception predisposition, preference, prejudice.
ant.- equality, fairness, impartiality.

Participate: associate, share, commune, cooperate, mingle, join, partake, unite.
ant.- abstain, boycott, forgo, passup.

Particle: atom, crumb, grain, bit, iota, jot, mite, molecule, scrap, shred, speck, whit.
ant.- aggregate, entirety, mass, total, whole.

Particular: characteristic, distinct, exclusive, peculiar, special, specific, unusual, exact, precise.
ant.- comprehensive, general, universal, usual, fallacious, ordinary.

Partisan: adherent, aide, ally, assistant, attendant, backer, devotee, disciple, follower, henchman, successor, votary, supporter.
ant.- chief, director, leader, master.

Partner: accomplice, ally, mate, associate, colleague, companion, comrade, crony, confederate, participant, co-worker, spouse, sharer, co-owner, copartner, silent partner.

ant.- adversary, enemy, foe, opponent.

Passable: acceptable, tolerable, adequate, admissible, allowable, average, ordinary, endurable, fair, mediocre, middling, so-so.

ant.- excellent, first class, first-rate, fine, great, good.

Passion: ardour, craving, desire, ecstasy, eroticism, excitement, fascination, fervour, frenzy, hunger, infatuation, intensity, lust, yearning.

ant.- calm, dispassion, frigidity, indifference, restraint, tranquillity.

Passionate: ardent, burning, excitable, extreme, fervent, fervid, feverish, fiery, hot, impetuous, intense, irascible, quickened, vehement.

ant.- apathetic, calm, cool, dull, impassive, phlegmatic.

Passive: cold, idle, inactive, indifferent, inert, submissive, non-resistant, quiet, receptive, relaxed, resigned, stoical, supine, unresisting.

ant.- active, dynamic, operative.

Patch: fix, mend, rebuild, adjust, reconstruct, renew, repair, restore, revamp, sew, ameliorate, better, correct, improve, rectify, remedy.

ant.- damage, destroy, impair, injure, ravage.

Patent: apparent, clear, conspicuous, evident, manifest, obvious, open, overt, plain, unconcealed, unmistakable.

ant.- concealed, covered, covert, hidden, obscure.

Pathetic: heart-rending, melting, moving, piteous, pitiable, pitiful, plaintive, poignant, saddening.

ant.- cheering, comical, funny, happy, joyful.

Patience: composure, calmness, endurance, forbearance, fortitude, cool, perseverance, persistence, resignation, submission, sufferance, tolerance.

ant.- disquietude, excitability, impatience, petulance, perturbation, rage.

Patient: calm, composed, enduring, forbearing, imperturbable, indulgent, lenient, long-suffering, placid, resigned, serene, stoical, submissive, tolerant, uncomplaining.

ant.- clamorous, hysterical, irritable, turbulent, ungovernable.

Pause: delay, desist, doubt, halt, hesitate, intermit, stop, waver, wait, discontinuance, break, cessation, hesitation, recess, intermission, interruption, lull, suspension, rest.
ant.- continue, persevere, proceed, resolve, continuance, continuity, extension.

Pay: allowance, compensation, fee, indemnity, payment, recompense, remuneration, reparation, retribution, wages, reward, salary, stipend, defray, expend, liquidate, offer, recompense, refund, reimburse, reward.
ant.- expenditure, expense, forfeiture, non-payment.

Peace: accord, agreement, amity, armistice, conciliation, concord, harmony, pacifism, quiescence, quiet, repose, serenity, silence, stillness, calm, tranquillity.
ant.- conflict, discord, disruption, fracas, uproar, warfare.

Peaceful: calm, complacent, composed, pacific, placid, quiet, unruffled, tranquil.
ant.- agitated, perturbed, noisy, turbulent, upset, violent.

Peak: acme, apex, climax, crest, culmination, height, high point, pinnacle, spire, summit, top, zenith.
ant.- abyss, base, bottom, lowest point, nadir.

Peculiar: abnormal, bizarre, eccentric, exceptional, extraordinary, idiosyncratic, odd, rare, singular, strange, queer, unusual, characteristic, distinctive, especial, particular, special, specific.
ant.- common, normal, visual, ordinary, regular.

Peculiarity: characteristic, eccentricity, oddity, feature, idiosyncrasy, mark, property, quality, singularity, trait.
ant.- formality, regularity, uniformity.

Pedantic: academic, bookish, erudite, formal, impractical, learned, precise, professorial, scholarly, scholastic, theoretical.
ant.- ignorant, practical, simple, interesting.

Peer: look alertly, gaze, stare, peep, colleague, companion, campier, equal, fellow,

match, mate, aristocrat, knight, lord, nobleman.
ant.- commoner, inferior.

Peevish: acrimonious, cross, cantankerous, fractious, fretful, grouchy, ill-natured, ill-tempered, irritable, moody, petulant, snappish, sulky, touchy, waspish, irascible, cranky.
ant.- affable, genial, gracious, pleasant, soothing.

Penalty: chastisement, fine, damages, handicap, amercement, forfeiture, punishment, retribution.
ant.- compensation, prize, forgiveness, reward.

Penetrating: acute, astute, discerning, piercing, sharp, shrill, stinging, pungent, pervasive, harsh, biting, subtle, penetrative.
ant.- shallow, blunt, dull, mild, muddled, obtuse.

Penitent: contrite, regretful, remorseful, repentant, rueful, sorrowful, sorry, regretting.
ant.- impenitent, uncontrite, obdurate, remorseless.

Penniless: destitute, empty-handed, fortuneless, poor, impecunious, indigent, needy, poverty-stricken, bankrupt.
ant.- affluent, opulent, rich, prosperous, wealthy.

Pensive: grave, melancholy, sad, dejected, introspective, meditative, musing, reflective, speculative, thoughtful.
ant.- careless, extroverted, heedless, thoughtless, unconcerned.

Penurious: close-fisted, stingy, niggardly, grasping, mercenary, miserly, parsimonious, tight, ungenerous.
ant.- extravagant, spendthrift, open-handed, altruistic, bountiful, charitable, generous, liberal.

Perceive: conceive, discern, note, notice, observe, see, sense, recognize, apprehend, comprehend, understand.
ant.- confuse, ignore, miss, overlook, misapprehend, misunderstand.

Perceptible: apparent, appreciable, apprehensible, discernible, noticeable, visible, observable, palpable, sensible, tangible.
ant.- absurd, impalpable, imperceptible, invisible.

Perceptive: discerning, aware, knowledgeable, observant, understanding, cognizant.

ant.- ignorant, mindless, dense, obtuse, unaware.

Perfect: absolute, complete, consummate, completed, entire, full, whole, blameless, faultless, flawless, immaculate, impeccable.
ant.- deficient, incomplete, lacking, unfinished, imperfect.

Perform: accomplish, achieve, act, do, effect, execute, fulfil.
ant.- fail, neglect, refrain, loaf, rest.

Perhaps: conceivably, maybe, mayhap, perchance, possibly.
ant.- certainly, definitely, impassably.

Peril: danger, exposure, hazard, vulnerability, insecurity, chance, jeopardy, menace, pitfall, risk, threat.
ant.- immunity, protection, safety, security.

Perimeter: ambit, border, edge, boundary, circle, circuit, circumference, compass, periphery, outline, contour, outside.
ant.- center, core, heart, hub, middle.

Perish: cease, crumble, decay, decease, depart, die, expire, pass away, succumb, vanish.
ant.- exist, flourish, live, survive, thrive.

Permanent: abiding, constant, durable, enduring, established, everlasting, fixed, indelible, indestructible, lasting, perpetual, persistent, unending, stable, unchangeable, unchanging, standing, settled, immovable, immutable, steadfast, eternal, lifelong, monotonous.
ant.- ephemeral, mutable, temporary, transitory, variable, vacillating.

Permission: allowance, permit, approval, authority, authorization, confirmation, consent, dispensation, enfranchisement, liberty, license, sanction, verification.
ant.- denial, opposition, prohibition, refusal, veto.

Permit: admit, allow, approve, authorize, empower, endorse, grant, let, sanction, charter, law, license, pass, passport, patent, permission, warrant.
ant.- forbid, inhibit, oppose, bar, restrain, ban, embargo, inhibition, injunction.

Perpendicular: erect, plumb, straight, upright, upstanding, vertical.
ant.- horizontal, oblique, slanting.

Perpetrate: accomplish, enact, commit, execute, inflict, perform, practise.
ant.- fail, miscarry, ignore, neglect.

Perpetual: continual, constant, deathless, endless, enduring, eternal, everlasting, immortal, incessant, infinite, interminable, lasting, permanent, timeless, unceasing, undying, uninterrupted, ageless, ever-living, unending, everflowing, ceaseless, never-ending.
ant.- ephemeral, evanescent, finite, fleeting, temporal.

Perplex: baffle, bewilder, confound, confuse, muddle, disconcert, dumbfound, mystify, puzzle, nonplus, distract.
ant.- clarify, explain, illumine, inform, instruct.

Perplexing: bewildering, complex, complicated, confusing, intricate, involved, mystifying, puzzling.
ant.- clear, lucid, manifest, obvious, plain, simple.

Persecute: afflict, aggrieve, annoy, badger, bother, tease, castigate, gall, harass, harry, hound, maltreat, oppress, pester, plague, rile, torment, torture, vex, victimize.
ant.- aid, assist, comfort gladden, nurture, support.

Persevere: abide, continue, endure, prevail, pursue, remain, survive, sustain.
ant.- cease, desist, surrender, vacillate, waver.

Perseverance: assiduity, constancy, determination, diligence, industry, persistence, persistency, pertinacity, resolution, steadfastness, tenacity.
ant.- cessation, idleness, inertia, laziness, procrastination, sloth.

Persistent: constant, fixed, determined, enduring, firm, immovable, indefatigable, persevering, resolute, steadfast, steady, tenacious, dogged, headstrong, insistent, obstinate, pertinacious, perverse.
ant.- dawdling, doubtful, hesitant, unsure, vacillating, wavering.

Perspicuity: clarity, clearness, discrimination, distinctness, explicitness, intelligibility, lucidity, preciseness.
ant.- confusion, mystification, obscurity, perplexity, vagueness.

Persuade: convince, incite, induce, influence, prevail upon, impel, satisfy, urge, win over.
ant.- deter, dissuade, divert, hinder, repress, restrain.

Pertinacious: constant, firm, contumacious, determined, dogged, headstrong, obstinate, immovable, inflexible, intractable, obdurate, persistent, resolute, stubborn, tenacious, unyielding, preserving.
ant.- compliant, docile, flexible, submissive, yielding.

Pertinent: applicable, appropriate, apropos, apt, fit, fitting, germane, material, proper, relevant, suited, apposite.
ant.- alien, extraneous, foreign, improper, irrelevant, unrelated.

Perturb: agitate, aggravate, annoy, bother, discommode, disquiet, harass, heckle, irk, irritate, perplex, pester, vex, plague, worry.
ant.- assist, calm, delight, help, please.

Perverse: cantankerous, dogged, contrary, contumacious, disobedient, fractious, intractable, irascible, obstinate, peevish, petulant, resolute, splenetic, stubborn, ungovernable, perverted, sinful, wayward, wicked.
ant.- agreeable, obliging, docile, tractable, angelic, saintly, virtuous.

Perversion: abasement, corruption, debasement, rebilling, degradation, depravity, desecration, falsification, humiliation, maltreatment, vitiation, outrage, misuse, profanation, wickedness.
ant.- elevation, enhancement, improvement, respect, veneration.

Pessimistic: cynical, gloomy, depressed, desolate, glum, despairing, despondent, rueful, doleful, downcast, foreboding, forlorn, hopeless, melancholy, misanthropic, spiritless.
ant.- bright, enthusiastic, hopeful, optimistic, trusting.

Pester: annoy, badger, bother, disturb, fret, harass, harry, heckle, inconvenience, irk, irritate, plague, tease, vex, torment, trouble.
ant.- accommodate, comfort, delight, gratify, soothe, support.

Petty: childish, frivolous, insignificant, negligible, puny, nugatory, paltry, shallow, slight, small, trifling, trivial, unimportant, worthless, weak.
ant.- important, momentous, serious, significant, vital.

Petulant: acrimonious, cross, choleric, cranky, crusty, fretful, ill-humoured, ill-natured, ill-tempered, surly, irascible, irritable, peevish, querulous, snappish, sullen, testy, touchy, unamiable, waspish.
ant.- affable, congenial, good-natured, pleasant, temperate.

Philanthropic: altruistic, beneficent, benevolent, charitable, compassionate, generous, gracious, humanitarian, liberal, magnanimous, munificent.
ant.- antisocial, merciless, cruel, selfish.

Phlegmatic: dispassionate, dull, apathetic, impassive, unexcitable, passionless, stoical, stolid, unemotional, unfeeling.
ant.- ardent, demonstrative, enthusiastic, passionate.

Phobia: aversion, dislike, distaste, fear, hatred, dread, revulsion, repulsion.
ant.- attraction, endurance, liking, love, tolerance.

Physical: anatomical, bodily, carnal, corporal, corporeal, material, substantial.
ant.- abstract, immaterial, incorporeal, spiritual, unreal.

Pick: collect, harvest, pluck, choose, cull, elect, gather, opt, prefer, select, single.
ant.- decline, refuse, reject.

Piece: bit, chunk, fraction, fragment, morsel, part, portion, scrap, section, segment, shred, slice.
ant.- all, entirety, sum, total, whole.

Pinnacle: acne, apex, chief, top, climax, crest, crown, summit, culmination, head, peak, zenith, spire.
ant.- base, bottom, depths, foot, foundation, nadir.

Pious: devotional, devout, divine, Godly, hallowed, holy, prayerful, religious, reverent, sacred, saintly, sanctified, seraphic, spiritual, unworldly.
ant.- blasphemous, evil, irreverent, wicked, profane, sacrilegious.

Pitch: cast, chuck, fling, heave, hurl, propel, sling, throw, thrust, toss.
ant.- catch, grab, receive.

Pitiful: clement, lenient, compassionate, merciful, tender, tender-hearted, sympathetic, lamentable, miserable, sad, mournful, piteous, sorrowful, tearful.
ant.- dignified, exalted, grand, joyful, noble, sublime.

Pity: charity, clemency, commiseration, compassion, condolence, empathy, kindness, mercy, philanthropy, sympathy, tenderness.
ant.- brutality, inhumanity, ruthlessness, vengeance.

Placid: calm, composed, equable, gentle, imperturbable, pacific, peaceful, quiet, serene, still, tranquil, undisturbed, unmoved, cool, unruffled, collected.
ant.- agitated, disturbed, excited, stormy, turbulent, wild.

Plain: even, flat, level, plane, smooth, apparent, clear, distinct, evident, exposed, lucid, manifest, obvious, palpable, perceptible, visible, recognizable, unmistakable.
ant.- broken, rough, uneven.

Plastic: ductile, flexible, pliant, formable, formative, resilient, impressible, impressionable, malleable, moldable.
ant.- brittle, hard, rigid, stiff.

Plausible: believable, credible, likely, probable, reasonable, specious.
ant.- implausible, impossible, incredible, unlikely, visionary.

Pleasant: attractive, charming, comforting, cordial, delightful, engaging, enjoyable, gratifying, honeyed, mellifluous, melodious, pleasing, pleasurable, suitable, winning, welcome.
ant.- disagreeable, hateful, obnoxious, offensive, painful, repellent, repulsive.

Pleasure: amusement, bliss, comfort, contentment, ease, delight, diversion, ecstasy, enjoyment, felicity, rapture, exhilaration, joy, gladness, gratification, happiness, light-heartedness, satisfaction.
ant.- affliction, distress, grief, hopelessness, suffering.

Pledge: affirmation, agreement, assertion assurance, commitment, contract, oath, covenant, declaration, pact, engagement, guarantee, vow, troth, promise, security, token, word.

ant.- break, faith, deceive, deny, renounce.

Plentiful: abundant, ample, bounteous, bountiful, copious, inexhaustible, lavish, liberal, luxurious, plenteous, profuse, replete, teeming, unsparing.

ant.- deficient, impoverished, scanty, scarce, stripped.

Pliable: compliant, docile, ductile, elastic, flexible, limber, manageable, pliant, resilient, supple, tractable, wavering, yielding.

ant.- brittle, intractable, rigid, stiff, unyielding.

Plump: buxom, chubby, puffy, corpulent, fleshy, paunchy portly, pudgy, rotund, stout.

ant.- emaciated, gaunt, lean, slender, slim.

Poignant: affecting, heart-rending, moving, pitiable, sad, tender, touching, acute, biting, penetrating, piercing, pungent, trenchant.

ant.- painless, pleasant, blunt, dull, insipid, numb, obtuse.

Pointed: acute, cutting, keen, knife-like, edged, sharp, spiky, spiked, sharpened, serrated, knife-edged, jagged, honed, barbed.

ant.- bland, unsharpened, dull, blunt.

Poisonous: deadly, fatal, toxic, noxious, pestilential, virulent, venomous.

ant.- curative, harmless, healthful, invigorating, nourishing, wholesome.

Polish: elegance, glaze, luster, refinement, smoothness, suavity, brighten, burnish, civilize, discipline, define, refinish, rub, shine, smooth, wax.

ant.- baseness, crudity, dull, mar, harshness, lowliness, roughness, debase, roughen, ruin.

Polite: civil, considerate, cordial, courteous, cultivated, refined, decorous, genteel, mannerly, polished, tactful, urbane, well-bred, well-mannered.

ant.- abusive, coarse, impudent, discourteous, offensive, rude.

Pollute: adulterate, befoul, foul, contaminate, corrupt, defile, demoralize, infect, poison, sully, taint, desecrate, vitiate.
ant.- clean, disinfect, purge, purify, sanitize.

Pomp: boasting, display, flourish, glory, grandeur, magnificence, ostentation, pageantry, parade, show, splendor, vaunting.
ant.- humility, modesty, plainness, shabbiness, simplicity, tawdriness.

Pompous: august, grand, imposing, lofty, magnificent, majestic, high-flown, bombastic, boastful, domineering, egotistical, flaunting, haughty, inflated, ostentatious, pretentious, swaggering.
ant.- common, humble, ordinary, modest, reserved, submissive.

Ponder: cogitate, contemplate, deliberate, devise, examine, investigate, mediate, muse, reflect, ruminate, scrutinize, study, weigh, think.
ant.- forget, ignore, neglect, overlook.

Ponderous: burdensome, dull, hefty, cumbersome, heavy, huge, massive, unwieldy, weighty, gloomy, grave, spiritless, bulky.
ant.- airy, fluffy, light, small, tiny, weightless.

Poor: destitute, impecunious, impoverished, bad, indigent, insolvent, needy, penniless, poverty-stricken, substandard, underprivileged, defective, deficient, inferior, insignificant, mediocre, miserable, shabby, unfavourable.
ant.- affluent, opulent, rich, solvent, wealthy.

Popular: noted, famed, well-known, famous, renowned, celebrated, common, familiar, plebeian, admired, favourite, liked.
ant.- disliked, disreputable, shunned, unpopular.

Pornographic: indecent, blue, lascivious, lecherous, lewd, obscene, prurient, smutty, coarse, corrupt, debauched, dirty, disgusting, filthy, gross, immoral.
ant.- chaste, decent, modest, pure, refined.

Portion: allotment, division, fraction, fragment, measure, morsel, parcel, part, piece, quota, ration, section, segment, share, slice, subdivision.

ant.- aggregation, entirety, mass, sum, total.

Positive: absolute, affirmative, assertive, assured, certain, concrete, decided, definite, dogmatic, emphatic, firm, fixed, incontrovertible, indubitable, unmistakable, unquestionable.

ant.- ambiguous, doubtful, dubious, hazy, questionable, uncertain.

Possess: control, dominate, own, have, hold, keep, obtain, occupy, reserve, retain, seize, take over.

ant.- abandon, lack, lose, need, renounce, surrender.

Possibility: chance, contingency, feasibility, happening, hope, occasion, occurrence, opportunity, plausibility, potentiality, likelihood, liability.

ant.- disadvantage, obstacle, impossibility, hindrance.

Possible: achievable, attainable, conceivable, contingent, liable, credible, feasible, imaginable, thinkable, reasonable, likely, obtainable, performable, plausible, potential, practical.

ant.- impossible, unlikely, inconceivable, incredible, unattainable, unreasonable.

Postpone: adjourn, defer, stay, delay, discontinue, interrupt, pigeonhole, procrastinate, protract, remand, retard, shelve, stall, suspend, table, waive.

ant.- accelerate, continue, maintain, persevere, persist, proceed.

Potent: forceful, forcible, great, hardy, influential, intense, irresistible, mighty, overpowering, powerful, puissant, robust, staunch, strong, sturdy, vigorous, virile.

ant.- delicate, enervated, fragile, impotent, weak.

Poverty: destitution, distress, hardship, penury, insolvency, indigence, necessity, need, pauperism, privation, want, impecuniousness.

ant.- abundance, affluence, opulence, riches, wealth.

Power: ability, capability, skill, capacity, competence, sway, efficacy, efficiency, vigour, endowment, potency, talent, energy, force, might, stamina, strength, authority, command, control, dominion, government, influence, jurisdiction, mastery, predominance, preponderance, sovereignty, superiority, supremacy.

ant.- impotence, inability, ineptitude, debility, infirmity, weakness.

Practical: balanced, down-to-earth, effective, feasible, functional, operative, useful, pragmatic, rational, realistic, reasonable, sensible, sound, unromantic, utilitarian.

ant.- idealistic, imperceptible, impractical, outlandish, useless.

Praise: acclaim, admire, applaud, approve, commend, compliment, exalt, extol, glorify, laud, magnify, eulogize.

ant.- admonish, berate, condemn, impugn, reproach, upbraid.

Precarious: critical, risky, dangerous, deadly, dubious, hazardous, insecure, usage, menacing, perlous, perilous, threatening, treacherous, unstable, doubtful, unassured, uncertain.

ant.- protected, safe, secure, stable, assured, certain, unquestionable.

Precious: costly, expensive, exquisite, dear, high-priced, inestimable, invaluable, priceless, profitable, select, superior, superlative, unequaled, useful, valuable, worthy.

ant.- cheap, insignificant, trifling, valueless, worthless.

Precipitate: hasty, headlong, impetuous, rash, accelerate, hasten, quicken, speed.

ant.- preclude, retard, slow.

Precise: accurate, correct, punctilious, definite, distinct, exact, meticulous, rigorous, scrupulous, strict, prim, prudish, rigid, stiff.

ant.- ambiguous, fallacious, inexact, negligent, slipshod, casual, informal, relaxed, loose.

Predicament: corner, crisis, fix, difficulty, dilemma, mess, muddle, perplexity, pinch, quandary, emergency, scrape.

ant.- comfort, ease, security, solace, tranquillity.

Predominant: cardinal, chief, controlling, distinguished, dominant, foremost, highest, leading, main, notable, paramount, preponderant, prevailing, prevalent, principal, ruling, supreme.

ant.- insignificant, minor, subordinate, subsidiary.

Preface: beginning, foreword, introduction, overture, preamble, prelude, prologue, preliminary.
ant.- addendum, afterword, conclusion, ending, epilogue.

Prejudice: bias, contempt, detriment, dislike, enmity, intolerance, objection, partiality, preconception, predilection, prejudgment, prepossession, pique, repugnance, revulsion, unfairness.
ant.- approval, benevolence, kindness, regard, respect, tolerance.

Premature: anticipatory, early, green, immature, incomplete, precipitate, unripe, precocious, raw, unfinished, unprepared, unseasonable, untimely, underripe, overhasty.
ant.- completed, expected, fully developed, matured, tardy.

Premeditated: calculated, deliberate, designed, intended, intentional, planned, plotted, prearranged, studied, predetermined.
ant.- accidental, casual, spontaneous, unforeseen, unplanned.

Preoccupied: absorbed, fixed, captivated, concentrating, engaged, fascinated, held, immersed, involved, lost, occupied, preoccupied, rapt, riveted, engrossed.
ant.- attentive, watchful.

Prepare: adjust, adapt, equip, anticipate, arm, arrange, concoct, develop, devise, fit, fix, foresee, form, furnish, outfit, plan, predispose, prime, provide, qualify, ready, settle.
ant.- forget, ignore, neglect, overlook.

Prerogative: authority, grant, birthright, claim, immunity, liberty, license, perquisite, privilege, right, franchise.
ant.- duty, injustice, limitation, obligation, violation.

Present: award, bestow, gift, confer, endow, introduce, proffer, propose, sacrifice, show, tender, boon, donation, grant, gratuity, favour, bonus, offering.
ant.- accept, receive, reject, spurn, take.

Preserve: conserve, defend, guard, keep, maintain, protect, rescue, safeguard, save, secure, shield, spare, retain, support, sustain, uphold.

ant.- abandon, abolish, abrogate, destroy, forego, waste.

Pressing: burning, serious, constraining, critical, crucial, crying, distressing, exigent, impelling, imperative, urgent, vital, important, importunate, insistent, necessary.
ant.- insignificant, petty, meaningless, superficial.

Pressure: burden, compression, encumbrance, force, stress, thrust, weight, affliction, coercion, strain, compulsion, constraint, exigency, obligation, persuasion, persuasiveness.
ant.- relief, release, assistance, ease, encouragement, leniency, relaxation.

Prestige: fame, glory, honour, influence, renown, repute, supremacy, dignity, weight, reputation, note, importance.
ant.- impotence, weakness, insignificance, unimportance.

Presume: assume, believe, guess, conclude, conjecture, consider, posit, hypothesize, imagine, presuppose, regard, speculate, suppose, surmise, theorize, think.
ant.- ascertain, confirm, demonstrate, manifest, prove.

Pretense: affectation, cloak, makeshift, deceit, disuse, dissimulation, garb, evasion, excuse, fabrication, mask, falsification, pomposity, pretension, ruse, pretext, prevarication, semblance, sham, show, simulation, subterfuge, trickery, wile.
ant.- candour, frankness, honesty, sincerity, truth.

Pretty: attractive, comely, fair, goodlooking, beautiful, lovely, charming, cute, graceful.
ant.- ugly, unattractive, unshapely, unsightly.

Prevalent: common, usual, comprehensive, controlling, familiar, frequent, general, ordinary, popular, predominant, prominent, prevailing, sweeping, ubiquitous, widespread, universal, worldwide.
ant.- exceptional, isolated, extraordinary, infrequent, sporadic.

Prevent: avert, block, check, foil, forestall, halt, hinder, impede, inhibit, interrupt,

obstruct, obviate, preclude, prohibit, repress, stop, thwart, restrain.
ant.- allow, assist, further, promote, stimulate.

Previous: aforesaid, earlier, antecedent, anterior, former, foregoing, preceding, prefatory, prior, preliminary, preparatory.
ant.- ensuing, latter, pursuant, subsequent, succeeding.

Pride: arrogance, conceit, egoism, egotism, haughtiness, loftiness, pomposity, pretension, self-esteem, self-glorification, self-love, vanity, self-respect, superciliousness.
ant.- humility, meekness.

Primary: basic, beginning, chief, earliest, elementary, first, fundamental, initial, prime, primeval, primitive, pristine, foremost.
ant.- following, hindmost, last, latest, inferior, least, secondary, subordinate.

Primeval: earliest, first, initial, original, prima, primordial, pristine, inventive.
ant.- derivative, subsequent, terminal, banal, trite.

Primitive: aboriginal, ancient, antiquated, archaic, old, primeval, primordial, pristine, crude, first, fundamental.
ant.- civilized, complex, sophisticated, modern, polished.

Principal: cardinal, chief, dominant, essential, first, foremost, highest, leading, main, paramount, predominant, prime, supreme, commander, director, executive, head, leader, master.
ant.- accessory, auxiliary, inferior, minor, negligible, unimportant.

Prior: previous, earlier, erst-while, preceding, ex-, former, forgoing.
ant.- later, following.

Private: clandestine, covert, concealed, hidden, latent, secluded, secret, surreptitious, unknown, unrevealed, individual, personal.
ant.- disclosed, exposed, known, open, public.

Privation: want, loss, poverty, indignance, deprivation.
ant.- richness.

Privilege: advantage, benefit, exemption, favour, immunity, liberty, franchise, license,

perquisite, prerogative, right, sanction, chance, event, occasion, opportunity.
ant.- depravation, disallowance, inhibition, limitation, prohibition, restriction.

Prize: accolade, award, bonus, bounty, citation, compensation, honour, premium, recompense, remuneration, reward, trophy, laurel, medal, decoration.
ant.- charge, punishment, earnings, forfeiture, penalty.

Problem: complication, plight, conundrum, difficulty, query, dilemma, enigma, intricacy, mystery, obstacle, perplexity, puzzle, quandary, question, riddle, poser.
ant.- answer, explanation, certainty, clarification, solution.

Proceed: advance, continue, forge, ahead, improve, move, progress, arise, thrive.
ant.- recede, regress, retire, retreat, withdraw.

Proceeds: earning, gain, gross, harvest, income, profits, receipts, result, return, yield, balance, issue, outcome.
ant.- costs, expenses, outlay.

Proclaim: advertise, affirm, divulge, announce, broadcast, circulate, declare, express, make known, profess, tell, promulgate, publish, reveal, state, voice, herald.
ant.- camouflage, conceal, mask, repress, suppress.

Procrastinate: adjourn, dally, dawdle, defer, delay, extend, loiter, postpone, prolong, stall, protract, retard, suspend.
ant.- accelerate, persevere, hasten, hurry, quicken.

Proficient: able, accomplished, adept, adroit, agile, clever, competent, cunning, deft, well-versed, expert, gifted, dexterous, ingenious, skilled, masterful, practiced, skillful, talented, versed.
ant.- bungling, incapable, incompetent, inept, maladroit, unskilled.

Profit: advantage, benefit, earnings, emoluments, gain, interest, proceeds, receipts, return.
ant.- destruction, detriment, failure, loss, ruin.

Profligate: abandored, corrupt, immoral, vicious, wicked, wanton, reckless, wild, intemperate.

ant.- chaste, moral, virtuous.

Profound: abstruse, recondite, subtle, heavy, abysmal, deep, consummate, erudite, solemn, heartfelt, mysterious, penetrating, scholarly, serious.

ant.- frivolous, shallow, superficial, trivial, unlearned, unenlightened.

Profuse: abundant, ample, copious, luxuriant, excessive, extravagant, exuberant, lavish, immoderate, improvident, redundant, liberal, overflowing, plentiful, prodigal, superfluous, wasteful.

ant.- barren, deficient, meager, inadequate, scanty.

Progress: advance, growth, advancement, attainment, betterment, development, headway, improvement, progression, increase.

ant.- deferment, moratorium, delay, regression, suspension.

Prohibit: ban, block, check, circumscribe, debar, deny, exclude, forbid, hinder, inhibit, interdict, preclude, prevent, proscribe, refuse, restrain, restrict, taboo, veto, withhold, disallow.

ant.- empower, endorse, license, permit, sanction, allow.

Prolific: bountiful, breeding, fecund, fertile, fruitful, luxuriant, plenteous, productive, propagating, rich, teeming.

ant.- barren, unproductive, sterile, unfruitful.

Prolong: amplify, augment, continue, elongate, extend, increase, lengthen, protract, stretch.

ant.- condense, curtail, shorten, shrink.

Prominent: celebrated, famous, conspicuous, distinguished, eminent, illustrious, influential, leading, salient, noteworthy, outstanding, popular, well-known, renowned, remarkable.

ant.- common, humble, obscure, ordinary, unknown.

Promote: advance, assist, aggrandize, aid, contribute, cultivate, improve, dignify, elevate, encourage, endow, exalt, facilitate, forward, foster, further, help, push, raise, urge.

ant.- degrade, discourage, hinder, impair, impede, obstruct.

Prompt: arouse, cause, evoke, incite, induce, inspire, make, motivate, occasion, originate, provoke, active, alert, direct, early, immediate, quick, ready, swift, timely, vigilant.
ant.- dilatory, late, overdue, slow, tardy.

Proof: affidavit, attestation, confirmation, corroboration, credentials, demonstration, evidence, facts, reasons, data, substantiation, test, testimony, verification, warrant, witness.
ant.- aberrancy, failure, fallacy, invalidity, misconception, untruth.

Propagate: beget, breed, grow, engender, generate, increase, multiply, originate, procreate, produce, publish, reproduce, raise, spread, broadcast.
ant.- annihilate, destroy, kill, exterminate, extinguish, ravage.

Propel: actuate, agitate, drive, force, impel, induce, instigate, move, persuade, push, start, thrust, urge, shove.
ant.- delay, discourage, drag, halt, hinder, stop.

Proper: appropriate, befitting, conventional, correct, fair, fit, formal, just, legitimate, meet, pertinent, respectable, right, seemly, suitable, individual, peculiar, special, fastidious, becoming.
ant.- improper, inaccurate, objectionable, unsuitable, unfit.

Proportion: dimension, ratio, extent, balance, composure, equilibrium, equivalence, poise, share, symmetry.
ant.- imbalance, inequality, fall.

Proposal: offer, presentation, proposition, recommendation, suggestion, tender, statement, overture, motion.
ant.- rejection, withdrawal, refusal.

Proprietor: heritor, deed-holder, keeper, landlady, landlord, master, possessor, titleholder, manager, owner.
ant.- renter, resident, servant, tenant.

Propriety: appropriateness, aptness, conventionality, fitness, correctness, decency, dignity, decorum, suitability, righteousness.
ant.- impropriety, misconduct, unfitness, unseemliness.

Prosper: achieve, advance, be fortunate, bloom, blossom, flourish, flower, gain, grow, multiply, increase, prevail, rise, succeed, thrive, win.
ant.- fail, lose, miscarry, miss, perish.

Prosperous: affluent, opulent, flourishing, luxurious, rich, moneyed, sumptuous, well-off, well-to-do, wealthy.
ant.- destitute, indigent, needy, poverty-stricken, poor.

Protect: defend, guard, shield, keep safe, preserve, save, secure, safeguard.
ant.- assail, assault, attack.

Protection: bulwark, covering, fence, refuge, safeguard, screen, shelter, shield, defense.
ant.- exposure, insecurity, fragility, frailty, weakness.

Protest: challenge, clamour, demonstration, difference, disagreement, dissentience, moratorium, non-compliance, non-conformity, objection, opposition, raucousness, rejection, dissent, remonstrance, tumult, turmoil, variance, complaint, contradiction, disapproval, expostulation.
ant.- acceptance, agreement, assent, compliance, peace, recongnition.

Protract: continue, drag on, drag out, draw out, spin out, stretch out, expand, extend, lengthen, elongate, postpone, procrastinate, spread.
ant.- abridge, condense, curtail, hasten, reduce, shorten.

Proud: arrogant, dignified, disdainful, exalted, haughty, imperious, lordly, majestic, overbearing, lofty, stately, supercilious, vain.
ant.- ashamed, humble, lowly, meek, modest.

Prove: confirm, corroborate, demonstrate, establish, justify, manifest, show, substantiate, test, try, verify, demonstrate, document.
ant.- contradict, disprove, deny, expose, refute.

Provide: afford, arm, cater, contribute, endow, equip, fit up, fit out, furnish, give, produce, purvey, replenish, stock, store, supply, yield, gear, accounter.
ant.- denude, deprive, divest, remove, strip, withhold.

Provident: careful, cautious, discret, economical, frugal, farsighted, prudent, thrifty, thoughtful, wise.
ant.- careless, short-sighted, heedless, negligent.

Provoke: among, excite, fire, evoke, irritate, arouse, incite, induce, inflame, inspire, kindle.
ant.- blunt, curb, ease, lull.

Proximate: adjacent, close, adjoining, besides, bordering, contiguous, handy, near, neighbouring, nigh.
ant.- distant, far, remote, removed.

Prudent: careful, cautious, circumspect, discerning, discreet, prudential, heedful, chary, judicious, reasonable, sensible, sound, vigilant, wary, watchful, wise, politic.
ant.- absurd, foolish, rash, impeteuous, reckless, stupid.

Prying: curious, inquisitive, interfering, meddling, nosy, peeping, peering, searching, seeking, snoopy, spying.
ant.- incurious, indifferent, aloof, nonchalant, uncaring, unconcerned.

Pseudo: artificial, bogus, quasi, counterfeit, fake, false, mock, imitation, phoney, sham, simulated, spurious.
ant.- actual, genuine, honest, real, sound, true.

Public: exposed, overt, known, open, unrestricted.
ant.- hidden, secret, secluded, unknown, unrevealed.

Pull: drag, draw, haul, lift, stretch, tow, tug, extract, pluck, remove, take out, wrench.
ant.- push, drive, thrust.

Punctual: dependable, early, exact, meticulous, precise, prompt, punctilious, ready, scrupulous, strict, timely, regular.
ant.- careless, desultory, dilatory, late, tardy.

Punish: castigate, chasten, chastise, correct, discipline, fine, flog, imprison, pummel, scold, strike, penalize.
ant.- acquit, exonerate, free, forgive, pardon, reward.

Puny: diminutive, dwarfish, tiny, faint, underized, pygmy, little, feeble, frail, small, stunted, undeveloped, weak, underdeveloped, undersized.
ant.- mighty, robust, strong, sturdy, vigorous.

Purchase: buying, emption, invest in, pay for, shop for.

ant.- auction, barter, retail, sale, selling, vendue, market.

Pure: clean, clear, genuine, immaculate, perfect, spotless, stainless, unadulterated, unblemished, unmixed, untainted, chaste, guiltless, modest, holy, incorrupt, unpolluted, underfiled, uncorrupted.

ant.- adulterated, polluted, foul, rotten, tainted, corrupt, defiled, licentious, immodest, obscene.

Purge: cleanse, clarify, flush, wash, clear.

ant.- foul, pollute.

Purify: chasten, clarify, clean, cleanse, filter, clear, correct, disinfect, fumigate, purge, rectify, refine, wash.

ant.- debase, dirty, pollute, stain, tarnish, vitiate.

Purpose: aim, determination, end, goal, inclination, intent, intention, object, objective, resolve, view, resolution.

ant.- accident, chance, fate, hazard.

Pursue: chase, follow, haunt, hound, hunt, persist, seek, shadow, track, harry.

ant.- abandon, elude, ignore.

Push: butt, compel, crowd, drive, elbow, force, impel, jostle, nudge, press, propel, shove, thrust.

ant.- drag, halt, pull, retreat, discourage, ignore.

Put: assign, deposit, establish, imbued, insert, install, lay, locate, lodge, place, plant, set.

ant.- displace, misplace, oust, remove, transfer.

Putrid: contaminated, corrupt, decayed, polluted, purulent, fetid, decomposed, rank, foul.

ant.- clean, fragrant, pure, wholesome, uncontaminated.

Puzzle: complexity, problem, complication, conundrum, enigma, intricacy, labyrinth, maze, mystery, perplexity, riddle, poser, mystification.

ant.- answer, key, solution, clarify, elucidate, explain, reveal, solve, unravel.

❑

Q

Quaint: curious, droll, eccentric, fanciful, odd, old-fashioned, peculiar, queer, strange, unique, unusual, whimsical.
ant.- common, familiar, usual, fashionable, regular.

Qualified: able, adequate, capable, clever, competent, efficient, eligible, talented, trained, experienced, fit, skilful.
ant.- incapable, ineffectual, inept, unfit, unqualified.

Quarrel: affray, altercation, argument, bickering, brawl, clash, contention, dissension, controversy, disagreement, dispute, feud, fray, fuse, row, spat, squabble, strife, tiff, wrangle.
ant.- agreement, armistice, harmony, peace, silence.

Queer: odd, peculiar, singular, remarkable, strange, unusual, uncommon.
ant.- common, normal, ordinary.

Query: ask, doubt, examine, inquiry, interrogate, question, quiz, search, seek.
ant.- answer, reply, respond, retort, state.

Question: query, interrogation, examination, inquiry.
ant.- answer, reply.

Quick: brisk, expeditious, fast, fleet, hasty, immediate, rapid, instantaneous, prompt, speedy, sudden, hurried, rash, swift, irascible, active.
ant.- slow, sluggish, retard.

Quiescent: abeyant, calm, dormant, inactive, latent, motionless, peaceful, placid, quiet, still, tranquil, moveless, fixed, stationary.
ant.- active, dynamic, manifest, spirited, stirring, vivacious.

Quiet: pacific, peaceful, placid, quiescent, secluded, serene, soundless, still, tranquil, undisturbed, calm, contented.
ant.- loud, noisy, strident, agitated, excited, impatient, perturbed, arouse, excite, incense, inflame, provoke.

❑

R

Radiant: beaming, bright, brilliant, dazzling, effulgent, glittering, glorious, glowing, luminous, lustrous, shining, resplendent, shimmering, sparkling.
ant.- cloudy, dark, dim, dull, obscure.

Radiate: broadcast, circulate, diffuse, disperse, disseminate, emanate, emit, gleam, glitter, illumine, propagate, shed, shine, spread.
ant.- absorb, concentrate, converge, gather.

Radical: basic, constitutional, essential, fundamental, inborn, ingrained, innate, inherent, inherited, irate, intrinsic, native, natural, organic, original.
ant.- extraneous, extrinsic, non-essential.

Rage: anger, animosity, choler, exasperation, frenzy, fury, indignation, ire, passion, resentment, temper, violence, wrath.
ant.- conciliation, patience, forbearance, peace, control, self-calm, tranquillity, placate, quiet.

Raise: elevate, erect, arouse, stir up, incite, exalt, heave, heighten, hoist, lift, uplift, cultivate, grow, produce, rear, collect, gather, aggrandize, amplify, augment, boost, increase, intensify, magnify, levy.
ant.- degrade, depreciate, destroy, lower, reduce.

Rapid: swift, speedy, fleet, prompt, quick, brisk, fast.
ant.- slow, tardy, unhurried.

Rapture: bliss, delight, ecstasy, exaltation, felicity, gladness, happiness, joy, transport.
ant.- depression, melancholy, misery, pain, grief, suffering.

Rare: infrequent, occasional, odd, peculiar, strange, choice, unusual, exceptional, unique, extraordinary, incomparable, precious, remarkable, scarce, singular, uncommon, sparse, unparalleled, unprecedented.
ant.- frequent, habitual, cheap, incessant, recurring, common, normal, ordinary, regular, typical, worthless.

Rash: incautious, giddy, wild, careless, indiscreet, reckless.
ant.- careful, cautious.

Rational: intelligent, judicious, logical, prudent, reasonable, sagacious, sensible, wise, lucid, sane, sound.
ant.- foolish, stupid, insane.

Ravenous: hungry, rapacious, famished, starved, starving.
ant.- full, glutted, satiated.

Raw: callow, coarse, crude, green, unrefined, immature, inexperienced, unprepared, rough, unripe, uncooled.
ant.- mature, polished, ripe, seasoned, well-prepared.

Raze: efface, erage, expunge, demolish, level, tear down, extirpate, extinguish, obliterate, rub out, wipe out.
ant.- build, construct, erect, raise, repair, restore.

Reach: arrive at, pass, get to, extend to, span, stretch, touch, accomplish, achieve, attain, earn, gain.
ant.- bangle, fail, fall, short, leave, miss.

React: act, answer, reciprocate, rejoin, reply, respond.
ant.- disregard, ignore, overlook.

Ready: available, complete, consummate, fit, disposed, quipped, finished, mature, mellow, prepared, ripe, seasonable, suitable, willing.
ant.- immature, unavailable, undeveloped, unready.

Real: actual, veritable, true, certain, authentic, sure, genuine, factual.
ant.- false, fake, feigned.

Reality: actuality, authenticity, entity, realness, genuineness, realism, factuality, fact, truth, verity.
ant.- fantasy, imagination, fiction, nonentity.

Realization: comprehension, appreciation, awareness, perception, understanding.
ant.- disregard, ignorance.

Reap: collect, cut, earn, gain, garner, gather, glean, harvest, hoard, mow, obtain, pick.
ant.- plant, seed, sow.

Reason: account, argument, aim, basis, cause, design, sake, foundation, ground, motive, object, purpose, view.
ant.- bewilder, fabricate, confuse, guess.

Reasonable: rational, logical, fair, fit, just, moderate, proper.
ant.- irrational, unfair.

Rebellion: insurrection, mutiny, outbreak, overthrow, revolt, revolution, insurgence,

riot, sedition, tumult, upheaval, uprising.
ant.- conciliation, law, order, peace.

Rebellious: contumacious, defiant, disobedient, unruly, insubordinate, intractable, rebel, mutinous, pugnacious, recalcitrant, insurgent.
ant.- docile, dutiful, manageable, obedient, subervient, tractable.

Rebuke: admonish, berate, censure, chide, condemn, criticize, reprimand, reproach, reprove, scold, upbraid.
ant.- approve, exonerate, laud, praise, reward.

Recall: recollect, remember, remind, reminisce, review.
ant.- forget, ignore, overlook.

Recede: abate, drawback, return, retrogress, regress, ebb, fall back, go back.
ant.- advance, approach, gain, increase, near, rise.

Receive: acquire, catch, gain, take, get, obtain, take in, win, admit.
ant.- bequeath, donate, give.

Recent: contemporary, fresh, late, latter, modern, new, novel.
ant.- ancient, antiquated, archaic, old-fashioned, obsolete.

Reckless: careless, daring, foolhardy, heedless, imprudent, precipitate, incautious, devil-may-care, rash, wild.
ant.- careful, heedful, wary, cautions, circumspect, prudent.

Recognize: distinguish, identify, know, perceive, realize, recollect, remember, accede, accept, acknowledge, admit, apprehend.
ant.- forget, ignore, overlook.

Recommend: advise, counsel, insinuate, offer, prescribe, propose, refer, suggest, urge, advocate, commend.
ant.- demand, dictate, insist, condemn, denigrate, disapprove.

Reconcile: accommodate, appease, accord, propitiate, adjust, arrange, conciliate, conform, harmonize, mediate, pacify, placate, rectify, settle, reunite.
ant.- alienate, annoy, brother, divide, irritate, separate.

Recover: cure, heal, mend, rally, get back, reclaim, get well, recuperate, revive, recapture, recoup, redeem, regain, renew, renovate, repossess, restore, retrieve, salvage.

ant.- perish, regress, relapse, wane, weaken, forfeit, lose, mislay.

Recreation: amusement, play, diversion, entertainment, frolic, fun, pastime, refreshment, game, relaxation, relief, sport.

ant.- drudgery, labour, task, toil, work.

Rectify: adjust, amend, correct, fix, improve, mend, purify, redren, refine, reform, revise, remedy, repair, right.

ant.- adulterate, debase, falsify, ruin, spoil.

Redeem: deliver, emancipate, extricate, liberate, propitiate, free, ransom, rescue, set free, save.

ant.- abandon, forfeit, ignore, neglect, overlook, shun.

Reduce: abate, abbreviate, thin, abridge, curtail, decrease, diminish, shorten, lessen, lower.

ant.- amplify, enlarge, increase, extend, magnify, strengthen.

Redundant: additional, spare, essential, accessory, supplementary, inordinate, unnecessary, unwanted, excessive, extra.

ant.- essential, necessary.

Refinement: clarification, cleansing, finishing, adorning, embellishing, purification, purity.

ant.- coarseness, crudity, rusticity, vulgarity.

Reform: amend, better, correct, improve, redress, renew, renovate, reoraganize, repair, restore, revise, right.

ant.- aggravate, corrupt, damage, impair, ruin.

Refrain: abstain, avoid, cease, desist, forbear, eschew, leave off, do without.

ant.- continue, indulge, presevere, persist.

Refresh: brace, cheer, enliven, freshen, reinvigorate, renew, renovate, revive, rejuvenate, revitalize, revivify, reanimate.

ant.- bore, exhaust, fatigue, tire, weary.

Refuge: asylum, fortress, harbour, haven, hideaway, protection, retreat, sanctuary, seclusion, shelter.

ant.- danger, exposure, hazard, jeopardy, pitfall, risk.

Refuse: decline, - deny, disavow, disown, negate, rebuff, veto, reject, renounce, repel, junk, repudiate, spurn, withhold, garbage, litter, rubbish, rubble, sweepings, trash, waste.

ant.- accept, consent, grant, present, sanction.

Refute: counter, confute, deny, dispute, controvert, disprove, discredit, negate, overthrow, parry, rebut.

ant.- confirm, substantiate, prove.

Regal: courtly, imperial, kingly, lordly, magnificent, majestic, monarchial, noble, princely, queenly, royal, sovereign, splendid, stately.

ant.- common, ignoble, lowly, ordinary, plebeian, servile.

Regard: attention, concern, view, consideration, notice, observe, observation, watch, believe, hold, imagine, reckon, suppose, think.

ant.- avoidance, neglect, antipathy, disgust.

Regression: backsliding, retrogradation, retroaction, retreat, recession, recidivism, retrogression, return, reversion, withdrawal.

ant.- advancement, headway, progress, progression.

Regret: repentance, attrition, compunction, contrition, grief, heartache, qualm, lamentation, penitence, remorse, repining, self-reproach, sorrow.

ant.- contentment, impenitence, induration, obduracy, satisfaction, tranquillity, celebrate, cheer, enjoy, exult, rejoice.

Regular: consistent, periodic, customary, even, methodical, constant, congruous, normal, orderly, ordinary, punctual, steady, symmetrical, systematic, uniform, unvarying, usual.

ant-. anomalous, erratic, rare, inconsistent, infrequent, strange, unusual.

Regulate: adjust, arrange, control, correct, direct, fix, govern, organize, rectify, rule, systematize.

ant.- confuse, disarrange, disorganize, entangle, jumble, sunder.

Reinforce: buttron, replenish, energize, fortify, invigorate, strengthen, support.

ant.- detract, weaken.

Reject: decline, deny, discard, dismiss, eject, eliminate, veto, exclude, rebuff, refuse, repel, renounce, repudiate, repulse, spurn, withhold.
ant.- accept, admit, choose, select, welcome.

Relaxation: ease, abatement, comfort, loosening, relief, repose, respite, suspension, diminution, easing, lessening, reduction, slackening.
ant.- drudgery, exertion, labour, striving, struggle, toil.

Release: deliver, discharge, give out, relinquish, emancipate, free, liberate, set free, acquittal, deliverance, discharge, dispensation, emancipation, exoneration, freedom, liberation.
ant.- confine, imprison, oppress, restriction, subjugation.

Relent: acquiesce, capitulate, mollify, mellow, melt, unbend, have pity, relax, soften, yield.
ant.- harden, stiffen.

Relentless: cruel, fierce, hard, implacable, inexorable, strict, inflexible, merciless, obdurate, pitiless, remorseless, rigid, rigorous, ruthless, stringent, unyielding.
ant.- compassionate, gentle, lenient, merciful.

Relevant: appropriate, apropos, applicable, apposite, fitting, pertinent, germane, suited.
ant.- inapplicable, inappropriate.

Reliable: credible, believable, dependable, stable, faithful, responsible, safe, tried and tested, sure, true, trusty, trustworthy, unimpeachable.
ant.- dubious, questionable, undependable, unreliable.

Relief: aid, alleviation, assuagement, balm, comfort, deliverance, mitigation, palliation.
ant.- aggravation, agitation, distress.

Relieve: deliver, discharge, disembarrass, disencumber, exempt, release, unburden, disburden, disentangle, ease, free, extricate, facilitate.
ant.- detain, engage, fasten.

Religious: believing, canonical, devout, divine, ecclesiastical, ethical, Godfearing, Godly, holy, ministerial, moral, pietistic,

pious, reverent, sacred, sanctimonious, spiritual, theological.
ant.- atheistic, freethinking, Godless, infidel, irreligious, immoral, impious, profane, secular.

Relinquish: abandon, abdicate, abjure, abnegate, let go, cede, spare, drop, give away, give up, dispose of, discard, spare, forego, renounce, resign, sacrifice, surrender, yield.
ant.- conquer, keep, persist, perpetuate, purse, retain.

Relish: taste, flavour, savour, spice, smack, tang, appetizer, seasoning, appreciation, enjoyment, gratification.
ant.- disflavour, distaste.

Reluctant: averse, backward, disinclined, loath, hesitant, indisposed, unready, revitent, recalcitrant, balky, unwilling.
ant.- amenable, disposed, eager, enthusiastic, ready, willing.

Rely: belief, confide, count, lean, depend, trust.
ant.- distrust, doubt.

Remain: abide, continue, dwell, endure, last, rest, survive.
ant.- depart, dissipate, go, leave, terminate.

Remarkable: distinguished, exceptional, extraordinary, impressive, notable, peculiar, prominent, rare, special, stirring, striking, wonderful, uncommon, unusual.
ant.- common, inconspicuous, normal, regular, unimpressive, usual.

Remedy: antidote, antitoxin, counterpoison, improve, counterirritant, counteragent, antibody, help, antiseptic, cure, mendicant, medication, nostrum, heal, panacea, redress, rectify, reform, mend, relive, renew, repair, restore.
ant.- ruination, aggravate, intensify, neglect, worsen.

Remember: memorize, recall, call up, look back, recollect, remind, reminisce, retain, retrace, review.
ant.- obliterate, overlook, forget.

Remembrance: recollection, commemoration, keepsake, memento, memoir, memorial, memory, reminiscence.
ant.- forgetfulness.

Remit: acquit, amnesty, condone, exculpate, exonerate, let off, excuse, exempt, forgive, relax, pardon, slacken.
ant.- fine, punish.

Remorseless: callous, cruel, hard, inhumane, merciless, impenitent, pitiless, hardened, hard-hearted, obdurate, ruthless.
ant.- kind, merciful.

Remote: alien, distant, foreign, faraway, removed, secluded, far, unconnected, unrelated.
ant.- adjacent, close, near, proximate, related.

Remove: depart, go away, dislodge, displace, evacuate, migrate, move, separate, shift, transfer, transport, discharge, dismiss, eject, evict, oust, unseat, eliminate, extract.
ant.- place, remain, establish, maintain, imbued, plant, root, preserve.

Renew: re-establish, refresh, regenerate, reiterate, repeat, renovate, replace, replenish, restore, resume, resuscitate, revive.
ant.- deplete, diminish, enfeeble, exhaust.

Renounce: abandon, abdicate, desert, drop, forego, forsake, abjure, give up, relinquish, resign, sacrifice, secede, quit, surrender, disclaim, disown, reject, repudiate, retract, revoke.
ant.- maintain, persevere, persist, remain, acknowledge, assert, claim.

Repair: amend, correct, darn, fix, mend, patch, rectify, refit, remedy, remodel, renew, renovate, replace, restore.
ant.- damage, destroy, mar, neglect, ruin.

Repeal: abolish, abrogate, annul, cancel, invalidate, nullify, quash, recall, rescind, revoke, vacate, veto.
ant.- continue, maintain, keep, renew, validate.

Repentance: compunction, contrition, penitence, regret, regretfulness, remorse, self-reproach.
ant.- callousness, impenitence, shamelessness.

Replace: reconstitute, refund, reconstruct, rehabilitate, reinstate, repay, restore, return, substitute, succeed, supplant, supersede.

ant.- alter, change, diversify, modify, transform.

Reply: acknowledge, answer, counter, echo, react, rejoin, respond, rejoinder, repartee, response, retort.

ant.- ask, disregard, ignore, question, examination, inquiry, summoning.

Report: advertise, announce, broadcast, recite, chronicle, communicate, declare, state, describe, detail, herald, tell, inform, mention, notify, proclaim, publish, relate, account, announcement, communication, description, news, dispatch, message, narrative, recital, record, statement, tidings, story.

ant.- conceal, delete, mask, screen, veil, concealment, evasion, deletion, reserve, secrecy, suppression.

Repose: calm, lie down, rest, comfort, ease, hush, leisure, peace, quiescence, quiet, quietude, respite, sleep, slumber, serenity, silence.

ant.- activity, disturbance, noise, tumult, turmoil.

Repress: check, curb, contial, stifle, crush, inhibit, restrain, overpower, quell, silence, smother, subdue, suppress.

ant.- advance, encourage, assist, exhilarate, invigorate, stimulate.

Reprimand: admonish, berate, blame, censure, reprove, chide, lecture, rebuke, scold, upbraid, vilify, vituperate.

ant.- applaud, commend, forgive, laud, praise, reward.

Reproach: rebuke, upbraid, condemn, censure, criticize, chide, blame.

ant.- praise, extol.

Reproduction: breeding, birth, generation, fructification, multiplication, re-enactment, begetting, bringing forth, parturition, labour, childbirth, delivery, travail, midwifery, obstetrics, procreation, propagation.

ant.- infertility, sterility.

Repugnant: averse, adverse, antagonistic, contrary, hostile, contradictory, inconsistent, inimical, disgusting, distasteful, invidious, obnoxious, offensive, opposed, repulsive, incompatible.

ant.- agreeable, appealing, conciliatory, harmonious, pleasant.

Repulsive: abhorrent, horrid, abominable, detestable, disgusting, hideous, nauseating, obnoxious, odious, offensive, repelling, ugly, loathsome, revolting, mawkish, repellent, repugnant.
ant.- alluring, captivating, enticing, inviting, pleasing.

Request: appeal, apply, ask, crave, beg, beseech, entreat, petition, plead, pray, seek, solicit, sue, supplicate.
ant.- command, order.

Requisite: compulsory, needed, essential, imperative, indispensable, mandatory, urgent, necessary, vital, obligatory, required.
ant.- accidental, expendable, extrinsic, non-essential, optional.

Rescue: deliver, disenthrall, extricate, set free, liberate, reclaim, recover, redeem, release, retrieve, save.
ant.- abandon, bind, enslave, hinder, incarcerate.

Resemblance: affinity, parity, analogy, facsimile, likeness, match, semblance, similarity, similitude.
ant.- contrast, deviation, dissimilarity, distinction, inconsistency, variance.

Resentment: anger, animosity, bitterness, displeasure, exasperation, huff, grudge, indignation, ire, irritation, pique, rancour, wrath.
ant.- affection, concord, geniality, happiness, harmony.

Reserved: cautious, demure, detached, diffident, distant, modest, restrained, reticent, retiring, taciturn, timorous, undemonstrative, preserved, saved.
ant.- affable, expansive, blatant, uninhibited, unreserved.

Resign: abandon, abdicate, quit, abjure, cede, eschew, forego, relinquish, renounce, retract, surrender, vacate, waive, withdraw, yield.
ant.- accept, receive, remain, retain, stay.

Resilient: buoyant, elastic, flexible, springy, supple, pliable, rubbery, tensile, ductile, malleable.
ant.- inflexible, unbending.

Resist: check, confront, defy, counteract, hinder, impede, impugn, obstruct, oppose, thwart, withstand.

ant.- acquiesce, collaborate, assist, comply, defer, submit, yield.

Resolution: constancy, energy, courage, decision, stamina, determination, willpower, earnestness, resoluteness, firmness, resolve, fortitude, persistence, steadfastness, zeal, pluck, grit backbone, morale, gumption.

ant.- cowardice, indecision, half-heartedness, uncertainty, vacillation.

Resolve: adjudicate, choose, fix, close, conclude, decide, decree, determine, elect, end, propose, settle, terminate.

ant.- hesitate, procrastinate, vacillate, waver.

Respect: admiration, regard, consideration, deference, esteem, honour, reverence, veneration, courtesy, attention, estimation.

ant.- contempt, disdain, scorn, irreverence, abuse, blame, censure, deride, despise.

Respectable: decorous, proper, estimable, honourable, upright, moderate, presentable, worthy, respected, venerable.

ant.- dishonourable, improper, indecent, reprehensible, scandalous, unworthy.

Resplendent: shining, lustrous, radiant, splendid, gleaming.

ant.- dark, cloud, dingy.

Respond: answer, reply, retort, rejoin, reciprocate.

ant.- ignore, remain, silent.

Responsible: accountable, amenable, answerable, liable, dependable, trustworthy, chargeable.

ant.- arbitrary, unbound, careless, irresponsible, lax, negligent, unreliable.

Restful: calm, comfortable, cozy, easy, mild, peaceful, placid, quiet, relaxing, reposeful, serene, soothing, tranquil, untroubled.

ant.- alarming, annoying, disconcerting, disturbing, upsetting.

Restless: agitated, anxious, uneasy, disquieted, disturbed, fidgety, irresolute, nervous, sleepless, unquiet, unsettled, worried.

ant.- calm, composed, placid, tranquil, unperturbed.

Restore: put back, reinstate, rehabilitate, re-establish,

re-install, reconstruct, rebuild, reorganize, reconstitute, renew, reconvert, renovate, regenerate, remodel.
ant.- demolish, scrap, wreck.

Restrain: check, restrict, debar, hinder, curb, control, govern, hold back.
ant.- assit, help.

Restrict: bind, bridle, check, confine, constrain, repress, curb, fence, hinder, impede, inhibit, limit, obstruct, restrain, stop, suppress.
ant.- enlarge, expand, free, extend, release.

Result: conclusion, effect, end, consequence, fruit, issue, outcome, product, resolution, resolve, termination, upshot.
ant.- origin, root, source, beginning.

Retain: detain, employ, engage, hold, keep, maintain, restrain, hold fast, hold light, preserve, reserve, secure, withhold.
ant.- discard, dismiss, relinquish, surrender.

Retaliate: avenge, match, punish, reciprocate, repay, requite, return, vindicate, retort.
ant.- forget, forgive, ignore, pardon.

Retard: defer, check, delay, loiter, linger, procrastinate, hinder, impede, postpone, hold up, dally, slow down.
ant.- accelerate, advance, hasten, speed.

Retract: abjure, abnegate, abrogate, annul, cancel, deny, disclaim, disown, nullify, recall, recant, withdraw, take back, disavow, repudiate, renounce, reverse, revoke.
ant.- affirm, confirm, ratify, endorse, uphold.

Retrogress: backslide, decline, degenerate, deteriorate, regress, relapse, retreat, retrograde, revert.
ant.- advance, develop, improve, proceed, progress.

Return: come back, go back, put back, bring back, rebound, recoil, turn back, reappear, recur, retreat, revert.
ant.- depart, disappear, go away, leave.

Reveal: disclose, divulge, display, exhibit, bare, explain, expose, express, publish, show, uncover, open, unfold, unmask, unveil.

ant.- conceal, deceive, mask, disguise, secrete.

Revenge: avenging, counter-attack, counterstroke, tit for tat, reciprocation, reciprocity, reprisal, requital, retaliation, retribution, vengeance.

ant.- forgiveness, pardon, reconciliation, remission.

Reverence: admiration, dignity, adoration, approbation, awe, deference, esteem, homage, honour, respect, veneration, worship.

ant.- contempt, execration, dishonour, derision, mockery, irreverence.

Revert: go back, recur, hark, turn, return, reverse, regress, restore.

ant.- advance, go forward, proceed.

Revive: animate, awaken, bring back, invigorate, reanimate, refresh, renew, renovate, reproduce, resuscitate, rouse, revivify.

ant.- decay, decline, fade, perish, waste, wither.

Revoke: recall, repeal, annul, rescind, withdraw, abrogate.

ant.- confirm, endorse, uphold, implement.

Revolting: repulsive, disgusting, repellant, loathsome.

ant.- pleasant, attractive.

Reward: recompense, prize, compensation, honorarium, remuneration, indemnity, meed, guerdon, reparation, quittance, indemnification, redress.

ant.- penalty, punishment, fine.

Riches: assets, wealth, fortune, opulence, money, affluence, richness, possession, wealthiness.

ant.- indigence, poverty, dearth, paucity.

Right: just, lawful, legal, fair, fit, suitable, proper, orderly.

ant.- improper, unfair, unjust, wrong.

Rigid: stiff, stiffened, inflexible, firm, hard, strict, unyielding, obdurate.

ant.- elastic, flexible, soft.

Ripe: mature, advanced, complete, grown, mellow, consummate, finished, prefect, perfected.

ant.- green, immature, unripe, undeveloped.

Rise: arise, climb, go or move, upward, ascend, mount, grow, increase.

ant.- decline, decrease, drop, unyielding, obdurate.

Rival: competitor, opponent, emulator, challenger, contender, antagonist, contestant.

ant.- ally, friend, helper, supporter.

Robust: strong, athletic, stout, muscular, vigorous, powerful, healthy, lusty, sturdy, stalwart, forceful.

ant.- feable, frail, infirm, weak.

Rough: uneven, rugged, cragged, jagged, stubby, vague, unfinished, shaggy, coarse.

ant.- even, level, smooth.

Routine: practice, custom, ordinary course, method, way.

ant.- abnormal, unusual, irregular.

Rude: rough, rugged, vulgar, boorish, unskilful, unskilled, barbarous, uncivil, blunt, bluff, impolite.

ant.- civilized, cultural, educated, elegant.

Ruin: destruction, demolition, wreck, ruination, demolish.

ant.- creation, preservation.

Run: race, step quickly, move swiftly, speed, go.

ant.- remain, stay.

Rural: rustic, pastoral, bucolic, countrified, arcadian.

ant.- urban, civic.

Ruthless: merciless, pitiless, cruel, unmerciful, barbarous, savage, ferocious, inhuman, hard-hearted, relentless.

ant.- forgiving, gentle, kind, humane, merciful, pitying.

❑

S

Sacred: sanctified, sacrosanct, holy, divine, consecrated, saintly, Godly, hallowed, dedicated, devoted.
ant.- lay, secular, temporal, worldly.

Sad: grave, gloomy, dismal, cheerless, downcast, woeful, dejected, unhappy, woebegone, depressed, disconsolate, melancholy, dismal, somber, sorrowful.
ant.- cheerful, glad, happy.

Safe: unharmed, undamaged, unhurt, secure.
ant.- risk, insecure.

Sage: wise, sagacious, acute, intelligent, prudent.
ant.- foolish, idiot.

Salable: vendible, marketable, merchantable, fit for sale.
ant.- purchasable.

Salute: greet, hail, welcome, congratulate.
ant.- insult.

Salvation: preservation, rescue, deliverance, redemption, reclamation, salvage.
ant.- hall, doom, perdition.

Sanity: saneness, soundness, mental balance, rationality, normality, sobriety, lucidity, senses, sound mind.
ant.- craziness, demention, folly, insanity, lunacy.

Satisfaction: compensation, enjoyment, atonement, redress, reparation, content, satiety, contentment.
ant.- discontent, dissatisfaction.

Save: rescue, preserve, deliver, salvage, safeguard.
ant.- assail, assault, attack.

Saver: rescuer, deliverer, saviour, preserver.
ant.- killer, slayer, murderer, assassin.

Scarce: deficient, wanting, rare, uncommon, scanty, few.
ant.- abundant, common, ample, plentiful.

Scornful: contemptuous, disdainful, insolent, insulting, scoffing.
ant.- commendatory, acclamatory.

Secret: hidden, concealed, veild, privy, clandestine, unrevealed, mysterious.
ant.- open, unconcealed, overt, disclosed.

Secure: sure, certain, assured, safe, insured, free of danger, protected.
ant.- endangered, insecure, unsafe.

Security: safety, protection, guard, safegaud, guarantee, warranty, bont, tie, pledge.
ant.- uncertainty, insecurity.

Seize: attach, distrain, gripe, grab, grip, grasp, snatch, clutch, capture, confiscate.
ant.- free, let go, let pass, loose, set free.

Seldom: rarely, infrequently, semi-occasionally, hardly ever.
ant.- frequently, again and again.

Select: appoint, choose, cull, decide, designate, elect, nominate, opt, pick, prefer, single out, specify.
ant.- eliminate, rebuff, refuse, reject.

Selfish: covetous, egoistic, egotistical, greedy, illiberal, mercenary, miserly, narrow, narrow-minded, parsimonious, rapacious, self-centered, self-indulgent, self-interested, self-seeking, uncharitable, stingy, ungenerous.
ant.- altruistic, charitable, generous, magnanimous, liberal, philanthropic.

Send: carry, cast, consign, convey, delegate, deliver, discharge, dispatch, drive, emit, fling, forward, hurl, impel, transfer, transmit.
ant.- get, hold, keep, receive, retain.

Senile: aged, ancient, decrepit, doddering, elderly, enfeebled, feeble, infirm, old.
ant.- alert, strong, young, youthful, vigorous.

Senior: advance, chief, dean, elder, older, superior.
ant.- inferior, junior, lower, subordinate.

Sensation: consciousness, excitement, feeling, passion, perception, espouse, sense, sensibility, sentiment.
ant.- apathy, insensibility, lethargy, narcosis, stupor.

Sense: apprehension, insight, consciousness, discernment, intent, judgment, meaning, notion, opinion, reason, sagacity, sensation, sensibility, sentiment, signification, sanity, intelligence, wit, gumption, wisdom, discrimination, understanding.
ant.- stupidity, folly, silliness, foolishness.

Senseless: absurd, brainless, dense, dull, dumb, fatuous, foolish, idiotic, insensible,

nonsensical, obtuse, unwise, ridiculous, witless, stupid, silly, unconscious.
ant.- alert, brilliant, clever, discerning, perceptive.

Sensibility: awareness, sense, consciousness, delicacy, discernment, emotion, feeling, impressibility, insight, sensation, sensitiveness, subtlety, sensitivity, susceptibility, response, sympathy, sympathetic.
ant.- anesthesia, coldness, detachment, indifference, insensitivity, nonchalance.

Sensible: apprehensible, awake, perceptible, attentive, aware, cognizant, comprehending, conscious, informed, perceiving, sentient, capable, careful, discreet, intelligent, judicious, keen, prudent, rational, reasonable, sharp, sagacious, shrewd, saber, sage, sound, sensitive, wise, sensuous, thoughtful.
ant.- foolish, inattentive, half-witted, insensitive, unaware.

Sensitive: conscious, delicate, impressionable, liable, painful, perceptive, predisposed, prone, responsive, sentient, sentimental, susceptible, sore, tender, irritable.
ant.- heartless, indifferent, unconscious, obdurate, unfeeling.

Sensual: carnal, debauched, erotic, lascivious, lecherous, epicurean, lewd, libidinous, lustful, licentious, salacious, sybaritic, sexual, voluptuous, sexy.
ant.- ascetic, moderate, self-controlled, spiritual, temperate, chaste.

Sentimental: dreamy, effusive, emotional, fanciful, gushing, idealistic, imaginative, languishing, maudlin, mushy, poetic, mawkish, romantic, overemotional, simpering, sappy, tender, unrealistic, visionary.
ant.- factual, literal, matter-of-fact, pragmatic, realistic.

Separate: detach, disconnect, disjoin, dissociate, disunite, divide, isolate, keep apart, part, segregate, sequester, sever, sunder, withdraw apart, disjoined, distinct, rend, disunited, divergent, parted, independent, unconnected, sift, screen.

ant.- assemble, attach, fuse, combine, intertwine, joined, associated, connected, mixed, united.

Separation: alienation, divorce, disconnection, disengagement, disjunction, disunion, division, insulation, isolation, partition, rupture, seclusion, segregation, sequestration, severance, withdrawal.
ant.- association, communion, connection, relationship, union.

Serene: calm, placid, tranquil, peaceful, unperturbed.
ant.- agitated, anxious, troubled.

Serenity: calmness, placidity, composure, quietness, stillness, tranquillity.
ant.- agitation, disquiet.

Series: sequence, succession, arrangement, chain, course, set, line, order, progression.
ant.- orderless, disorder, derangement.

Serious: humourless, sober, momentous, grave, profound, sedate, solemn, somber, staid, thoughtful.
ant.- jolly, joyful, flippant, relaxed, mirthful.

Serve: aid, assist, attend, contribute, help, promote, requite, satisfy, succour, suffice, support, treat, uphold, wait on.
ant.- resist, obstruct, thwart, hamper, handicap.

Serviceable: advantageous, applicable, beneficial, conducive, contributive, favourable, helpful, profitable, salutary, usable, useful, valuable, wholesome.
ant.- deleterious, detrimental, impractical, ineffective, useless.

Settle: adjudicate, close, conclude, confirm, decide, determine, dispose, end, reconcile, resolve, terminate, calm, pacify, quiet, tranquillize, colonize, domesticate.
ant.- suspend, vacillate, ruin, waver, anger, antagonize, roil, stir, destroy, disestablish, raze, unsettle, confuse, disarrange, disorganize, disrupt, etangle.

Sever: cut-off, cleave, separate, part, sunder, disjoin, disunite, rend.
ant.- attach, connect, join, unite.

Several: manifold, many, quite a few, numerous, separate, sundry, unlike, various.
ant.- one, none.

Severe: acute, arduous, austere, despotic, distressing, drastic, exacting, extreme, hard, harsh, inflexible, pitiless, merciless, intense, obdurate, relentless, rigid, rigorous, stern, stiff, strict, stringent, uncompromising, unmitigated, unrelenting, unyielding.
ant.- compassionate, gentle, courteous, lenient, placid, beautified, decorated, embellished.

Sew: baste, bind, fasten, fix, mend, patch, refit, repair, seam, stitch, tailor.
ant.- deface, destroy, hurt, rend, ruin.

Shabby: dilapidated, seedy, rundown, poor, ragged, tatty, threadbare, scruffy, tattered, worn-out.
ant.- fair, well-dressed, net, new.

Shade: shadow, umbrage, shadiness, darkness, cloud, dimness, duskiness, darken, haziness, mistiness, dim, eclipse, obscure.
ant.- brighten, illuminate, manifest, reveal.

Shallow: shoal, depthless, flat, shoaly, shelf, bank, sandbank, sandbar.
ant.- bottomless, deep, profound, unfathomable, depth, pit.

Sham: affect, assume, feign, dissimulate, imitate, fakery, personate, pretend, simulate, counterfeit, fake, fraud, ruse, humbug, imitation, mockery, pretense, pretext, stratagem, trick, wile.
ant.- actuality, fact, reality, substance, truth.

Shame: abashment, chagrin, discomfiture, embarrassment, humiliation, mortification, ignominy, shamefacedness, remorse, baseness, contempt, disfavour, disgrace, dishonour, disrepute, infamy.
ant.- contentment, serenity, impenitence, satisfaction, tranquillity, dignity, glory.

Shape: appearance, aspect, build, cast, configuration, conformation, construction, contour, cut, figure, form, frame, guise, image, mold, outline, pattern.
ant.- contortion, deformity, distortion, malformation, mutilation.

Shapeless: amorphous, vague, deformed, disfigured, formless, irregular, misshapen, ill-defined, unshapely, unsymmetrical.

ant.- proportionate, shapely, proportioned, well-formed, symmetrical.

Share: allotment, bit, helping, contingent, dividend, division, dole, dose, fraction, fragment, parcel, part, piece, portion, quota, ration, section.

ant.- bulk, entirety, sum, totality, whole, aggregate, amass.

Sharp: acute, honed, keen, jagged, cutting, pointed, razor-edged, sharpened, wily, brilliant, clever, cunning, discerning, witty, incisive, intelligent, sagacious, wise, shrewd.

ant.- blunt, dull, pointless, unsharpened.

Shattered: broken, collapsed, crushed, demolished, destroyed, fractured, ruptured, separated, smashed, splintered, wrecked.

ant.- intact, integral, repaired, sound, united.

Shelter: asylum, harbour, lee, haven, refuge, retreat, sanctuary, cover, defense, safety, protection, screen, security, shield, cloak.

ant.- endanger expose, danger, exposure, ignore, hazard, jeopardy, menace, threat, neglect, uncover.

Shift: displace, exchange, remove, substitute, adapt, adjust, alter, change, convert, moderate, modify, move, stir, turn, transfigure, transform, vary, veer.

ant.- keep, retain, continue, establish, preserve, stabilize, cease, halt, rest, stop.

Shining: beaming, bright, gleaming, glittering, radiant, sparkling, brilliant.

ant.- hazy, misty, foggy, cloudy.

Shocking: horrible, ghastly, frightful, fearful, horrendous.

ant.- delightful, laudable, decent.

Short: compact, diminutive, little, low, slight, small, tiny, abbreviated, abridged, pithy, abrupt, compendious, brief, compressed, terse, concise, condensed, laconic, precise, succinct, summary.

ant.- colossal, enormous, titanic, gigantic, towering.

Shorten: abbreviate, abridge, curtail, decrease, dimish, lessen.

ant.- expand, increase, lengthen.

Shout: bawl, bellow, call out, cry, cry out, ejaculate, shriek, exclaim, howl, roar, scream, screech, vociferate, yell, yelp.
ant.- intimate, murmur, mutter, suggest, whisper.

Shove: butt, crowd, drive, elbow, force, hustle, impel ,jostle, press, propel, push, ram, shoulder, thrust.
ant.- drag, halt, pull, stop.

Showy: artificial, ceremonious, dramatic, flashy, gaudy, glaring, histrionic, ornate, pompous, melodramatic, theatrical, tinseled.
ant.- genuine, humble, modest, subdued, unaffected.

Shred: bit, fragment, frazzle, jot, mite, particle, remnant, snippet, scrap, rag, smidgen, speck, strip, tatter.
ant.- aggregate, bulk, mass, quantity, volume.

Shrewd: artful, crafty, cunning, foxy, furtive, guileful, tricky, insidious, sly, surreptitious, wily, underhand, acute, alert, astute, careful, clever, sharp, stealthy, ingenious, intelligent, perspicacious, prudent.
ant.- frivolous, ignorant, impetuous, undiscerning.

Shrill: sharp, piercing, piping, strident, ear-piercing, ear-splitting.
ant.- mellifluous, dulcet, soft, soothing.

Shrink: compress, reduce, contract, cringe, decline, decrease, deflate, diminish, droop, dwindle, fail, flinch, languish, lessen, quail, recoil, shrivel, weaken, wilt, wince, withdraw, wither.
ant.- expand, grow, enlarge, dilate.

Shut: close, lock, seal, exclude, confine, immure, imprison, incarcerate.
ant.- open, unbar, unlock, clear, free, liberate, release, commence, initiate, start.

Shy: bashful, reserved, retiring, demure, cautious, suspicious, wary, timid, skittish, fearful, short, lacking.
ant.- bold, brash, fearless.

Sick: ailing, confined, feeble, indisposed, ill, diseased, morbid, sickly, unhealthy, unwell.
ant.- hale, hardy, healthy, robust, vigorous.

Significant: critical, emphatic, consequential, expressive, grave, important, indicative, meaningful, momentous, vital, notable, outstanding,

prominent, remarkable, serious, weighty, worthy.
ant.- inconsequential, insignificant, petty, shallow, trivial.

Signify: denote, designate, disclose, express, imply, import, indicate, intimate, manifest, mean, purport, reveal, specify, suggest, show.
ant.- conceal, cover, hide, obscure, withhold.

Silent: calm, hushed, mute, noiseless, peaceful, placid, quiescent, quiet, reserved, reticent, still, taciturn, tight-lipped, uncommunicative, tranquil.
ant.- clamorous, communicate, loquacious, noisy, raucous, voluble.

Similar: alike, allied, analogous, comparable, correlative, like, corresponding, parallel, reciprocal, resembling.
ant.- different, dissimilar, alien, divergent, opposed, unlike.

Similarity: affinity, analogy, concordance, conformity, correlation, correspondence, homogeneity, likeness, parity, parallelism, resemblance, semblance, sameness.
ant.- difference, disparity, distinction, divergence.

Simple: apparent, effortless, elementary, facile, mere, obvious, pure, simplistic, single, unblended, uncompounded, unmixed, homely, humble, modest, artless, frank, naive, unpretentious, easy, unsophisticated.
ant.- complicated, complex, difficult, intricate.

Simultaneous: accompanying, coincident, concomitant, concurrent, contemporaneous, synchronal, synchronous.
ant.- foregoing, following, preceding, prior, subsequent.

Sincere: artless, bona fide, frank, candid, conscientious, genuine, guileless, heartfelt, honest, ingenuous, open, straightforward, true, trustworthy, truthful, unaffected, upright, undisguised, unfeigned, unreserved, veracious.
ant.- deceitful, deceptive, evasive, false, hypocritical, untrustworthy.

Sinewy: athletic, brawny, burly, energetic, firm, hardy,

husky, mighty, muscular, powerful, stout, robust, stalwart, steely, strapping, strong, sturdy, virile, wiry.
ant.- delicate, emaciated, feeble, penny, weak.

Sinful: bad, corrupt, criminal, guilty, immoral, unrighteous, wicked.
ant.- sinless, honest, virtuous, upright.

Single: celibate, distinct, individual, isolated, marked, one, only, separate, simple, singular, sole, solitary, special, specific, unaccompanied, unique, unmixed, unwed.
ant.- associated, multiple.

Singular: unique, individual, peculiar, unusual, eccentric, odd, exceptional.
ant.- common, conventional, familiar, normal.

Sinister: adverse, corrupt, deleterious, dire, disastrous, dishonest, evil, foreboding, harmful, hostile, malefic, mischievous, unfavourable, ominous, pernicious, unlucky, perverse, threatening.
ant.- righteous, auspicious, expedient, favourable, good, opportune, propitious.

Sink: be submerge, engulf, go down, immerse, touch bottom, collapse, decline, decrease, descend, diminish, drop, fall, slump, subside, extend, hang, downward.
ant.- float, rise, stay, afloat, swim.

Skeptic: agnostic, doubter, free-thinker, infidel, questioner, schismatic, doubting, unbeliever.
ant.- believer, devotee, disciple, evangelist, worshipper.

Skepticism: agnosticism, disbelief, distrust, doubting, hesitation, infidelity, mistrust, questioning, suspicion.
ant.- certainty, conviction, faith, belief, reliance, trust.

Skill: professionalism, mastery, mastership, skilfulness, facility, dexterousness, expertise, dexterity.
ant.- inability, incompetence, ineptitude, unhandiness.

Skilful: able, accomplished, adept, adroit, apt, clever, deft, dexterous, expert, handy, ingenious, master, practised, proficient, skilled, talented, trained, versed.

ant.- awkward, blundering, clumsy, inept, inexperienced.

Slack: lax, limp, loose, relaxed, slow, stagnant, careless, dilatory, dissolute, heedless, indifferent, negligent, remiss, tardy, unrestrained, wanton.
ant.- alert, careful, dutiful, disciplined, restrained.

Slander: scandal, aspersion, defamation, disparagement, calumny.
ant.- acclaim, acclamation, praise, laudation.

Slant: bent, bias, inclination, leaning, tendency, declivity, obliquity, slope, declination, tilt, pitch.
ant.- ascending, mounting, rising.

Slavery: serfdom, thralldom, vassalage, bondage, servitude, captivity.
ant.- freedom, liberty.

Sleazy: feeble, flabby, flimsy, gauzy, fragile, limp, tenuous, thin, trashy, weak.
ant.- excellent, fine, firm, forceful, strong.

Sleek: glossy, lustrous, oily, polished, satiny, shiny, silky, slick, smooth, velvety.
ant.- coarse, dry, dull, harsh, rough.

Slender: attenuated, feeble, lank, lean, narrow, scanty, scrawny, skinny, slight, slim, tenuous, thin.
ant.- broad, bulky, fat, strong, thick, wide.

Slight: disregard, ignore, snub, light, rebuff, scamp, neglect, omit, overlook, skip.
ant.- flatter, praise.

Slip: blunder, bloomer, error, fallacy, fault, inaccuracy, fluff, indiscretion, lapse, misstep, mistake.
ant.- accuracy, perfection, precision, truth.

Slothful: lazy, idle, inactive, indolent, inert.
ant.- active, energetic, diligent.

Slow: crawling, creeping, dawdling, deliberate, dull, gradual, laggard, languid, leisurely, loitering, slack, torpid, unready, apathetic, dilatory, idle, indolent, lazy, lethargic.
ant.- quick, rapid, speedy, swift.

Sluggish: indolent, inactive, stagnant, torpid, slow, lazy, dull.
ant.- swift, vigorous, dynamic.

Sly: artful, astute, covert, crafty, cunning, deceitful, designing, foxy, furtive, guileful, insidious, mischievous, scheming, shifty, shrewd, stealthy, subtle, tricky, surreptitious, traitorous, underhand, wily.
ant.- artless, candid, frank, genuine, open, sincere.

Small: diminutive, microscopic, little, miniature, minute, petty, penny, short, dwarfish, weak, undersized, pygmy, scanty, slender, slight, tiny, trivial, ungenerous, wee, young.
ant.- enormous, immense, huge.

Smart: adroit, apt, clever, quick, alert, dexterous, quick-witted, skilful, talented, witty, acute, bright, intelligent.
ant.- dull, stupid, unintelligent.

Smooth: glossy, polished, silky, sleek, slick, soft, shiny, even, velvety, flat, flush, level, plane.
ant.- rough, rugged, blunt.

Snare: ambush, spring, gin, catch, clutch, grasp, grip, net, seize, trap, pitfall, ruse, stratagem, noose, wire, trick.
ant.- free, liberate, release, unchain, unshackle.

Snub: cut, discomfit, disdain, disregard, humble, humiliate, ignore, neglect, rebuke, slight, rebuff.
ant.- comfort, honour, love, regard, respect.

Snug: comfortable, sheltered, intimate, comfy, homely, cozy, warm.
ant.- uncomfortable.

Soar: flutter, fly, glide, fly high, tiwer, hover, mount, ascend, escalate, remain, aloft, sail, swoop, wing.
ant.- descend, fall, plummet, sink, topple.

Sober: abstemious, abstinent, austere, calm, dispassionate, earnest, grave, moderate, quiet, reasonable, sedate, serious, solemn, staid, steady, temperate, unintoxicated, unruffled.
ant.- boisterous, dissipated, drunk, excited, immoderate, joyful, overwrought.

Soft: elastic, flaccid, flexible, fluffy, gentle, impressible, pliable, pliant, silky, smooth, spongy, subdued, supple, tender, tractable, yielding.
ant.- unyielding.

Soften: abate, allay, alleviate, diminish, dissolve, extenuate, mollify, mellow, melt, mitigate, moderate, relax, relieve, thaw, solace, soothe, tenderize.

ant.- aggravate, agitate, augment, increase, lengthen.

Sole: alone, deserted, desolate, isolated, lonely, secluded, individual, lone, one, only, single, solitary.

ant.- accompanied, attended, surrounded, collective, multiple, public, social.

Solemn: august, awe-inspiring, ceremonious, formal, imposing, impressive, majestic, momentous, precise, regular, reverential, austere, earnest, ritualistic.

ant.- informal, insignificant, ordinary, transitory, uneventful.

Solid: compact, concrete, dense, hard, rigid, massed, firm, sturdy, stable, substantial.

ant.- liquid, porous, vaporous, vulnerable, weak.

Solitary: alone, lonesome, sole, single, individual, lone.

ant.- companionable, cordial, convivial, sociable.

Solitude: isolation, loneliness, retirement, seclusion.

ant.- exposure, notoriety, publicity, tumult.

Solve: decipher, discover, elucidate, explain, interpret, resolve, unfold, untangle.

ant.- complicate, involve.

Somatic: bodily, carnal, corporal, corporeal, fleshly, material, physical, unspiritual, substantial.

ant.- ethereal, mental, spiritual.

Sombre: bleak, dull, funereal, gloomy, dark, overcast, sad, leaden, depressing, mournful, doleful, dismal.

ant.- bright, cheerful.

Soon: early, instantly, promptly, immediately, quickly, shortly.

ant.- late, overdue, slow, tardy.

Soothe: allay, alleviate, calm, assuage, comfort, compose, quiet, console, ease, mollify, pacify, mitigate, tranquillize, relieve, solace.

ant.- afflict, annoy, distress, vex, antagonize.

Sophisticated: astute, blase, cultivated, cultured, experienced, knowledgeable, wise, polished, refined.

ant.- artless, crude, immature, ingenuous, naive.

Sordid: base, debased, foul, depraved, dirty, loathsome, odious, vicious, vile, vulgar, wicked, abject, contemptible, degraded, mean, despicable, worthless, wretched, ignoble, low.
ant.- attractive, charming, decent, laudable, upright, noble, distinguished, eminent.

Sorrow: affliction, contrition, distress, grief, mourning, penitence, remorse, sadness.
ant.- comfort, happiness, joy, delight, solace.

Sorrowful: dismal, sombre, gloomy, woeful, cheerless.
ant.- happy, gay, joyous.

Sort: category, character, type, class, description, variety, kind, nature, species, group.

Sound: twang, intonation, resonance, audibility, voice, din, noise, tone.
ant.- hush, quiet, stillness, silence.

Sour: acid, acrid, acrimonious, subacid, acidulous, acetic, acerbic, acetous, acetose, sourish, soured, astringent, bitter, curdled, rancid, spoiled, tart, vinegary.
ant.- sugary, sweet.

Source: agent, determinant, incentive, inducement, cause, motive, principle, reason, beginning, commencement, birth, derivation, foundation, fountain, fountainhead, fount, inception, incipience, origin, primogenitor, root, spring, start, wellspring.
ant.- consequence, effect, result, harvest, outcome, issue, product, termination.

Spacious: roomy, capacious, ample, commodious, broad, worldwide, large, vast.
ant.- narrow, small, close.

Spare: extra, additional, free, inreserve, leftover, surplus, emergency, unused.
ant.- necessary, needed.

Special: distinctive, exceptional, exclusive, extraordinary, rare, individual, particular, peculiar, restricted, singular, specific, uncommon, unique, unusual.
ant.- broad, commonplace, ecumenical, prevalent, universal.

Specific: distinguishing, exact, characteristic, concrete, distinct, definite, especial,

precise, explicit, particular, peculiar, special.
ant.- general, indefinite, uncertain, vague.

Specify: denominate, designate, entitle, individualize, mention, name, particularize, stipulate, identify, enumerate, indicate, define, itemize, detail.
ant.- discard, generalize, hint, miscall, misname, reject.

Speculate: conjecture, guess, consider, deduce, imagine, think, mediate, muse, ponder, presume, reflect, suppose, theorize, surmise.
ant.- ascertain, conclude, demonstrate, substantiate.

Spiritual: divine, ecclesiastical, insubstantial, fleshless, holy, ethereal, ghostly, immaterial, incorporeal, sacred, supernatural.
ant.- corporeal, material, carnal, physical, worldly.

Spite: malevolence, malice, ill-will, malignity, animosity, grudge, spitefulness.
ant.- benevolence, charity, goodwill, kindness.

Spiteful: antagonistic, hostile, disagreeable, ill-natured, vicious, malevolent, malicious, malignant, rancorous, surly, vengeful, venomous, vindictive.
ant.- forgiving, friendly, generous, helpful, merciful.

Splendid: brilliant, bright, dazzling, effulgent, eminent, excellent, glorious, gorgeous, grand, illustrious, magnificent, radiant, refulgent, resplendent, shining, showy, sumptuous.
ant.- drab, dull, mediocre, unimpressive.

Splendour: brilliance, radiance, grandeur, brightness, dazzle, glory, luster.
ant.- dullness, ignominy, lack lusterness.

Spoil: decay, decompose, ruin, disintegrate, putrefy, waste, corrupt, damage, debase, rot, destroy, disfigure, impair, harm, injure, vitiate.
ant.- flourish, grow, increase, luxuriate, thrive, enhance, improve, mend, perfect, repair.

Spoken: announced, vocal, expressed, oral, unwritten, uttered, verbal, voiced, told, phonetic, said, viva voce.

ant.- documentary, written, non-verbal, recorded.

Spontaneous: automatic, casual, extemporaneous, impulsive, instinctive, involuntary, offhand, unbidden, uninhibited, natural, unforced, unintentional.

ant.- deliberate, designed, intended, planned, arranged, premeditated, rehearsed.

Spread: circulate, diffuse, open, dispense, disperse, disseminate, distribute, exhibit, expand, extend, promulgate, propagate, radiate, scatter, sow, stretch, strew, unfold, unroll.

ant.- condense, suppress, collect, tighten.

Sprightly: agile, animated, blithe, brisk, lively, buoyant, cheerful, debonair, elated, jocund, spirited, sportive, vivacious.

ant.- dejected, depressed, despondent, gloomy, pessimistic.

Sprout: bud, burgeon, develop, germinate, grow, shoot.

ant.- decrease, shrink, wither.

Spry: active, agile, alacritous, brisk, frisky, lively, nimble, alert, quick, sprightly, supple, vivacious.

ant.- inactive, lethargic, sluggish, torpid.

Squalid: dirty, filthy, repulsive, degraded, foul, grimy, muddy, soiled, sordid, unclean, base, contemptible, despicable, low, mean, miserable, pitiful, poor, shabby, unkempt, wretched.

ant.- clean, immaculate, pure, spotless, appealing, attractive.

Squander: consume, dissipate, exhaust, expend, lavish, misspend, misuse, scatter, spend, waste.

ant.- economize, hoard, save, store, preserve, retain.

Squeamish: delicate, fastidious, finicky, prissy, punctilious, scrupulous.

ant.- bold, brassy, brazen.

Stability: immutability, fixture, constancy, firmness, steadiness, unchangeableness, permanence.

ant.- changeableness, fickleness, fragility, instability, unsteadiness.

Stable: balanced, constant, durable, enduring, equable, established, unchangeable, unaltered, unalterable, steady, changeless, durable, firm, fixed, immovable, permanent, steadfast, unwavering.

ant.- erratic, fluctuating, mercurial, mutable, vacillating.

Staid: earnest, grave, demure, settled, inexcitable, reserved, sedate, serious, sober, solemn, steady.

ant.- boisterous, flighty, frivolous, impulsive, volatile.

Stain: blot, defile, discolour, mark, soil, spot, sully, taint, tarnish, colour, dye, tinge, tint.

ant.- cleanse, decorate, purify, blanch, bleach, whiten.

Stale: rancid, tasteless, insipid, dried up, flat, vapid.

ant.- fresh, unfaded, unjaded.

Stand: be upright, be vertical, erect, mount, place, position, put, rise, set.

ant.- bent, flaccid, leaning.

Start: launch, inaugurate, begin, commence, set out, create, initiate, set up.

ant.- end, finish, stop, wind up.

Startle: alarm, amaze, stun, astonish, astound, bewilder, confound, daze, dumbfound, flabbergast, petrify, shock, surprise, frighten, unsettle.

ant.- caution, forewarn, prepare, signal, warn.

Staunch: reliable, trusty, loyal, stanch, faithful, constant.

ant.- unbelievable, untrustworthy.

Stay: abide, delay, halt, linger, lodge, pause, sojourn, stand, stop, tarry, wait, check.

ant.- dart, hasten, leave, progress, scurry, encourage, assist, facilitate, promote, sustain.

Steady: inflexible, fixed, firm, secure, stable, immovable, unyielding.

ant.- fluctuating, changeable, fickle.

Steep: abrupt, angular, craggy, hilly, perpendicular, precipitous, rugged, sharp, sheer, vertical, upright.

ant.- flat, gradual, horizontal, level.

Sterile: arid, barren, childless, fallow, fruitless, impotent, infecund, unfertile, unfruitful, unproductive, unprolific.

ant.- fecund, fertile, fruitful, generative, prolific, proliferous.

Stern: uncompromising, rigorous, oustere, strict, harsh.
ant.- gentle, compassionate, kind.

Stiff: firm, hard, hardened, inflexible, petrified, rigid, solid, tense, unbending, sever, strong, brisk.
ant.- bendable, flexible, pliable.

Still: hushed, inaudible, inert, motionless, mum, mute, noiseless, quiet, quiescent, soundless, silent, stagnant, stationary, undisturbed, unruffled, calm, gentle, meek, mild, passive, peaceful, patient, placid, tranquil.
ant.- clamorous, disturbed, loud, piercing, stirring, tumultuous, aggressive.

Stilted: affected, artificial, bombastic, fustian, grandiose, grandiloquent, high-flown, high-sounding, magniloquent, pompous, pretentious.
ant.- natural, unaffected, unpretentious.

Stimulate: animate, arouse, energize, excite, impel, incite, instigate, invigorate, provoke, rouse, stir up, spur, exhilarate, stir, urge.
ant.- calm, deaden, pacify, quell, tranquillize.

Stingy: miser, niggard, churl, skinflint, scrimp, lickpenny, harpy, penurious, miserly, niggardly, curmudgeon.
ant.- generous, liberal.

Stop: be over, break off, close, impede, pause, pull up, cease, halt, hinder, interrupt.
ant.- begin, continue, going.

Storm: cyclone, hurricane, tornado, whirlwind, blizzard, gale, gust, squall, tempest.
ant.- calm, peace, placidity, repose, serenity, tranquillity, pacify.

Stormy: blustery, boisterous, squally, gusty, raging, rough, tempestuous, turbulent, windy.
ant.- calm, clear, composed, peaceful, tranquil.

Stout: sturdy, muscular, strong, stalwart, robust, brawny, firm, vigorous.
ant.- lean, slim, lanky, feeble.

Straight: direct, erect, even, level, perpendicular, rectilinear, right, unbent, vertical, upright.

ant.- circuitous, crooked, bent, distorted, swerving.

Strain: distend, draw, tight, extend, stretch, tauten, tighten.

ant.- loose, relax, slacken.

Strange: abnormal, alien, curious, eccentric, exotic, extraordinary, fantastic, foreign, irregular, odd, peculiar, queer, extraneous, singular, surprising, uncommon, unfamiliar, wonderful, unusual, remarkable.

ant.- conventional, familiar, ordinary, prevailing, regular, typical.

Stranger: alien, foreigner, drifter, immigrant, outlander, unknown, newcomer, outsider, visitor.

ant.- acquaintance, associate, companion, friend, neighbour, peer.

Strength: fortitude, stamina, sturdiness, energy, vigour, might, brawn, muscle, muscularity, toughness, power.

ant.- feebleness, infirmity, frailty, weakness.

Strengthen: corroborate, brace, fortify, harden, steel, invigorate, reinforce, enlarge, extend, heighten, caseharden, toughen, indurate, intensify, sharpen.

ant.- enervate, weaken.

Strict: austere, firm, harsh, rigid, rigorous, stern, rough, rugged, severe.

ant.- flexible, mild, soft.

Striking: affecting, august, remarkable, grandiose, overpowering, impressive.

ant.- average, indifferent, dull, undistinguished.

Stripped: naked, uncovered, bare, unclothed, nude, unclad, unappareled.

ant.- clothed, concealed, covered, dressed, wrapped up.

Strong: athletic, healthy, robust, durable, forcible, fortified, hale, impregnable, resistant, resolute, solid, strenuous, tough, mighty, sinewy.

ant.- feeble, frail, weak.

Stubborn: adamant, dogged, contumacious, determined, headstrong, immovable, inflexible, intractable, mulish, obdurate, obstinate, pertinacious, perverse, persistent, recalcitrant, refractory, uncompromising, ungovernable, unyielding.

ant.- amenable, compliant, reasonable, submissive, tractable, yielding.

Stumble: fall, pitch, slide, slip, sprawl, tilt, topple, tumble, trip.
ant.- arise, ascend, mount, soar.

Stupid: asinine, brainless, crass, dense, dull, dumb, feeble-minded, foolish, inane, inept, moronic, obtuse, slow-witted, senseless, witless.
ant.- clever, discerning, perspicacious, saga, wise.

Stupor: apathy, coma, daze, drowsiness, inertness, torpor, insensibility, languor, lethargy, narcosis, numbness, unconsciousness.
ant.- activity, consciousness, liveliness, sensibility, vivacity.

Sturdy: mighty, robust, hardy, stalwart, husky, sinewy, strong.
ant.- weak, feeble, infirm, puny.

Suave: affable, amiable, bland, courteous, cultured, debonair, gallant, genteel, glib, gracious, pleasing, polished, polite, smooth, sophisticated, well-bred, tactful, urbane.
ant.- brusque, displeasing, crude, inept, rude.

Subdue: conquer, control, defeat, master, moderate, overcome, quell, restrain, rout, subjugate, surmount, tame, temper, vanquish.
ant.- awaken, enrage, incite, rouse, stimulate.

Sublime: elevated, glorious, lofty, noble, exalted, superb, magnificent, supreme, grand, eminent, great.
ant.- bad, poor, ordinary.

Submit: offer, present, propose, suggest, proffer, tender, prefer, advance.
ant.- defy, obstruct, resist, withstand, deny, refuse, reject, retain, withhold.

Subordinate: ancillary, dependent, inferior, junior, lower, minor, secondary, subject, subservient, subsidiary, subjugate.
ant.- dominant, excellent, leading, superior, dignify, chief.

Subsequent: after, posterior, consequent, later, next, ensuing, succeeding, following, successive.
ant.- antecedent, anterior, earlier, preceding, prior.

Subside: descend, drop, abate, descent, decrease, lessen,

ebb, lower, fall, sink, droop, extend, downward, hang, collapse, decline, heighten.
ant.- grow, mount, escalate, rise.

Substantiate: evidence, prove, confirm, corroborate, affirm, demonstrate, verify, bear out, attest to, validate.
ant.- confute, invalidate, disprove.

Subtract: deduct, subduct, remove, take away, detract, curtail, deduce, withdraw, take off, decrease, lessen.
ant.- add, append, increase by, supplement.

Subvert: demolish, depress, destroy, extinguish, invert, overthrow, overturn, upset, ruin, overwhelm, pervert, reverse, supplant, topple, fell, raze.
ant.- conserve, establish, perpetuate, preserve, sustain.

Succeed: achieve, accomplish, attain, conquer, defeat, flourish, gain, prevail, prosper, surmount, thrive, triumph, vanquish, win.
ant.- lose, miscarry, miss.

Succinct: compendious, curt, terse, brief, crisp, laconic, meaty, pithy, sententious, concise.
ant.- prolix, long-winded.

Sudden: quick, abrupt, rapid, immediate, unpremeditated, precipitate, instantaneous, unexpected, hasty, hurried.
ant.- expected, slow, unhasty, gradual.

Suffer: encounter, bear, endure, experience, sustain, tolerate, feel, agonize, undergo, ache.
ant.- avoid, resist, surrender, deny, disallow, prohibit, refuse, heal, rally, overcome, recover, revive.

Sufficient: abundant, adequate, ample, commensurate, enough, fitting, full, complete, plentiful, plenteous, plenty, satisfactory.
ant.- deficient, inadequate, insufficient, lacking, scant.

Suit: accommodate, adapt, adjust, alter, conform, fit, revise, fill, gratify, please, satisfy.
ant.- misapply, misfit, annoy, disturb, vex.

Suitable: acceptable, just, meet, accordant, adapted, agreeable, applicable, fitting, appropriate, becoming, conformable, congruous, consonant, eligible, expedient, gratifying, pertinent, relevant.

ant.- disagreeable, improper, incongruous, irrelevant, obnoxious, reprehensible.

Sullen: crabbed, dismal, dour, fretful, gloomy, glum, moody, morose, peevish, irascible, sour, stubborn, sulky, surly.

ant.- amiable, cheerful, genial, jovial, sociable.

Sum: aggregate, amount, bulk, collection, entirety, entity, everything, gross, lump, total, totality, unity, value, whole, worth.

ant.- fraction, ingredient, part, portion.

Summit: apex, crest, crown, cap, culmination, head, height, peak, pinnacle, tip, top, vertex, zenith.

ant.- base, bottom, foot, foundation, nadir.

Sunny; bright, brilliant, clear, cloudless, dazzling, fair, gleaming, shining, shiny, splendid, sunlit.

ant.- cloudy, dark, dull, foul, overcast.

Superficial: cursory, exterior, dilettante, slender, trivial, inane, external, flimsy, ignorant, imperfect, outward, shallow, short-sighted, slight, surface, unenlightened.

ant.- careful, deep, deliberate, learned, profound.

Superfluous: abounding, extra, exaggerated, excessive, exorbitant, extreme, lavish, needless, overmuch, profuse, redundant, superabundant, spare, unnecessary.

ant.- inadequate, insufficient, scanty, scarce.

Superior: above, better, distinguished, excellent, finer, greater, higher, preferred, sovereign, unsurpassed, supreme, upper.

ant.- below, deficient, inferior, minor, substandard.

Supple: elastic, limber, lithe, pliant, flexible.

ant.- firm, rigid, stiff.

Support: base, basis, bolster, brace, buttress, foundation, fulcrum, groundwork, prop, shore, stanchion, stay.

ant.- groundless, ungrounded, baseless, unfounded.

Supporter: advocate, pillar, defender, devotee, sustainer, upholder, votary, follower.

ant.- opponent, competitor, rival, adversary, antagonist.

Suppress: lower, moderate, quell, subdue, repress, put down, restrain, quash, check, lessen.
ant.- rouse, stirup, promote, whip up.

Supreme: best, cardinal, chief, dominant, essential, final, first, foremost, greatest, highest, leading, main, paramount, peerless, predominant, prime, principal, ultimate, utmost.
ant.- auxiliary, inferior, subordinate, subsidiary, supplemental.

Sure: certain, positive, assured, undebatable, safe, dependable, trustworthy, convinced, inevitable, secure, definite, undeniable, unquestionable.
ant.- distrustful, doubtful, insecure, unsure.

Surplus: surplusage, excess, oversupply, profit, balance, glut.
ant.- deficit, lack, paucity, shortage.

Surprise: miracle, amazement, astonishment, bewilderment, wonder, wonderment, alarm, amaze, astonish, astound, bewilder, confound, dazzle, awe, disconcert, dumbfound, flabbergast, overwhelm, shock, startle, stun.
ant.- familiarity, habit, routine, triviality, anticipation, apathy, expectation.

Surrender: acquiesce, cede, forgo, renounce, yield, give up, capitulate, relinquish, resign, sacrifice, submit.
ant.- defy, oppose, resist, fight.

Suspect: disbelieve, discredit, be doubtful, suspense, guess, distrust, doubt, mistrust, waver, assume, imagine, presume, speculate, suppose, theorize.
ant.- believe, confide in, rely on, trust.

Suspend: adjourn, cease, defer, delay, desist, discontinue, interrupt, postpone, stay, append, dangle, hang, hitch, poise, sling, swing.
ant.- accelerate, continue, expedite, persist, proceed, support.

Swallow: absorb, assimilate, bear, consume, devour, endure, engulf, envelop, ingest, gulp, retract.
ant.- discharge, emit, expel, reject.

Swarthy: brown, dark, dusky, swart, darkcomplexioned, sable, tawny.
ant.- bright, fair, light.

Sweet: honeyed, mellifluous, melodious, dulcet, lush, candied, sweetened, honey, candy, sirupy, saccharine, sugary, luscious.
ant.- bitter, shap, sour, tart, acid, acerbic.

Swell: bulge, dilate, distend, expand, heave, increase, inflate, intensify, billow, grow, surge, protrude, puff up, rise, tumefy.
ant.- compress, contract, diminish, shrink, shrivel.

Swift: fast, quick, rapid, fleet, speedy, expeditious.
ant.- slow, sluggish, tardy, unhurried.

Symmetry: agreement, arrangement, balance, equality, form, equilibrium, equivalence, harmony, congruity, parallelism, uniformity, correspondence, eurythmy, proportion, regularity, order, shapeliness.
ant.- disagreement, disparity, distortion, irregularity.

Sympathetic: forbearing, kindly, tender, thoughtful, affectionate, caring, feeling, pitying, compassionate.
ant.- apathetic, disdainful, inhumane.

Sympathize: commiserate, feel for, sorrow for, condole, feel sorry for.
ant.- disagree, disregard, misunderstand.

Sympathy: accord, affinity, pity, agreement, condolence, congeniality, consolation, harmony, commiseration, fellow-feeling, warmth. compassion, empathy.
ant.- antipathy, harshness, indifference, insensitivity, malevolence.

Synthetic: artificial, man-made, unnatural, ersatz, fake, feigned, fictitious, phony, unreal, counterfeit, pseudo, sham.
ant.- authentic, genuine, real, natural.

❑

T

Tact: adroitness, dexterity, diplomacy, discretion, savior, fire, discrimination, finesse, consideration, perception, skill, knack, perspicacity.
ant.- indiscretion, insensitivity, tactlessness.

Tactful: discreet, discriminating, judicious, politic, diplomatic, careful, prudent, thoughtful.
ant.- indiscreet, tactless.

Take: catch, clasp, clutch, grasp, grip, procure, seize, appropriate, arrogate.
ant.- give, give back.

Talkative: voluble, garrulous, talky, verbose, chatty, big-mouthed, gabby, gossipy, loquacious, mouthy, wordy.
ant.- quiet, reserved, silent, tight-lipped.

Tall: high, lofty, towering, long, long-limbed, elongated.
ant.- short, small, tiny.

Tame: domestic, tamed, gentle, domesticated, obedient, docile, subdued.
ant.- untamed, wild, undomesticated.

Tangible: palpable, corporeal, actual, concrete, discernible, solid, perceptible, real.
ant.- ethereal, impalpable, intangible, unreal.

Tangle: complicate, confuse, ensnare, entrap, hinder, interlace, interline, mat, knot, trap, ennesh, embroil, involve, jumble, muddle, snare, snarl.
ant.- disentangle, unravel, free, untangle.

Tardy: detained, lax, overdue, behind, time, slow, dilatory, sluggish, retarded, slack, late.
ant. quick, prompt, speedy.

Tarnish: befoul, besmirch, blemish, blot, defile, discolour, smirch, smudge, soil, spot, stain, sully, taint.
ant.- brighten, cleanse, shine, polish up.

Tart: acid, sour, acerbic, snappy, sharp, astringent.
ant.- honeyed, sugary, sweet, syrupy.

Taste: flavour, gusto, piquancy, relish, savour, tang, zest, smack, sapidity, savoriness, sapor, tastiness, palatability.
ant.- indelicacy, insipidity, distaste, tasteless.

Taut: bound up, constricted, tense, strained, firm, fixed, snug, stretched, unbending, tight, unyielding, flexed, rigid.

ant.- lax, loose, relaxed, shaky, slack.

Tax: assessment, custom, dues, duty, excise, impost, levy, rate, tariff, toll, tithe, income tax, interval, revenue.

ant.- gift, grant, present, remuneration, reward.

Teach: advise, coach, direct, educate, enlighten, explain, expound, imbue inculcate, indoctrinate, inform, instill, instruct, interpret, lecture, guide, nurture, interpret, school, train, tutor.

ant.- follow, imbibe, learn, misguide, misinform.

Tedious: boring, dreary, dull, fatiguing, humdrum, irksome, monotonous, soporific, tiresome, uninteresting, wearing, dry, dry-as-dust, wearisome, prosy.

ant.- enjoyable, exciting, animating, exhilarating, fascinating, inspiring.

Teeming: abounding, abundant, ample, bountiful, copious, overflowing, plenteous, plentiful, profuse, prolific, swarming, crowded, chockfull, jam-packed.

ant.- deficient, inadequate, meager, scant, scarce.

Temperate: abstemious, abstinent, ascetic, cautious, continent, frugal, moderate, self-restrained, sober, mild, unruffled.

ant.- excessive, immoderate, impetuous, tempestuous, uncontrolled.

Temporal: carnal, earthly, ephemeral, lay, mundane, profane, secular, terrestrial, sublunary, worldly.

ant.- ecclesiastical, eternal, everlasting, spiritual.

Temporary: brief, changeable, cyclical, ephemeral, fleeting evanescent, impermanent, momentary, passing, short-lived, provisional, irregular, seasonal, transient, transitory.

ant.- abiding, durable, endless, permanent, perpetual, timeless.

Tempt: cajole, seduce, allure, bait, captivate, attract, charm, coax, decoy, entice, fascinate, incite, induce, inveigle, lure.

ant.- deter, discourage, dissuade, hinder.

Tend: mind, attend, escort, care for, guard, keep, manage, nurse, protect, serve, watch, gravitate, incline, lean.
ant.- disregard, ignore, neglect, overlook.

Tendency: aptness, aptitude, predilection, turn, tenour, penchant, bent, inclination, leaning, mood, predisposition, bias, proclivity, proneness, propensity, susceptibility, tone.
ant.- disinclination, aversion, apathy, deviation, opposition.

Tender: feeble, fragile, weak, immature, delicate, frail, soft, benevolent, loving, delicate, merciful, responsive, sympathetic.
ant.- strong, tough.

Tense: nervous, overwrought, restless, troubled, firm, rigid, stiff, high-strung, strained, taut, tight, edgy, high, strung.
ant.- lax, limp, loose, slack.

Tentative: experimental, conditional, makeshift, probationary, provisional, temporary.
ant.- conclusive, decisive, definitive, final, permanent.

Terminate: abolish, cease, close, complete, conclude, end, expire, finish, perfect, stop.
ant.- begin, commence, inaugurate, initiate, start.

Terrible: alarming, appalling, awesome, awful, dreadful, fearful, frightful, gruesome, hideous, horrible, horrid, shocking, terrifying.
ant.- appealing, attractive, captivating, happy, pleasing.

Terse: brief, compact, concise, condensed, crisp, incisive, laconic, pithy, sententious, short, succinct, summary.
ant.- profuse, rambling, redundant, verbose, wordy.

Thankful: appreciative, grateful, pleased, beholden, gratified, much obliged, indebted.
ant.- ungrateful, thankless, unappreciative.

Thaw: deliquesced, dissolve, flow, defrost, infreeze, liquefy, melt.
ant.- chill, congeal, freeze, solidify.

Theoretical: analytical, ideal, scholastic, speculative, hypothetical, conjectural, learned.

ant.- factual, experimental, realistic.

Theory: assumption, attribution, doctrine, opinion, perception, presupposition, speculation, surmise, thesis, viewpoint, plea, hypothesis.
ant.- fact, reality, certainty.

Thick: close, compact, dense, compressed, condensed, crowded, packed, populous, profuse, solid, coagulated, curdled, gelatinous, glutinous, gummy, muddy, solidified, viscid, viscous, broad, stout, fat, mire, massive, squat, thickset.
ant.- clear, transparent, thin, watery, diluted, runny.

Thin: scrawny, skeletal, leam, narrow, threadlike, gaunt, slender, bony, skinny, slim.
ant.- bulky, corpulent, fat, heavy, obese, stout.

Thorough: absolute, accurate, complete, concluded, entire, consummate, ended, exact, exhaustive, finished, full, painstaking, perfect, plenary, thoroughgoing, unbroken, total, undivided, unmitigated.
ant.- deficient, incomplete, perfunctory, sketchy, superficial, imperfect.

Thought: cerebration, cogitation, conception, consideration, contemplation, deliberation, imagination, impression, judgement, lucubration, meditation, memory, notion, opinion, perception, recollection, reflection, sentiment, speculation, thoughtfulness, view.
ant.- emptiness, fatuity, inanity, vacancy, vacuity.

Thoughtful: attentive, careful, charitable, concerned, prudent, considerate, empathic, heedful, kind, sympathetic, cogitative, contemplative, engrossed, introspective, meditative, pensive, philosophic, speculative, studious.
ant.- careless, heedless, indifferent, negligent, thoughtless, fatuous, idiotic, inane, obtuse, vacuous.

Threatening: menacing, intimidative, denunciatory, fulminatory, bullying, warning, cautionary, dangerous, perilous, jeopardous.
ant.- encouraging, comforting, auspicious.

Thrift: conservation, economy, frugality, parsimony, saving, providence, prudence.
ant.- extravagance, prodigality, shiftlessness, waste.

Thrill: excitement, flutter, stir, sensation, shock, tingling, tremor, affect, agitate, tingle, electrify, stimulation, strike, tremble, vibration.
ant.- boredom, dullness, monotony.

Thrive: advance, batten, grow, bloom, flourish, luxuriate, improve, increase, prosper, flower, succeed.
ant.- decline, fail, fall, lose.

Throng: aggregation, crowd, assemblage, assembly, bevy, concourse, crush, gang, host, horde, legion, masses, mob, multitude, populace.
ant.- dispel, disperse, scatter, separate.

Throw: cast, chuck, fling, hurl, unhorse, unseat, pitch, project, propel, sling, thrust, toss.
ant.- catch, draw, haul, hold, retain.

Thrust: drive, force, impel, jostle, penetrate, pierce, press, propel, lunge, ram, plunge, push, shove, impact.
ant.- drag, falter, halt, retreat, impede, obstruct, oppose, debility.

Thwart: block, defeat, oppose, baffle, frustate, contravene, foil.
ant.- aid, assist, help, support.

Tidy: clean, cleanly, methodical, neat, orderly, shipshape, prim, well-groomed, well-kept, spruce, systematic, trim.
ant.- deranged, disheveled, littered, slovenly, unkempt.

Tie: attach, bind, confine, connect, constrain, engage, fasten, fetter, hitch, interlace, knat, lash, rope, join, link, moor, obligate, restrain, restrict, secure, shackle, tether, unite.
ant.- detach, free, loosen, unbind, separate.

Tight: close, close-fitting, taut, compact, contracted, narrow, tense, penny-pinching, fast, firm, fixed.
ant.- lax, loose, relaxed, slack.

Timely: appropriate, convenient, opportune, prompt, propitious, punctual, seasonable, suitable, well-timed.

ant.- inopportune, ill-timed, late, tardy, untimely.

Timid: abashed, afraid, bashful, faint-hearted, shrinking, coy, daunted, diffident, embarrassed, faltering, fearful, irresolute, modest, recoiling, scared, shamefaced, sheepish, shy, skulking, spiritless, terrified, timorous, unaspirated, vacillating, wavering.

ant.- adventurous, courageous, dauntless, determined, gregarious, intrepid.

Tiny: dwarfish, minute, pigmy, little, miniature, diminutive, microscopic, puny, wee, small.

ant.- colossal, enormous, huge, giant, titanic.

Tire: bore, drain, exhaust, fag, fatigue, jade, overtax, pall, overwork, wear out, weary.

ant.- amuse, energize, invigorate, refresh, restore.

Tired: drained, drooping, drowsy, exhausted, faint, fatigued, jaded, spent, weary, wearied, worn out.

ant.- active, energetic, fresh, invigorated, lively.

Toil: exhaustion, hard work, donkey-work, pains, drudgery, effort, labour, task, travail, work.

ant.- leisure, recreation, rest, relaxation, repose, idleness, laziness.

Tolerant: enduring, patient, fair, forbearing, lenient, liberal, open-minded, sympathetic, unprejudiced, unbigoted, understanding.

ant.- bigoted, discriminatory, intolerant, prejudiced, stern, unyielding, strict.

Tolerate: allow, condone, stand, sanction, permit, abide, bear, brook, endure, stomach, swallow, undergo.

ant.- bar, forbid, hinder, inhibit, veto.

Top: acme, apex, chief, crest, crown, culmination, head, peak, pinnacle, summit, vertex, zenith.

ant.- bottom, foundation, foot, base, nadir.

Torment: agony, anguish, distress, languish, excruciation, misery, pain, suffering, torture, woe, badger, bait, bother, distress, disturb, grill, gull, harass, harry, hurt, irritate, nag, oppress, pester.

ant.- comfort, mitigation, ease, relief, solace, console, help, mollify, please, relieve, soothe.

Torrid: hot, scalding, parched, sizzling, burning, arid, warm, scorching, sweltering.
ant.- cold, chill, iciness.

Torture: anguish, agony, pain, excruciation, torment.
ant.- comfort, console, ease, relieve, solace, soothe.

Touchy: choleric, fiery, hasty, fretful, petulant, peevish, sensitive, snappish, irritable.
ant.- cheerful, genial, sweet, sunny.

Tough: firm, hardened, hardy, seasoned, stalwart, strong, sturdy, tenacious, wiry, difficult, formidable, hard, intricate, laborious, puzzling, rigorous, troublesome, incorrigible, intractable, obdurate, obstinate, raging, savage, stubborn, turbulent, unmanageable, fierce, unyielding, vicious.
ant.- easy, effortless, facile, elementary, simple, amenable, compliant, deferential, docile, passive, tractable, yielding.

Trace: mark, scar, stain, stigma, tinge, characteristic, clue, evidence, feature, fragment, trait, impression, indication, memorial, property, record, sign, symptom, vestige.
ant.- deletion, effacement, extinction, non-existence, obliteration.

Tractable: adaptable, dutiful, amenable, compliant, docile, governable, manageable, obedient, pliant, submissive, willing, yielding.
ant.- insubordinate, stubborn, intractable, obstinate, rebellious.

Traitorous: apostate, recreant, backslider, turncoat, deserter, disloyal, faithless, false, insidious, mutinous, perfidious, rebellious, renegade, seditious, treacherous, treasonable.
ant.- flag-waver, patriot, chauvinist, devoted, faithful, loyal.

Transmit: broadcast, convey, communicate, disclose, mail, dispatch, forward, impart, pass on, relay, send, post, wire, telegraph, land down, transfer.
ant.- conceal, hide, mask, secrete.

Transparent: translucent, transpicuous, diaphanous, lucid, pellucid, lucent, limpid, glassy, hyaline, hyaloid, vitreous, flimsy, crystalline, thin.
ant.- cloudy, hidden, muddy, opaque, unclear.

Trash: debris, dregs, dross, garbage, junk, leavings, litter, rags, refuse, riffraff, rubbish, rubble, scourings, offal, scrap, slag, sweepings, trumpery, waste.
ant.- advantages, benefits, goods, perquisites, valuables.

Treacherous: deceitful, false, disloyal, faithless, perfidious, traitorous, treasonable, unfaithful, unreliable.
ant.- dependable, faithful, honest, reliable, trustworthy.

Treason: betrayal, disloyalty, faithlessness, traitorousness, duplicity, mutiny, perfidy, sedition, treachery.
ant.- faithfulness, loyalty, patriotism.

Treat: negotiate, review, deal, bargain, parley.
ant.- ignore, neglect, offend, overlook, annoy, bore, irritate, vex.

Tremendous: awful, appalling, awesome, colossal, great, enormous, gigantic, huge, monstrous, prodigious, vast, stupendous.
ant.- insignificant, miniature, tiny, trivial, unimportant.

Trespass: encroach, infringe, intrude, invade, penetrate, poach, transgress, violate.
ant.- abandon, evacuate, guard, protect, relinquish, vacate.

Tribulation: adversity, agony, affliction, anguish, distress, grief, misery, sorrow, trouble, suffering, wretchedness, woe.
ant.- consolation, delight, elation, joy, peace.

Trick: antic, artifice, caper, cheat, deceit, deception, device, fraud, guile, hoax, ruse, humbug, illusion, imposture, maneuver, ploy, stratagem, stunt, subterfuge, swindle, wile.
ant.- candour, honesty, justness, openness, sincerity.

Tricky: tricklish, intricate, foxy, guileful, insidious, evasive, artful, deceitful, shifty, crafty, cunning, stealthy, subtle, shrewd.
ant.- artless, honest, truthful.

Trim: shipshape, spruce, tidy, neat, well-ordered, embellish, cut, lop, prune, scissor, shave, shear, snip, nice, orderly.
ant.- disorderly, messy, untidy.

Trite: banal, bromidic, common, dull, hackneyed, humdrum, ordinary, commonplace, boring, tedious, stale, old, stereotyped, uninspiring.
ant.- fresh, new, bracing, effectual, novel, original, rousing.

Triumph: achievement, victory, ascendancy, celebration, conquest, exultation, joy, jubilation, mastery, success, trophy, succeed, win.
ant.- adversity, defeat, downfall, failure, subjugation, default, fail, flounder, lose, quit, succumb.

Trivial: beggarly, diminutive, dribbling, frivolous, useless, picayune, inappreciable, inconsiderable, insignificant, little, meager, minute, mean, piddling, paltry, petty, scanty, small, trifling, unessential, unimportant, valueless, worthless.
ant.- paramount, precious, significant, valuable, vital, weighty.

Trouble: afflict, agitate, annoy, bother, concern, distract, distress, disturb, inconvenience, irk, irritate, molest, perturb, pester, plague, tease, upset, vex, worry, affliction, ailment, bind, crisis, difficulty, distress, grief, hardship, illness, ordeal, pain, sorrow, woe, annoyance, embarrassment, worry, irritation, torment, predicament, problem.
ant.- happiness, joy, pleasure, comfort, gratification, peace, quietude, repose, satisfaction, security, solace, tranquillity.

Troublesome: afflictive, difficult, annoying, bothersome, burdensome, damaging, distressing, disturbing, galling, harassing, irksome, tedious, upsetting, wearisome.
ant.- comfortable, facile, gratifying, smooth, manageable.

True: absolute, accurate, actual, authentic, correct, definite, exact, factual, genuine, legal, legitimate, valid, faithful, real, uncontradictable, incorrupt, honest, honourable, just, loyal, reliable, righteous, scrupulous, sincere, steadfast, straight, trustworthy, upright.

ant.- erroneous, false, fictional, imaginary, inaccurate, invalid, mythical.

Trust: assurance, belief, faith, certainty, certitude, credit, confidence, conviction, credence, reassurance, reliance, security.

ant.- disbelief, incredibility, misgiving, skepticism, suspicion.

Trustworthy: constant, loyal, dependable, faithful, reliable, sincere, steadfast, truthful, upright, believable, credible, responsible, trusty, veracious, true.

ant.- deceitful, perfidious, sneaking, traitorous, underhand, unfaithful.

Truth: accuracy, actuality, authenticity, fact, candour, constancy, correctness, exactness, fidelity, honesty, honour, ingenuousness, verity, rectitude, rightness, sincerity, truthfulness, uprightness, veracity, verisimilitude.

ant.- duplicity, evasion, fabrication, falsehood, hypocrisy.

Truthful: candid, frank, honest, reliable, sincere, true, pure, trustworthy, veracious, exact, accurate, correct, factual, guileless, bonafide, true-blue, legitimate, verifiable.

ant.- deceitful, misleading, sly, venal, fictitious, inaccurate, incorrect, inexact.

Try: aim, aspire, attempt, design, endeavour, essay, exert, intend, labour, seek, strive, struggle, tackle, undertake.

ant.- abandon, decline, ignore, neglect, omit.

Trying: aggravating, annoying, bothersome, disquieting, distressing, disturbing, galling, irksome, irritating, troublesome, upsetting, vexatious, burdensome, painful, strenuous.

ant.- accommodating, encouraging, gratifying, pleasing, soothing, easy, facile, simple.

Tumult: disarray, hubbub, jumble, turbulence, agitation, stir, commotion, disorder.
ant.- calm, hush, peace, quiet, silence.

Turbulent: agitated, blustery, brawling, disturbed, gusty, insurgent, obstreperous, wild, riotous, roaring, stormy, tempestuous, tumultuous, windy, violent.
ant.- calm, orderly, peaceful, placid, tranquil.

Twist: bend, bow, coil, contort, convolve, crook, curve, deflect, distort, interlace, encircle, gnarl, incline, pervert, rotate, screw, squirm, turn, twine, wind, wrench, wring, writhe.
ant.- uncoil, straighten, unravel, unroll.

Typical: accustomed, average, common, conventional, ideal, customary, figurative, modal, habitual, illustrative, model, indicative, middling, normal, ordinary, plain, regular, usual, representative, symbolic.
ant.- aberrant, atypical, rare, deviant, distinctive.

Tyrannous: authoritative, dictatorial, domineering, imperious, oppressive, cruel, despotic.
ant.- liberal, tolerant, kind.

❑

U

Ugly: deformed, homely, boul, beautiless, dingy, unbeautiful, unlovely, unseemly, unsightly, bullying.
ant.- beautiful, captivating, dazzling, exquisite, magnificent, agreeable, charming, gentle, inviting, loving, pleasant.

Ultimate: greatest, highest, paramount, topmost, utmost, eventual, extreme, farthest, final, maximum, terminal, last, conclusive.
ant.- beginning, first, initial, opening, preliminary, primary.

Unadulterated: clean, clear, true, simple, pure, undiluted, genuine, immaculate.
ant.- impure, unclean, foul.

Unanimity: accord, concert, agreement, apposition, concord, concordance, conformity, congruence, harmony, unity.
ant.- disagreement, discord, dissonance, division.

Unassuming: compliant, plain, simple, submissive, modest, humble, meek, unassertive.
ant.- assuming, pretentious.

Unbecoming: gauche, improper, inappropriate, indecent, indecorous, ugly, maladroit, unbefitting, unseemly, ill-suited, unfitting, unattractive, inharmonious, unsuitable .
ant.- appropriate, becoming, fitting, proper, suitable.

Unbiased: equitable, fair, honest, impartial, judicial, just, neutral, objective, reasonable, unimpassioned, unjaundiced, dispassionate, unprejudiced.
ant.- biased, prejudiced, partial, slanted, unfair.

Uncertain: ambiguous, hazy, doubtful, dubious, indefinite, indistinct, insecure, irresolute, questionable, unclear, vague, undecided, undetermined, unsettled, unstable, unsure, vacillating.
ant.- certain, definite, explicit, lucid, precise, specific.

Uncertainty: ambiguity, doubt, indecision, qualm, quandary, vagueness, distrust.
ant.- assurance, certainty, decision.

Uncivilized: discourteous, gross, uncultured, unenlightened, boorish, brutish, churlish, uncouth, uneducated, unmannered, unsophisticated, vulgar.
ant.- civilized, polite, mannerly, civil.

Unclad: naked, nude, bare, exposed, stripped, unclothed, unappareled.
ant.- clothed, concealed, covered, dressed.

Unclean: dirty, fetid, filthy, foul, grimy, impure, smutty, soiled, sooty, squalid, unwashed.
ant.- clean, immaculate, impeccable, pure.

Uncommon: different, rare, exceptional, extraordinary, infrequent, noteworthy, odd, occasional, remarkable, sporadic, scarce, strange, singular, unconventional, unique, unusual, unwanted.
ant.- typical, usual, conventional, customary, expected.

Uncompromising: confirmed, contumacious, determined, dogged, firm, headstrong, fixed, immovable, inflexible, intractable, intransient, obdurate, pertinacious, rigid, stiff, strict, stubborn, tough, unyielding.
ant.- adaptable, amenable, compliant, flexible, yielding, submissive.

Unconditional: absolute, carte, blanched, certain, entire, full, genuine, positive, thorough, unequivocal, unlimited, unqualified, unrestricted, whole, unreserved, plenary.
ant.- conditional, limited, partial, qualified.

Uncouth: awkward, clumsy, coarse, crass, crude, gawky, graceless, harsh, rough, rude, rustic, ungainly, ungraceful, unpolished, unrefined, vulgar, common, boorish, uncultivated, ill-mannered, gauche.
ant.- cultivated, civilized, courteous, elegant, graceful, refined.

Uncover: open, unclose, unseal, disclose, discover, bare, reveal, laybare, expose, undress, denude.
ant.- clothe, conceal, cover, hide.

Under: below, beneath, following, inferior, subject to, subordinate, underneath.
ant.- above, over, superior.

Understanding: appreciation, awareness, comprehension, discernment, grasp, insight, intellect, intelligence, knowledge, perception, perspicacity, rationality, reason, reasoning, sapience, wisdom.

ant.- foolishness, imbecility, incapacity, stupidity.

Undertaking: business, matter in hand, emprise, endeavour, enterprise, project, venture, work.

ant.- inertia, laziness, negligence, passivity, shiftlessness.

Undisguised: genuine, open, real, true, uncovered, evident, obvious, candid, frank.

ant.- disguised, feigned, hidden.

Undivided: intact, integral, unpaired, complete, united, single, entire, concentrated, exclusive, whole.

ant.- divided, separated, detached, disconnected, segregated.

Undying: eternal, everlasting, permanent, imperishable, deathless, unending, immortal, perennial.

ant.- mortal, perishable, finite.

Uneasy: anxious, jittery, apprehensive, disturbed, fearful, fidgety, nervous, peevish, petulant, restless, shaky, troubled, restive, perturbed, jumpy, disquieted, constrained, uncomfortable, unquiet, wakeful, worried.

ant.- calm, content, peaceful, serene, undismayed.

Uneducated: untaught, untutored, uninformed, illiterate, unlettered, unschooled, ignorant.

ant.- educated, taught, literate, schooled.

Unemployed: idle, out of job, workless, jobless, free, loafing, out of work, unoccupied.

ant.- active, busy, employed, industrious, occupied.

Unequal: disparate, odd, ill-matched, uneven, inequitable, one-sided, unbalanced, unlike, disproportionate, inadequate, mismatched, unfair, unparalleled.

ant.- balanced, coequal, even, matched, uniform.

Uneven: jagged, broken, odd, lumpy, notched, rough, rugged, spasmodic, unequal, variable.

ant.- even, matched, regular, smooth.

Unexpected: amazing, abrupt, astonishing, immediate, instantaneous, raid, sudden,

surprise, accidental, coincidental, contingent, chance, surprising, unforeseen, awaited.
ant.- expected, planned, anticipated.

Unfair: biased, disingenuous, inequitable, unjust, partial, prejudiced, slanted, unethical, unreasonable, unsporting.
ant.- ethical, fair, honest, just, unbiased.

Unfavourable: counteractive, adverse, disadvantageous, inauspicious, unpropitious, unfriendly, antagonistic, negative, contrary, inclement, inopportune, untimely, disastrous, unlucky.
ant.- amicable, favourable, friendly, positive.

Unfeeling: apathetic, callous, cold, cruel, hard, harsh, inconsiderable, insensate, insensible, merciless, pitiless, rigorous, senseless, severe, stony, hard-hearted, cold-blooded, heartless, inhuman, dispassionate, unmerciful, relentless, adamant, unkind, numb, unsympathetic.
ant.- compassionate, empathic, merciful, responsive, sympathetic.

Unfit: improper, inappropriate, incapable, incompetent, inexpert, objectionable, unconditioned, unhealthy, unqualified, unsuitable.
ant.- capable, competent, fit, skilled, suitable.

Unfold: spread out, unravel, unwarp, unfurl, stretch out, expose, open, unroll, smooth out, disclose.
ant.- fold, bend, crease.

Unfortunate: calamitous, ill-fated, disastrous, doomed, ill-starred, inopportune, unlucky, unsuccessful, hapless, star-crossed, luckless.
ant.- advantageous, beneficial, fortunate, opportune, propitious.

Unhappy: calamitous, dejected, despondent, disconsolate, dismal, distressed, dolorous, gloomy, heartsick, grievous, inconsolable, sad, joyless, inappropriate, miserable, mournful, sorrowful.
ant.- contented, delighted, exhilarated, gratified, peaceful, satisfied.

Uniform: alike, consistent, constant, customary, equable, equal, even, harmonious, homogeneous, homologous, orderly, proportionate, regular, symmetrical, systematic, unchanging, monotonous, invariable, undeviating, undiversified, unvaried, unvarying.

ant.- amorphous, disordered, distorted, diversified, erratic, irregular, unsystematic.

Unify: ally, amalgamate, blend, combine, concentrate, merge, conjoin, connect, consolidate, entwine, join, mix, organize, solidify, strengthen, unite.

ant.- disperse, disrupt, divide, separate, split.

Unimportant: commonplace, immaterial, incidental, slight, inconsequential, inferior, irrelevant, mediocre, nugatory, ordinary, picayune, poor, trivial.

ant.- important, essential, grave, major, significant.

Uninformed: unacquainted, ignorant, unknowing, unaware, incognizant.

ant.- aware, informed, wise.

Unintelligible: cloudy, dim, dusky, indistinct, vague, mysterious, undecipherable, unexplained, illegible, inarticulate, incoherent.

ant.- intelligible, legible, understandable.

Uninteresting: boring, dreary, burdensome, dull, tedious, humdrum, sluggish, monotonous.

ant.- interesting, exciting, inspiring.

Union: amalgamation, joining, annexation, coalescence, unity, unison, attachment, blending, combination, commixture, conjunction, connection, coupling, fusion, junction, merging, mingling, solidarity, unification, uniting, concord, unanimity, alliance, association, coalition, federation.

ant.- disconnection, dispersion, division, separation, dissociation, segregation.

Unique: distinctive, exceptional, matchless, only, peculiar, rare, remarkable, single, singular, solitary, uncommon, sole, unequalled, unmatched, unparalleled, unprecedented, unrivalled, unusual, suigeneris.

ant.- commonplace, familiar, convectional, ordinary.

Unite: affiliate, ally, amalgamate, annex, associate, attach, blend, coalesce, combine, conjoin, confederate, connect, mingle, consolidate, couple, embody, entwine, fuse, join, merge, mix, unify.

ant.- disconnect, divide, part, separate, sever.

Unity: continuity, oneness, isolation, seclusion, amalgamation, individuality, indivisibility, integrality, inseparability, homogeneity, solitude, fusion, consolidation, integration, coalescence, junction, singleness, solidarity, union, unification, uniformity.

ant.- discord, dissimilarity, diversity, multiplicity, variety.

Universal: all, all-embracing, catholic, comprehensive, cosmic, cosmopolitan, entire, ecumenical, prevailing, whole, worldwide, unlimited.

ant.- distinctive, individual, partial, singular.

Unlawful: invalidate, illegal, outlawed, illicit, lawless, illegitimate.

ant.- legal, lawful, validate.

Unlike: contrary, different, separate, distinct, dissimilar, diverse, disparate.

ant.- like, equal, similar, matched.

Unlimited: limitless, unconfined, unconstrained, undefined, unrestrained, indefinite, boundless, uncounted, full, absolute, unconstricted, unrestricted, infinite.

ant.- limited, bounded, confined, constrained.

Unlocked: ajar, disengaged, exposed, unclosed, unlatched, free, passable, unobstructed.

ant.- closed, locked, sealed, barred, blocked, impassable, inaccessible, obstructed, shut, unobtainable.

Unmistakable: evident, clear, manifest, patent, apparent, plain, open, obvious.

ant.- mistakable, doubtful, unclear, unsure, ambiguous.

Unpretentious: candid, frank, modest, open, plain, simple, sincere, unobtrusive, unostentatious, unpretending.

ant.- deceitful, hypocritical, false, ostentatious, pompous.

Unqualified: ineligible, inept, incapable, incompetent, unfit, ineligible, inexperienced, unprepared, unsuited.

ant.- eligible, experienced, qualified.

Unreasonable: absurd, foolish, illogical, irrational, mindless, nonsensical, preposterous, ridiculous, senseless, silly, stupid.
ant.- consistent, judicious, rational, reasonable, sensible, wise.

Unrestricted: allowable, clear, available, exposed, passable, free, open, permitted, public, sanctioned, unobstructed, welcoming.
ant.- denied, forbidden, private, prohibited, refused, restricted.

Unruly: disobedient, fractious, headstrong lawless, mutinous, obstreperous, rebellious, recalcitrant, refractory, balky, unmanageable, insubordinate, turbulent, boisterous, violent, ungovernable, wanton, wailful.
ant.- docile, law-abiding, manageable, obedient, tractable.

Unsafe: dangerous, hazardous, insecure, menacing, perilous, precarious, risky, threatening, treacherous, unreliable, unstable.
ant.- firm, harmless, safe, protected, secure.

Unscrupulous: corrupt, crooked, roguish, immoral, unethical, knavish, dishonest, conscienceless.
ant.- honest, ethical, principled, moral.

Unseemly: boorish, brutish, depraved, disgraceful, gross, disorderly, dissolute, dowdy, improper, inappropriate, unfit, indecorous, objectionable, rowdy, unfitting, indecent, slovenly, unbecoming, ungraceful, unkempt, unpolished, unsightly, unsuitable, vulgar, worthless.
ant.- commendable, cultivated, fitting, polished, proper, suave.

Unselfish: disinterested, selfless, benevolent, altruistic, charitable, liberal, noble-minded, magnanimous, large-hearted, generous.
ant.- self-indulgence, self-interest, selfishness.

Unsettled: adrift, unsteady, apprehensive, vacillating, unstable, fickle, wavering, changeable, inconstant, nervous, perturbed, restless, stirred, troubled, unhinged, unnerved.
ant.- calm, certain, constant,

peaceful, secure, inhabited, settled.

Unskilled: awkward, clumsy, ungainly, inexpert, bungling, unskilful, lubberly, gauche, gangling, unqualified, inept, amateur, ill-qualified, unfit, incompetent, inexperienced, maladroit, unpracticed.
ant.- accomplished, efficient, competent, expert, trained.

Unsophisticated: artless, guanine, guileless, ingenuous, innocent, naive, natural, simple, true, unaffected, undesigning, unspoiled, unstudied, unvitiated.
ant.- experienced, guileful, initiated, sophisticated.

Unstable: fickle, irregular, fluctuating, unsteady, inconstant, vacillating, changeable, variable.
ant.- stable, fixed, secure.

Unusual: aberrant, abnormal, anomalous, atypical, curious, distinguished, exceptional, extraordinary, rare, strange, odd, uncommon, unique, unparalleled.
ant.- common, normal, usual, ordinary, regular.

Unyielding: immovable, firm, unbending, rigid, inflexible, indomitable, obdurate, stubborn, relentless, uncompromising.
ant.- flexible, movable, yielding.

Upbraid: reprove, chide, rebuke, reprimand, admonish, scold.
ant.- applaud, acclaim, extol, laud, praise.

Upright: direct, right, erect, undeviating, unswerving, standing, straight, unbent, perpendicular, on end, vertical, conscientious, ethical, fair, faithful, honest, honourable, incorruptible.
ant.- deviating, indirect, bent, swerving, horizontal.

Urge: solicit, plead, importune, advocate, exhort, incite, instigate.
ant.- caution, deter, warn, discourage, dissuade.

Urgent: compelling, critical, demanded, exigent, imperative, important, serious, importunate, insistent, necessary, pressing, required.
ant.- common, insignificant, petty, trivial, unessential, uneventful.

Useful: advantageous, fruitful, applicable, beneficial,

gainful, helpful, practical, profitable, remunerative, salutary, serviceable, suitable, utilitarian, valuable, wholesome.

ant.- deleterious, destructive, detrimental, harmful, noxious.

Useless: abortive, empty, fruitless, futile, inadequate, ineffective, ineffectual, inutile, inefficacious, bootless, effete, unprofitable, null and void, unavailing, unproductive, unserviceable, vain, valueless, vapid, worthless.

ant.- beneficial, effective, potent, profitable, valuable.

Usual: accustomed, common, commonplace, conventional, customary, everyday, wonted, expected, familiar, general, habitual, normal, ordinary, regular.

ant.- abnormal, exceptional, extraordinary, rare, unconventional.

Utility: adequacy, expediency, advantageousness, avail, benefit, convenience, efficacy, efficiency, productiveness, profit, service, serviceableness, usefulness, utilitarianism, value, worth.

ant.- disadvantage, futility, inefficacy, uselessness, worthlessness.

Utilize: adopt, appropriate, avail, employ, exercise, exert, exploit, occupy, practise, use.

ant.- discard, discharge, expel, refuse, reject.

Utmost: absolute, chief, total, extreme, furthest, final, full, unlimited, complete, farthest, greatest, highest, last, main, maximum, most, ultimate, uttermost.

ant.- closest, least, merest, minimum, nearest.

Utopian: chimerical, faultless, exemplary, fabulous, fancied, fantastic, ideal, idealistic, optimistic, unrealistic, illusory, imaginary, perfect, supreme, unreal, visionary.

ant.- casual, faulty, imperfect, substantial, tangible, visible.

Utter: complete, entire, total, finished, full, perfect, ideal, thorough, whole absolute, consummate, excellent, pure, superlative, supreme, sheer.

ant.- imperfect, incomplete, lacking, partial, unfinished, inferior, lesser, negligible, poor.

❑

V

Vacant: abandoned, bare, idle, barren, blank, depleted, void, deserted, empty, hollow, tenantless, unfilled, uninhabited, unoccupied, untenanted, unused, vacuous.
ant.- filled, full, inhabited, occupied, overflowing.

Vacate: abandon, abdicate, move out, decamp, abjure, depart, desert, empty, evacuate, leave, quit, relinquish, resign, surrender, waive.
ant.- fill, stock, store, supply, pack.

Vacillate: change, oscillate, vary, waver, swing, veer, seesaw, shift, fluctuate, falter, shilly shally, undulate, hesitate.
ant.- fix, firm, stable.

Vacillation: changeableness, faltering, fluctuation, hesitation, inconstancy, oscillation, reeling, rocking, swaying, shallying, uncertainty, unsteadiness, wavering.
ant.- certainty, constancy, dependability.

Vagrant: aimless, wayward, beggar, bum, hobo, idler, loafer, ramble, rogue, rover, straggler, tramp, truant, vagabond, wanderer, erratic, homeless, itinerant, nomadic, peripatetic, roaming, roving, straying, wandering.
ant.- gentleman, labourer, toiler, worker.

Vague: doubtful, dubious, unclear, blurred, blurry, amorphous, shapeless, undefined, formless, imprecise, nebulous, indefinite.
ant.- clear, distinct, exact, lucid, precise.

Vain: abortive, bootless, delusive, empty, fleeting, frivolous, fruitless, futile, hollow, idle, ineffective, ineffectual, nugatory, pointless, shadowy, trifling, trivial, unavailing, unprofitable, useless, valueless, worthless.
ant.- advantageous, effective, portent, profitable, valuable, demure, genuine.

Valiant: adventurous, brave, audacious, bold, chivalrous, courageous, daring, strong, dauntless, fearless, gallant, lionhearted, noteworthy, heroic, indomitable, intrepid, plucky, spirited, unafraid, valorous, venturesome.

ant.- cowardly, craven, fearful, timid, timorous, weak.

Valid: accurate, actual, just, authentic, bona-fide, binding, definite, efficient, factual, genuine, legal, lawful, legally, well-grounded, legitimate, logical, real, solid, sound, tested, true, weighty.

ant.- counterfeit, erroneous, fallacious, invalid, spares.

Valour: boldness, bravery, chivalry, manliness, prowess, spiritedness, courage, daring, gallantry, intrepidity, heroism, fearlessness, derring-do.

ant.- fear, cowardice, timidity.

Valuable: costly, meritorious, expensive, high-priced, dear, precious, worthy, profitable, serviceable, useful, estimable.

ant.- cheap, unmarketable, common, worthless.

Value: account, evaluate, rate, esteem, prize, treasure, price, appraise, assess, compute, worth, estimate.

ant.- abandon, despise, ignore, neglect, overlook, reject.

Vandalism: barbarism, pillage, sabotage, looting, burning, depredation, plundering, mutilation, defacement, deseration, profanation, damage, destruction, piracy, spoliation, wasting, wrecking.

ant.- appear, preservation, protection, replacement, appear.

Vanish: cease, depart, fade out, disappear, dissolve, evaporate, go away, decamp, vamoose, sink.

ant.- emerge, reappear, appear.

Vanity: arrogance, conceit, self-love, conceitedness, egotism, pretension, self-laudation, vainglory, self-esteem, self-praise, complacency, pride, smugness, airs, egoism.

ant.- bashfulness, diffidence, humility, modesty, meekness.

Vapid: banal, bland, dry, dull, flat, hackneyed, inane, insipid, lifeless, prosaic, spiritless, trite, tasteless, flavourless, savourless, uninteresting, watery.

ant.- bright, fresh, original, pungent, stimulating, striking.

Variable: fickle, unstable, changeable, alterable, inconstant, wavering, vacillating.
ant.- firm, fixed, stable, steady.

Variation: aberration, alteration, change, contrariety, departure, deviation, difference, variety, dissimilarity, dissimilitude, distinction, diversity, innovation, modification, diversification, variance, divergence.
ant.- congruity, homogeneity, permanence, stability, uniformity.

Variety: change, difference, dissimilarity, diversification, diversity, heterogeneity, class, miscellany, mixture, multifariousness, variance, brand, category, variation, assortment, kind, vaudeville, divisions.
ant.- homogeneity, likeness, monotony, unity, sameness, uniformity.

Various: assorted, different, disparate, divergent, diverse, manifold, many, miscellaneous, numerous, several, sundry, diversified, multiform.
ant.- alike, congruous, same, identical, uniform.

Vast: huge, immense, ample, capacious, immeasurable, enormous, extensive, large, big, boundless, colossal.
ant.- small, microscopic, puny, tiny.

Vehement: ardent, burning, eager, enthusiastic, excitable, fervent, fervid, fiery, hot, impetuous, intense, irascible, passionate.
ant.- apathetic, calm, cool, indifferent, lukewarm.

Velocity: alacrity, celerity, impetus, pace, quickness, rapidity, speed, expedition, speediness, promptness, swiftness.
ant.- slowness, tardiness, delay.

Venerable: esteemed, honoured, patriarchal, respected, revered, superannuated, timeworn, venerated, worshipped.
ant.- dishonour, scorn, mock.

Venerate: admire, adore, cherish, esteem, honour, respect, regard, revere, worship.
ant.- abhor, despise, dislike, loathe, scorn.

Vengeance: reprisal, requital, retaliation, vengefulness, retribution, nemesis, revenge, spitefulness.
ant.- forgiveness, pardon, forbearance.

Venom: poison, bane, toxin, gall, virus, toxicity, acerbity, hate, bitterness, contempt, enmity, malevolence, malice, rancor, malignity, resentment.
ant.- ambrosia, nectar.

Vent: belch, breathe, discharge, eject, emanate, emit, expel, explode, shoot, ventilate, airhole, emission, escape, hole inlet, loophole, vent out, let off, mouth, nostril, opening, spurt, passage.
ant.- bottle-up, curb, inhibit, quash, quell.

Veracity: accuracy, candour, credibility, exactitude, fidelity, frankness, honesty, probity, reality, sincerity, truth, truthfulness.
ant.- chicanery, deception, duplicity, falsehood, misrepresentation.

Verbal: announced, lingual, communicated, expressed, literal, oral, sounded, spoken, told, unwritten, uttered, vocal, verbatim, word-for-word, voiced.
ant.- documentary, printed, unspoken, written.

Verbose: chattering, chatty, fluent, garrulous, long-winded, gossipy, voluble, loquacious, redundant, prolix, repetitive, talkative, verbal, wordy.
ant.- reticent, close-mouthed, tight-lipped, silent, stammering, taciturn, uncommunicative.

Verge: border, boundary, brim, brink, edge, end, extreme, limit, lip, margin, rim, skirt, marge.
ant.- body, bulk, center, inside.

Verification: affirmation, attestation, authentication, confirmation, corroboration, proof, evidence, validation, recognition, testimony.
ant.- contradiction, denial, failure, fallacy, invalidity.

Verify: affirm, approve, assure, attest, authenticate, certify, corroborate, confirm, ratify, validate, establish, prove, identify, substantiate, make certain.
ant.- contradict, disprove, deny, invalidate, repudiate.

Versed: acquainted, aware, cognizant, conversant, skilled, familiar, knowing, proficient, skilful, trained, accomplished.
ant.- unaware, unfamiliar, unknowing.

Versatile: multifaceted, all purpose, all round, many-sided, movable, variable, ready.
ant.- awkward, limited, unadaptable, unchanging.

Vertical: erect, perpendicular, plumb, standing, straight, upright.
ant.- flat, horizontal, inclined, oblique, prone.

Vex: tease, plague, harass, fret, torment, chafe, annoy, nettle, aggravate, irritate.
ant.- console, please, quiet, soothe.

Vice: blemish, carnality, sin, debauchery, defect, fault, evil, impropriety, impurity, crime, viciousness, evil-doing, wrongdoing, wickedness, offense, sinfulness, iniquity, criminality, perversity, ungodliness.
ant.- morality, virtue.

Vicinity: environment, environs, locality, neighbourhood, adjacency, nearness, proximity, vicinage.
ant.- outskirts, distance, remoteness.

Vicious: bad, base, corrupt, vile, debased, degenerate, demoralized, depraved, evil, malignant, obnoxious, wrong, wicked, pernicious, unruly, profligate, sinful, iniquitous, immoral, debauched, criminal, evil-minded.
ant.- admirable, exemplary, honourable, noble, upright, virtuous.

Victim: dupe, gull, martyr, prey, sacrifice, scapegoat, cat's-paw, sufferer.
ant.- culprit, evildoer, felon, swindler.

Victor: champion, conqueror, vanquisher, winner.
ant.- failure, loser, vanquished, flop.

Victory: conquest, defeating, mastery, overcoming, success, superiority, supremacy, triumph, win, winning.
ant.- collapse, defeat, failure, overthrow.

View: aim, belief, conception, examination, glance, glimpse, goal, impression, inception, judgment, look, object, vista, observation, opinion, outlook, panorama, vision, picture, prospect, range, regard, sight, perspective, scene, survey, theory.
ant.- avert, disregard, ignore, miss, overlook, sidetrack.

Vigilant: alert, attentive, careful, heedful, cautious, wary, circumspect, guarded, unsleeping, observant, wakeful, watchful, wide-awake.
ant.- careless, foolhardy, negligent, rash, reckless.

Vigour: energy, force, spirit, virility, hardihood, potency, efficacy, might, vim, power, verve, activity, warmth, health liveliness, strength, vitality, robustness.
ant.- exhaustion, langour, lassitude, listlessness.

Vigorous: active, energetic, forceful, healthy, lusty, powerful, robust, mighty, potent, mettlesome, hardy, hearty, hale, sound, sturdy, stalwart, muscular, buxom, spirited, strenuous, strong, virile.
ant.- debilitated, feeble, frail, inactive, lethargic.

Vile: base, brutish, debased, contemptible, depraved, evil, foul, gross, ignoble, impure, iniquitous, loathsome, low, lowly, nasty, paltry, villainous, corrupt, mean, obscene, ugly, odious, repulsive, sinful, sordid, vicious, vulgar, wicked, wretched.
ant.- attractive, decent, elevated, honourable, laudable, valuable.

Vilify: abuse, asperse, revile, defame, scandalize, vilipend, calumniate, traduce, slander, libel, decry, belittle, malign, slur.
ant.- adore, comment, exalt, esteem, praise.

Villainous: bad, unwholesome, deleterious, iniquitous, base, evil.
ant.- angelic, humane, moral, noble, saintly, justify, acquit, exculpate.

Vindicate: advocate, assert, defend, excuse, maintain, support, uphold, whitewash, extenuate, pilliate, excuse,

set right, soften, exonerate.
ant.- accuse, condemn, blame.

Vindictive: avenging, grudgeful, implacable, revengeful, malicious, spiteful, bitter, rancorous, resentful, unforgiving, vengeful.
ant.- conciliatory, excusing, forgiving, placable.

Violate: break, disobey, disregard, encroach, infringe, transgress, debauch, defile, deflower, desecrate, breach, dishonour, outrage, profane, rape, desecrate, ravish.
ant.- honour, obey, respect, uphold.

Violence: assault, intensity, outrage, vehemence, riot, row, fury, rumpus, turmoil, violation, wildness, force.
ant.- non-violence.

Violent: fierce, fiery, frenzied, furious, passionate, raging, riotous, savage, turbulent, ungovernable, ungentle, untamed, barbaric, boisterous, frenetic, bestial, vehement, wild.
ant.- composed, kind, pacific, peaceful, tranquil.

Virgin: maiden, miss, celibate, vestal, spinster, girl, lass, chaste, clean, immaculate, innocent, modest, pure, spotless, stainless, untamed, unblemished, undefiled, new, unsullied, untainted, fresh, genuine, natural, original, untouched.
ant.- corrupt, shameless, foul, defiled, used.

Virile: hardy, lusty, vigorous, manly, macho, potent, fully-sexed, masculine.
ant.- feminine, effeminate, emasculate, impotent.

Virtue: chastity, decency, goodness, honesty, impeccability, innocence, integrity, morality, probity, prudence, purity, rectitude, sanity, uprightness, value, virginity, effectiveness, excellence, merit, superiority, worth.
ant.- corruption, depravity, vileness, wickedness, debility, enervation, infirmity, weakness, deficiency, inferiority, inutility, uselessness, worthlessness.

Virtuous: decent, honourable, just, right, scrupulous, chaste, ethical, good,

innocent, pure, meritorious, deserving, worthy, correct, dutiful, duteous, moral, righteous, right-minded, well-intentioned, creditable, noble, laudable, commendable, praiseworthy, excellency, admirable, exemplary, saintly, heaven-born, angelic, seraphic.
ant.- corrupt, debauched, evil, sinful, unchaste.

Vision: sight, optics, eyesight, seeing, look, espial, glance.
ant.- blindness, eyelessness, sightlessness.

Visionary: chimerical, ideal, delusory, dreamy, fancied, fanciful, illusory, imaginary, imaginative, remonetize, unreal, utopian.
ant.- actual, material, real, substantial.

Vital: alive, animate, existing, vibrant, living, basic, cardinal, essential, fundamental, important, indispensable, necessary, paramount, requisite, urgent.
ant.- dead, inanimate, lifeless.

Vitality: being, existence, life, animation, buoyancy, energy, intensive, liveliness, spirit, verve, vigour, vim, vivacity, virility, viability.
ant.- death, demise, lethargy, extinction, apathy, lassitude, passivity.

Vitiate: adulterate, debase, contaminate, corrupt, poison, deteriorate, impair, infect, lower, nullify, pervert, pollute, spoil, weaken, void.
ant.- clean, enhance, purify, improve, revive, vitalize.

Vivid: energetic, flamboyant, active, dynamic, spirited, animated, unfaded, glowing, vital, bright, brilliant, expressive, fresh, graphic, intense, life-like, lively, pictorial, picturesque, realistic, sprightly, striking, strong, telling, vibrant.
ant.- cloudy, dreary, dull, vague, weak.

Vocal: announced, articulate, communicated, expressed, expressive, choral, lyric, musical, oral, spoken, sung, uttered, verbal, vocalized, voiced, callable.
ant.- printed, quiet, silent, unspoken, written.

Vocation: art, business, calling, commerce, employment, job, enterprise, field, life-work, mission, occupation, office, profession, pursuit, role, trade, trading, undertaking, work.

ant.- avocation, diversion, entertainment, hobby, pastime.

Void: blank, deplete, deflate, vacuous, exhaust, evaculate, drain, discharge, unload, empty.

ant.- replete, filled, full.

Volition: choice, decision, determination, election, will, intention, voluntariness, willingness, resolution.

ant.- coercion, compulsion, force, persuasion, pressure.

Voluntary: deliberate, free, intentional, self-determining, uncoerced, volitional, willed, spontaneous, voluntered, freewill, unsaked, unforced, wilful, willing.

ant.- compulsory, enforced, forced, instinctive, involuntary, mandatory, required.

Vouch: affirm, assert, test, back, avow, certify, confirm, declare, guarantee, support, attest, swear, testify, uphold, warrant, witness, answer for.

ant.- abnegate, controvert, deny, disavow, repudiate.

Vulgar: abusive, base, brutish, cheap, coarse, common, crass, disgusting, general, gross, ignorant, ill-bred, indecent, inelegant, low, obscene, odious, offensive, profane, ribald, rough, rowdy, rude, tawdry, uncouth, uncultured, unpolished, unrefined.

ant.- aristocratic, charming, cultured, elegant, polished.

Vulnerable: assailable, defenseless, exposed, unprotected, unsafe, susceptible, insecure.

ant.- guarded, immune, well-protected, unassailable.

❑

W

Wages: compensation, fee, pay, income, earnings, payment, recompense, remuneration, salary, stipend, hire.
ant.- donation, gift, gratuity.

Wait: abide, bide, delay, dally, procrastinate, look for, linger, remain, rest, stay, tarry, await, expect.
ant.- act, depart, hasten, leave, proceed, heat up, warm up.

Waive: relinquish, forgo, give up, disclaim, surrender, defer, renounce.
ant.- uphold, insist, pursue.

Wake: activate, animate, call, arouse, awake, awaken, prod, enkindle, excite, kindle, revive, rouse, stimulate, stir, wake.
ant.- catnap, doze, hibernate, sleep, snooze.

Wander: deviate, digress, err, diverge, drift, journey, travel, straggle, saunter, meander, peregrinate, ramble, range, roam, stray, stroll, tour, traipse, walk.
ant.- halt, pause, remain, stay.

Want: aspire, covet, crave, desire, long for, wish, hunger for, require, lack, need, dearth, deficiency, depletion, destitution, exigency, inadequacy, indigence, insufficiency, pauperism, penury, poverty, scarcity.
ant.- abhor, detest, dislike, enjoy.

Warfare: armed, struggle, war, arms, strife, battle, blows, discord, combat, conflict, contest, fighting, hostilities, military operations.
ant.- accord, harmony, peace, truce.

Wariness: alertness, attention, care, watchfulness, caution, carefulness, heedfulness.
ant.- carelessness, inattention, heedlessness.

Warlike: aggressive, bellicose, belligerent, hostile, combative.
ant.- pacific, peaceful, placid.

Warm: balmy, thermal, heated, lukewarm, melting, mild, sunny, temperate, tepid, heat, incite, melt, thaw, summery, hot.
ant.- cold, cool, freezing, icy, frosty, calm, chill.

Wary: attentive, alert, awake, aware, careful, cautious, circumspect, discreet, guarded, heedful, scrupulous, vigilant, watchful.

ant.- foolhardy, unwary, rash, careless, unguarded.

Wash: bathe, clean, cleanse, douse, immerse, launder, rinse, scour, scrub, soak, swab, deterge, lave, soap, wet, wipe.

ant.- dirty, foul, soil, stain.

Wasteful: dissipated, reckless, extravagant, improvident, spendthrift, lavish, prodigal, profligate, profuse, ruinous, squandering, thriftless.

ant.- economical, money, parsimonious, saving, hoarding, mercenary, thrifty.

Watchful: alert, attentive, wary, vigilant, wakeful, careful, cautious, circumspect, wide-awake, guarded, heedful, observant, prudent.

ant.- careless, inattentive, lax, neglectful, oblivious.

Waver: dilly-dally, falter, flicker, fluctuate, flutter, hesitate, oscillate, quiver, reel, shake, totter, vacillate, vibrate.

ant.- determine, stand firm.

Weak: faint, fragile, frail, debilitated, feeble, decrepit, enervated, exhausted, infirm.

ant.- rigid, strong, unyielding, animated, healthy, robust, vigorous.

Weaken: debilitate, devitalize, emasculate, dilute, diminish, enervate, enfeeble, impair, reduce, thin, undermine.

ant.- brace, energize, fortify, invigorate, strengthen.

Weakness: infirmity, feebleness, debelitation, decrepitude, debility, inanition.

ant.- sturding, strength, vitality, potency.

Wealth: affluence, property, assets, means, capital, fortune, money, opulence, plenty, possessions, stock, prosperity, treasure, riches, resources.

ant.- indigence, poverty, need, privation, want.

Wear: bear, be clothed in, be dressed in, carry, clothe, don, dress in, have on, put on.

ant.- put off.

Weariness: ennui, exhaustion, faintness, fatigue, languor, lassitude, lethargy, prostration, tedium, tiredness.

ant.- alertness, amusement, energy, strength, vim.

Weary: bored, exhausted, faint, fatigued, jaded, spent, tired, wearied.
ant.- animated, invigorated, refreshed, rested, arouse, brace, energize, enliven, revise, strenghten.

Weight: ballast, burden, contents, density, gravity, heaviness, load, mass, tonnage, pressure, authority, consequence, sway, domination, emphasis, import, importance, stress, influence, moment, power, seriousness, significance, value.
ant.- airiness, buoyancy, levity, lightens.

Weird: curious, mysterious, odd, peculiar, spooky, strange, eerie, supernatural, uncanny, unearthly.
ant.- common, normal, usual, ordinary, regular.

Welcome: accept, address, admit, embrace, entertain, greet, hail, hug, receive, take in, recognize, salute, shelter.
ant.- discharge, ignore, reject, snub, turn, away.

Well: adequately, admirably, competently, expertly, extremely, rightly, properly, favourably, satisfactorily, strongly, suitably.
ant.- badly, coldly, gracelessly, poorly.

Well-being: advancement, felicity, fortune, gladness, happiness, health, pleasure, prosperity, satisfaction, serenity, welfare, wholeness.
ant.- depression, distress, illness, suffering, trouble.

Well-bred: polished, suave, well-behaved, polite, hoble, well-borne, gentle, courteous.
ant.- bad-mannered, base, rude, uncivilized, uncultured, uncouth.

Well-known: familiar, famous, recognized, celebrated, notable, renowned, popular.
ant.- notorious, infamous.

Whole: absolute, all, complete, entire, full, integral, perfect, total, everything, aggregate, on and all, unabridged, unbroken, undivided.
ant.- defective, fragmentary, imperfect, incomplete.

Wholesome: good, beneficial, nourishing, nutritive, nutritious, health-giving, healthful, hygienic, healthy.
ant.- unhealthy, unhygienic, unwholesome.

Wicked: atrocious, base, evil, corrupt, criminal, delirious, disorderly, disreputable, fiendish, immoral, nefarious, noxious, pernicious, scandalous, sinful, unrighteous, vicious, vile, villainous.
ant.- admirable, honourable, commendable, moral, noble, praiseworthy, virtuous.

Wide: broad, comprehensive, expanded, extensive, general, large, roomy, widespreading, spacious, sweeping, vast.
ant.- confined, hampered, limited, narrow, restricted.

Wild: undomesticated, giddy, untamed, rough, uncultivated, impetuous, irregular, turbulent, wayward, extravagant, foolish, boisterous.
ant.- domesticated, lawful.

Will: choice, conviction, desire, decision, determination, inclination, intent, intention, mind, preference, purpose, resolution, willingness, wish, volition.
ant.- coercion, compulsion, doubt, indecision, wavering.

Wilful: intentional, intended, premeditated, deliberate, self-willed, arbitrary, willed, volitional, voluntary.
ant.- unintentional, unwitting, unplanned.

Win: conquest, success, victory, triumph.
ant.- beating, defeat, failure, downfall, loss.

Winding: bending, coiling, crooked, curving, devious, involuted, meandering, sinuous, twining, twisting.
ant.- direct, plain, straight.

Wisdom: astuteness, comprehension, discernment, discretion, discrimination, enlightenment, erudition, foresight, insight, intelligence, judgment, knowledge, learning, prudence, reason, sense, understanding, sagacity.
ant.- absurdity, foolishness, imprudence, misjudgment, ignorance.

Wise: astute, deep, discerning, discreet, enlightened, erudite, foresighted, informed, intelligent, judicious, profound, well-advised, learned, sage, prudent, rational, sagacious, sane, sensible, sound.

ant.- foolish, silly, unwise, unintelligent.

Wish: appetite, aspiration, bid, will, hankering, intention, want, craving, desire, thirst, hungering, longing, inclination, liking, urge, whim.

ant.- aversion, reluctance, dislike, yearning.

Wit: comprehension, intellect, intelligence, mind, perception, perspicacity, reason, sagacity, sense, understanding.

ant.- dullness, stupidity, folly, foolishness.

Withdraw: abandon, abjure, abstract, deduct, depart, desert, dissociate, disengage, draw, off, forsake, give up, go, leave, quit, recall, recant, relinquish, remove, renounce, retire, retreat, separate, drop out, subduct, subtract, back out, rescind, resign, abdicate, decamp, shrink, vacate.

ant.- abide, introduce, stay, remain, return, tarry.

Withhold: abstain, check, conceal, deny, desist, detain, forbear, hide, hinder, keep, back, refrain, refuse, retain, reserve, hold back, repress, restrain, suppress.

ant.- accord, concede, grant, indulge, persist, yield.

Withstand: combat, confront, contradict, counteract, defy, fight off, oppose, face, hinder, hold out, obstruct, resist, thwart.

ant.- acquiesce, consent, yield, submit, succumb.

Witty: quick-witted, pert, clever, skilful, talented.

ant.- fool, foolish.

Woe: disaster, misery, trouble, unhappiness, tribulation, grief, sorrow.

ant.- pleasure, joy, happiness.

Wonder: curiosity, marvel, miracle, oddity, phenomenon, portent, prodigy, rarity, sight, sign, spectacle, admiration, amazement, astonishment, bewilderment, fascination, surprise, wonderment.

ant.- commonness, familiarity, triviality.

Wordy: diffuse, discursive, garrulous, long-winded, prolix, loquacious, rambling, verbose, redundant, talkative, voluble.

ant.- brief, concise, succinct, laconic, terse.

Work: action, business, calling, deed, drudgery, duty, effort, employment, trade, stint, moil, grind, routine, exertion, job, labour, occupation, office, opus, performance, production, profession, pursuit, travail.
ant.- ease, idleness, leisure, recreation, relaxation.

Worldly: carnal, corporeal, secular, earthly, irreligious, materialistic, mundane, opportunistic, practical, profane, mercenary, unspiritual, sensual, temporal, terrestrial, ungodly.
ant.- incorporeal, intellectual, refined, spiritual.

Worn: tattered, ragged, tatty, jaded, shabby, threadbare, tired, shopworn, second wasted, wearied, weary, used, hand.
ant.- fresh, invigorated, new, rested, unused.

Worry: anxiety, apprehension, care, concern, disquiet, fear, trouble, uneasiness, mental anguish.
ant.- contentment, ease, peace, satisfaction, serenity.

Worship: adore, rever, inspire, aspire, be devout, idolize, reverence.
ant.- blaspheme, deride, despise, disdain.

Worthless: insignificant, poor, meritless, pointless, nothing, futile, profitless, unimportant, useless, no good, good-for-valueless, unproductive.
ant.- fruitful, useful, valuable, worthwhile, worthy.

Worthy: charitable, creditable, dependable, deserving, good, honourable, meritorious, worthwhile, decent, reliable, estimable, honest, upright, reputable, righteous, virtuous.
ant.- corrupt, dishonourable, iniquitous, vicious, villainous.

Wrap: bundle, cloak, clothe, roll, conceal, cover, enclose, fold, enfold, envelop, hide, lap, swaddle, muffle, package, shroud, swathe, wind.
ant.- bare, divulge, expose, open, reveal, unfold.

Wreck: annihilate, demolish, break, damage, destroy,

devastate, eradicate, exterminate, extinguish, obliterate, ravage, raze, ruin, shatter, crack up, tear down, smash, crash.

ant.- conserve, construct, establish, preserve, repair.

Wretched: baggarly, worthless, miserable, paltry, mean, pitiful, unhappy, unfortunate, woebegone, tormented, disreputable, deplorable.

ant.- admirable, cheerful, happy, contended, jovial.

Wrong: amiss, askew, awry, erroneous, fallacious, false, faulty, inaccurate, incorrect, inexact, mistaken, untrue, improper, inappropriate, unsuitable.

ant.- accurate, correct, right, exact, precise, appropriate, becoming, fitting, suitable.

❑

Y

Yearning: longing, craving, lankering, wish, coveting, solicitude.
ant.- abhorrenea, disgust, loathing.

Yield: crop, fruit, harvest, bear, product, reaping, result, breed, generate, impart, produce, supply, allow, bestow, concede, confer, permit, sanction, store, grant.
ant.- consumption, input, loss.

Young: adolescent, blooming, green, growing, immature, inexperienced, juvenile, pubescent, puerile, vigorous, youthful, teenage.
ant.- aged, ancient, elderly, experienced, mature.

❑

Z

Zeal: ardour, dedication, earnestness, verve, zealotry, devotion, eagerness, energy, enthusiasm, excitement, fanaticism, fervency, fervour, intensity, intentness, passion, perseverance, vehemence, keenness, zest, warmth, willingness.

ant.- apathy, detachment, indifference, nonchalance, ennui.

Zealot: adherent, devotee, bigot, dogmatist, dreamer, enthusiast, extremist, fanatic, martyr, opinionist, partisan, patriot, visionary.

ant.- dawdler, idler, shirker, slacker.

Zealous: afire, ardent, burning, brisk, bustling, diligent, fervid, fiery, hustling, indefatigable, passionate, resolute, sedulous, steadfast, vivacious.

ant.- apathetic, cold, cool.

Zenith: acme, apex, apogee, cap, climax, crest, crown, culmination, height, pinnacle, maximum, peak, summit, top.

ant.- base, bottom, floor, foundation, nadir.

Zero: blank, cipher, naught, nil, none, nobody, nonentity, nothing, nullity.

ant.- corporeality, matter, existence, object, substance.

Zest: ardour, delight, desire, enhancement, enjoyment, enthusiasm, appetite, thrill, titillation, twang, sauce, exhilaration, gusto, passion, pleasure, relish, spirit, flavour, energy, piquancy, pungency, savouriness, sharpness, tang, savour, taste.

ant.- apathy, aversion, loathing, weariness.

Zigzag: askew, awry, bent, cringed, crooked, curved, devious, diagonal, erratic, fluctuating, forked, inclined, indirect, jagged, meandering, oblique, osculating, rambling, serrated, sinuous, sloping, spiral, straggling, transverse, twisted, undulatory, vibratory, waggling, wry.

ant.- direct, even, rectilinear, straight, unbent.

❑❑❑